Ideas in America's Cultures

Ideas in America's Cultures

FROM REPUBLIC TO MASS SOCIETY

EDITED BY
Hamilton Cravens

INTRODUCTION BY
Merle Curti

IOWA STATE UNIVERSITY PRESS, AMES

© 1982 The Iowa State University Press. All rights reserved

Composed and printed by The Iowa State University Press, Ames, Iowa 50010

First edition, 1982

Library of Congress Cataloging in Publication Data
Main entry under title:

Ideas in America's cultures from Republic to mass society.

Includes bibliographical references and index.
Contents: Stow Persons as a historian of American intellectual life / Merle Curti—The godly and virtuous republic of John Witherspoon / Roger Fechner—Horace Bushnell, gentleman theologian / Howard A. Barnes—[etc.]
1. United States—Intellectual life—Addresses, essays, lectures. 2. United States—Civilization—Addresses, essays, lectures. 3. Persons, Stow, 1913–   —Addresses, essays, lectures. I. Cravens, Hamilton.
E169.1.I34   973   81–15577
ISBN 0–8138–0081–1   AACR2

CONTENTS

PREFACE

THE PURPOSE of this book is to commemorate the contributions Stow Persons has made to scholarship in American intellectual history and to graduate education at the University of Iowa. The contributors and editor assume that it is important to recognize publicly those high standards of the historical craft that Persons has always exemplified, and, by honoring his achievements, to affirm that excellence is the only meaningful justification of the scholarly enterprise.

American intellectual history is, relatively speaking, a newcomer among the myriad specialties of American history; younger, certainly, than such conventional fields as frontier, colonial, or Civil War and Reconstruction. It might be said that Persons's career, spanning as it has more than four decades, developed along with American intellectual history itself. Although there were pioneers writing American intellectual history before Persons entered the profession, most notably Merle Curti, Ralph Henry Gabriel, and Perry Miller, it was the accomplishment of Persons's generation of intellectual historians to establish intellectual history as a recognized collegiate course across the nation and less certainly as a research field in which the work of current practitioners served as the basis for research by future scholars.

American intellectual history has existed long enough as a self-conscious academic specialty to have already acquired a monographic account of its past. According to Robert A. Skotheim, American intellectual historians have approached the history of American intellectual life in one of two ways. So-called internalist intellectual historians have focused upon the history of ideas and their intellectual antecedents, whereas externalist intellectual historians have emphasized the material bases and circumstances of intellectual life.[1] Whether or not Skotheim's schematic diagrams possess some ultimate validity, many within and without the field have easily accepted this binary formulation as an accurate description of what American intellectual historians have done and are currently doing.

And more is the pity. Doubtless such a bifurcation has been harmful to the historical reconstruction and explanation of intellectual life. Neither approach is articulated and elaborated from a genuinely *historicist* consciousness. Neither is the stuff of historical thinking, properly conceived. Most likely both are a legacy from the confused and bewildered controversies in late nineteenth-century American social science and, beyond that, from more general popular tendencies of thought which have appeared from time to time in the nation's past. A rigid pursuit of a genetic and abstract history of ideas without consideration of historical context can be just as intellectually impoverishing as a dogmatic insistence upon the reductionist and mechanistic implications of the external approach in which ideas and even ideologies are presented as pale reflections of ineluctable social and economic forces.

The 1940s and 1950s were the salad days of American intellectual history, as undergraduates flocked to lecture courses in the field, and more and more freshly minted Ph.D.s in American intellectual history entered the historical profession. Such collateral fields as the history of science and American studies grew also in those years. For a few years it appeared that the future of the profession belonged to intellectual historians of one stripe or another. Since the early and middle 1960s, however, the bloom has come off the rose; in the past fifteen or so years, a mood of debilitating pessimism has swept the ranks of intellectual historians. The reasons for this mood have been multiple and complex.[2] In retrospect the internalist versus externalist dichotomy has played a crucial role, for it has highlighted and indeed overexaggerated problems of historical reconstruction and interpretation in intellectual history as compared with other fields of history. For those who accept this dichotomy as meaningful, it has suggested that intellectual historians are caught on the horns of an intractable dilemma. To emphasize ideas seems to remove reconstruction and analysis from human behavior and historical context; to stress behavior and context apparently threatens to diminish or even negate the role of ideas in history. In this view intellectal historians are faced with methodological and conceptual problems that historians in other fields are not, although proponents of this position have never explained why this should be so.

Perhaps such a question has not been posed because of the terrific heat, not to say light, that the new social historians and the new left historians have generated in the historical profession since the early 1960s. Although these groups constitute but a small fraction of the profession, and they are strikingly dissimilar in many ways, their impact upon intellectual historians has been devastating. From very different points of view, they have questioned the importance and causal significance of elites, especially cultural and intellectual elites. Often they have written history without reference to ideas or have redefined ideas in such ways as to offer cold comfort to intellectal historians.

It is hardly astonishing that scholars insist upon the importance of the phenomena they study. Nor is it noteworthy that the leaders of a new academic field or movement often exaggerate their claims and lustily attack established groups. But it has been remarkable, to say the least, that many intellectual historians have accepted their critics' indictments without so much as a whimper of protest. Here one likely reason has been the internalist-externalist dichotomy, which implies to some intellectual historians that their methodological and conceptual difficulties are extraordinarily and perhaps uniquely difficult. The proper and sensible yardstick for the validity of any field of scholarship ought to be the results of the research done; on these grounds, intellectual historians have little to fear from comparison with historians in other fields. Doubtless intellectual historians have no easy handles to grasp, as, for example, the chronologies of regimes and elections, or the dramatic events of war and peace. In the final analysis all historians, regardless of field of specialization, character of phenomena emphasized, or applicable research methods and technologies, face common kinds of problems in research, conceptualization, generalization, and interpretation.

Persons's most important contribution to the writing and the teaching of American intellectual history is that he has never lost sight of his primary intellectual identity as a *historian*. As a practicing historian his chief interest has been in ideas in their cultural and historical context. His work has been grounded in a profoundly historicist consciousness. It cannot be facilely labeled as either internalist or externalist. And he has enriched it with conceptual insights from the disciplines of the humanities and the social sciences. Merle Curti has suggested in the introduction that the hallmarks of Persons's scholarship, broadly defined, have been its interdisciplinary orientation and its perceptive analyses of ideas set in their cultural historical contexts. Persons has taken ideas seriously, on their own terms, as historical phenomena. His technical mastery of ideas has been authoritative, acute, and penetrating, showing a close familiarity with difficult ideas in theology, science, and the social disciplines without contamination by presentist or other ahistorical considerations. From his start as an assistant professor in the 1940s, he sought to define coherent patterns of ideas and establish their interrelationships, which could then be contrasted with the dominant patterns of other areas.[3] If Persons has followed the methodological dictum that the sources of ideas are always, strictly speaking, antecedent ideas, this has not meant that he has restricted himself to a kind of abstract genetic and unilinear approach. On the contrary, it has always been one of the strengths of his precise analyses of ideas to show how much ideas can become transformed and new ideas become forged from a variety of antecedents in a new cultural historical context.

Persons has consistently incorporated into his explanations of American intellectual life discussions and analyses of the larger historical context. Naturally the density of contextual detail presented depended upon the problem selected for investigation and the angle of vision employed. In his genuinely *monographic* work he created richly detailed and lively narrative as context for analysis of ideas. For example, in *Free Religion* (1947), he discussed the emergence of the new liberal Unitarianism within the context of the concrete phenomena germane to the ferment of doctrine and belief. Yet the bulk of his work has actually been on a different level of discourse; that is, bold analysis of patterns of ideas superimposed over a narrative structure often implicit in the design of explanation and exposition. Most of his publications could be described as historical syntheses rooted in extensive research in primary source materials. From this perspective it has not been necessary, or even desirable, to present the kind of detailed narrative of historical events and phenomena associated with the traditional, historical monograph. For Persons, consideration of historical context has not signified the ritualistic application of vague historical cliches, such as urbanization or industrialization, to explain a specific cluster of ideas. It meant rather something far more rigorous and sophisticated: the precise analysis of a pattern of ideas and ultimately a broadening and extending of such reconstruction and analysis to those particular historical circumstances and cultural contexts appropriate to the ideas.

Increasingly Persons identified particular clusters of ideas, not simply with individuals, or even groups of individuals who articulated those ideas, but with larger subcultures within the population in given historical epochs. Such interest had been evident in his earliest work and in the dissertations he directed on various aspects of American religious history in the 1950s and early 1960s. Certainly by the early 1960s he had become increasingly impressed by the importance of the dynamics of cultural class conflict, although in retrospect such reformulation probably flowed from his earlier emphases upon those patterns of ideas that constituted "social minds." In the 1960s his growing stress on the clusters of ideas and values of culture-bearing classes, groups, and subcultures became an important and integral part of his own work, most notably on the consequences for modern cultural life of the decline of the gentry class and the rise of mass society. Certainly these new emphases emerged in the revised edition of *American Minds* (1975), although it would be inaccurate to assume that such concern was absent from the original edition published in 1958. In many respects Persons's approach could be likened to that of the modern cultural anthropologist, but such a label, if applied literally, would be a distortion. In reality Persons has been eclectic and has employed, with proper modifications for historical investigation, methods and conceptual tools from other disciplines as well, such as textual analysis and the theory of mass society, when he has deemed it appropriate. At the same time, his discussions of methods and concepts from other disciplines consistently turned back to specific questions of historical circumstance and reality.

The question arises in a book of this character of the impact of master upon apprentices. In this instance it has been largely indirect. Unfortunately we cannot describe, let alone analyze, Persons's impact upon the several hundred graduate students on whose committees he served, not to mention the thousands of undergraduates who took his heavily enrolled lecture courses in intellectual history, eighteenth-century American society, and science in America. We can only evaluate his influence upon the thirty-seven men and women who finished their doctorates with him in slightly more than three decades. The doctoral students usually arrived and departed in ones, twos, or threes. They have been widely separated by age, geography, and other attributes. They have been more commonly aware of one another by word of mouth than personal or professional contact. More importantly, Persons allowed the greatest possible student initiative, interest, and latitude in professional self-definition. Thus it was not his custom to dispense ready-made dissertation topics. Rather, students brought proposals to him for further definition and refinement. Nor did he structure his graduate seminar around a specific theme. Above all, he encouraged students to become independent investigators.

Yet the imprint exists. A recurring theme of Persons's work has been his interest in and explanation of those cultural forms, ideas, values, and social structures characteristic of early Anglo-American culture and their eventual transformation, in sharply altered ways under new and different circumstances, into the elements of the modern culture and society. He has not been usually thought of as a historian of modernization, and so much the better; that trendy conception, like many others which practitioners of one discipline cheerfully borrow from another, in time will become self-evidently limiting and stultifying as scholars discover that again they must redefine what they appropriate from other fields in ways that are truly useful for the research they do in their disciplines. Nevertheless his work might be of more than passing interest to historians enthusiastically engaged in applying modernization theory to the American past. In the main, Persons's work has centered on various historical problems commonly associated with modern American culture: the role of religion in modern culture; the group dynamics and cultural contexts of ethnic life; the impact of evolutionary ideas in America; the influence (or lack thereof) of the many varieties of socialism in America; the decline of gentility and the rise of mass society and culture; and in recent years the ideas of the Chicago school of sociology on mass society and ethnic pluralism.

What interested Persons appealed strongly to his doctoral students. His interpretations of historical problems were routinely grounded in deep, insightful reading of primary sources, whether expressed in his lecture courses, graduate seminars, or publications. Especially to students nurtured upon the progressive historians, Frederick Jackson Turner, Charles A. Beard, and Vernon Louis Parrington, the topics Persons touched upon were often new and explained in fresh and original ways. Virtually all doctoral students selected research problems from the eighteenth century to the present. Some gravitated to church history and religious ideas, others to the history of social thought, a handful to the history of science. Virtually all linked the history of ideas as a research problem to particular individuals representative of larger groups, or to such groups themselves, such as clergymen, social thinkers, denominations, ideological movements, the gentry class, scientists, and articulate champions of certain dissenting and minority groups. Individual students selected research topics inspired in one way or another by Persons's work, often his current research. Among the graduates there has been both a mutual interest in certain historical questions and in particular lines of attack upon such questions, evident both in the dissertations and in the considerable work conducted and published since graduation. If because students seemed to go their own ways in their work an impression was created that there was no general impact upon several generations of Ph.D.s, this supposition probably resulted from Persons's style as a graduate teacher, which was the product of his personal and professional integrity and iron-clad commitment to independent investigation.

Yet there has been a larger mosaic of influence, as became clear in the negotiations that I commenced thirteen months ago with the graduates, resulting in the current volume. The impact appropriately reflected Persons's approach to graduate education. The corpus of the graduates' work, long after each had received the doctorate, showed how each had taken up issues and problems that Persons had pioneered or introduced and developed them on their own, often with strikingly different emphases and explanations than his might have been. Among the graduates, there has been an emphasis upon clusters and patterns of ideas and values, expressed by culturally defined groups within the national population, sometimes in conflict with one another. Always there is a precise definition of historical context. There has been strong, continuing interest in problems in the history of religious thought, social ideas, or a blending of the two, as well as the premise—introduced or reinforced by Persons—of the continuing importance of religion in American culture. Furthermore, there has been a conception of the main or major theme of American history from the middle of the eighteenth to the middle of our own century as the transformation from republican culture to the modern culture or the mass society. That intellectual legacy, which itself is complex and diverse in some respects, is nevertheless a striking portrait of the history of the ideas of the cultures of America. The organization of this book reflects that legacy. It is a fitting tribute to say that Persons provided intellectual leadership of the highest order, leadership by inspiration and example.

As editor it is my pleasant task to thank those individuals who assisted me in the complex tasks of carrying through the effort that has resulted in the publication of this book. A large number of graduates could not meet the Draconian deadlines I had to impose at various stages but nevertheless offered indispensable encouragement and moral support. Harold B. Wohl graciously prepared the comprehensive bibliography, current as of January 1, 1981. Special thanks go to Merle Curti, who generously consented to prepare the introduction, even though this necessitated the interruption of other pressing obligations. Other friends eased my chores and responsibilities considerably; above all, Lawrence E. Gelfand, who supplied the original list of graduates and facilitated many other matters, but scarcely less importantly, Charles A. Hale, John Bell Henneman, Richard Lowitt, Alan I. Marcus, David W. Noble, Robert E. Schofield, Henry D. Shapiro, John Simmons, and Albert E. Stone. A grant in aid of publication by the Learned Publications Fund of the University of Iowa Graduate College is gratefully acknowledged. The directors, editors, and staff of the Iowa State University Press were unfailingly cooperative. Circumstances dictated that the organization and coordination of the project be centralized in my hands alone, and I cheerfully accept responsibility for all such decisions.

H. C.

Ames, Iowa
December 17, 1980

INTRODUCTION

Stow Persons as a Historian of American Intellectual Life

MERLE CURTI

SINCE the preface to this volume and the essays by former students bear witness to the skill and other gifts of Stow Persons as a teacher and director of research, my comments will be confined to an effort to record the significance of his publications, thus far, in American intellectal history.

Both in reviews of his books in professional journals and in writings on the historiography of the field Persons's work has been respectfully and appreciatively, though sometimes critically, received. Some have referred to the likely influence on his work of his New England clerical background and of Arthur O. Lovejoy, Perry Miller, and his mentor during his graduate study at Yale, Ralph H. Gabriel.[1] He may also have been influenced by the emphasis of Moses Coit Tyler and Samuel Eliot Morison as well as Gabriel on timeless values that have survived changing circumstances. He himself has spoken of his early appreciation of Woodbridge Riley, a too little known but technically competent pioneer historian of American philosophy. Persons obviously has a first-hand acquaintance with the work of such scholars as Max Weber, Ernst Troeltsch, Karl Mannheim, and sociologists concerned with mass society. Whatever his intellectual debts, Persons has been an independent and original scholar.

Before turning to his writings something should also be said about his Princeton experience which, early in his career, throws light on his contributions to the cooperative and interdisciplinary approach in American studies. As a member, codirector, and director of the Princeton Conference on American Civilization during the 1940s, he both learned from and contributed a good deal to the program. His first essay

MERLE CURTI is Frederick Jackson Turner Professor, Emeritus, University of Wisconsin-Madison.

in this connection, "The Americanization of the Immigrant," appeared in the volume his colleague David F. Bowers edited, *Foreign Influences in American Life* (1944). Persons edited, with colleagues, *Evolutionary Thought in America* (1950) and *Socialism and American Life* (1952). His contributions to these volumes reflected an interest in themes later to be developed in his work—the role of religion, moral values, community, ethnicity, science, and the social disciplines. His editorial work and illuminating essays in still other volumes, *Social Darwinism: Selected Essays of William Graham Sumner* (1963) and *The Cooperative Commonwealth* (1965) likewise reflected a continuing interest in themes examined in the Princeton program. Limited to undergraduates, the Princeton conference nevertheless influenced, both as a pioneer example of teaching and research, the developing American studies movement. By involving Persons in interdisciplinary studies with emphasis on both the humanistic and social science approach, the Princeton experience seems also to have been a formative influence on his later work.

Just as Persons's contributions were interdisciplinary, all of them in greater or lesser measure reflect a similarly nonparochial character in treating the intellectual relations of Europe and America. "In its formal thought even more than in its institutions," he wrote, "the United States lies at the periphery of Western culture, and its major intellectual stimuli have at least until most recent times been derived from Western Europe. This is as true of the theory of organic evolution as it is of the social ideas of the Enlightenment or of the literary attitudes of romanticism, influences which preceded and conditioned the reception of evolution. The problem for the student of American culture," he continued, "is to lay bare the context in which the new ideas asserted themselves and to examine the compromises and adjustments which necessarily resulted from the merging of the new with the old."[2]

Though this awareness is touched on rather than developed in *The Decline of American Gentility* (1973), it is very clear in *American Minds* (1958), a major synthesis of the intellectual history of the United States from the early seventeenth century to the midtwentieth century. Here we see how the new problems posed by the migration to America almost imperceptibly affected the institutions and outlook of New England Puritans. That a minority party now became a majority and that specific practical situations led to an emphasis on community and to the reluctant concession of toleration with the growth of dissent and secularism was of course only one example of what happened in the transfer and accommodation of ideas and values from the Old World to the New. Thus Roger Williams espoused the idea that even with religious differences, the covenant or contract made possible a stable, united life in civil affairs though, to be sure, Rhode Island for a time came far from demonstrating the principle in practice.

An even more striking example was the effect of a new situation and experience on the ideas of individualism and progress. While individualism was not an American invention, the westward movement intensified it without making drastic changes in institutions. Similarly, though the sources of the doctrine of progress, a dominant faith in nineteenth-century America, were in antecedent ideas, "the material conditions of American life provided the setting within which the belief in progress could flourish. The idea," Persons went on, "was certainly an appropriate assumption for an active, dynamic society engaged in exploiting the resources of a continent." American conditions, in short, explained how such constituent ideas in the concept of progress as millenialism, Christian perfectionism, and its science-based counterpart coalesced in the burning faith in progress.

Similarly, the popularity of the optimistic romantic temperament, rooted in the Old World, flourished with the rapid growth of the country,the rising standard of living, and the prevailing sense of military and intellectual security.

On the other hand, indigenous conditions sometimes explained why ideas or movements of thought European in origin, such as many in the Enlightenment, appealed to elites rather than becoming quickly assimilated throughout the community. Persons's discussion of naturalism, evolution, and socialism reflected and supported the basic thesis of borrowing or transference and Americanization in transatlantic intellectual relations.

The examples cited in this process disprove the contention that *American Minds* and, to a lesser extent, *Free Religion* (1947) treated ideas in a social vacuum. It is true that he believed that "the sources of ideas are, strictly speaking, to be found in antecedent ideas rather than in material facts and circumstances." Yet in explicit statements as well as in his use of social context he took account, as we have seen, of the new and the changing character of American society in explaining the historical careers of given ideas and movements of thought. In other words, Persons tried to strike a balance between a treatment of the history of ideas that completely divorced the discussion from social context and that which gave prime importance to material conditions as the source or at least mainspring of the ideas themselves.

Within this broad frame Stow Persons succinctly defined his view of American intellectual history. He wrote in the preface to his first book, *Free Religion*, that the dissidents within Unitarianism—Transcendentalists, scientific empiricists, and social activists—had not received their due. This seemed enough. It was not the place to draw lessons. In noting this, Sidney Mead felt the story itself was ''a lesson for those precious liberals who make individual freedom their only basic principle in protest against an overweening authoritarianism.''[3]

A more considered statement of Persons's view of intellectual history came a decade later. The purpose of this book, he wrote in the preface to *American Minds,*

> is to describe the principal focal concentrations of ideas, or ''minds,'' that have determined the profile of American intellectual life during its historical development. . . . A social mind is the cluster of ideas and attitudes that gives to a society whatever uniqueness or individuality it may have as an epoch in the history of thought. It binds together in an intellectual community those who share its beliefs.

The book was thus concerned mainly with ''the intellectual functions of the social mind.'' Its object was ''to indicate the leading characteristics of each successive social mind and to illustrate them with discussion of representative thinkers and movements. The method might be described as cross sectional rather than chronological or systematic.'' It made no effort ''to explore the formation or dissolution of these systems of ideas or to trace the transitions between them.'' He identified five roughly chronological minds or clusters of ideas and attitudes: the colonial religious mind, the Enlightenment, the mind of nineteenth-century Democracy, the naturalistic mind, and the contemporary neo-Democratic mind. If in our early history long gaps separated social minds successively from each other, this has been far less true in recent times because of the increasing tempo of thought.

In introducing *The Decline of American Gentility* Persons extended his view of the purpose of writing intellectual history. This book explored the factors involved in successive modifications of the functions of the social type embodying the values of gentility which had flourished in the Western world for more than three centuries. This involved an analysis of the factors that explained the final disappearance of a clearly defined social type and its related views and values in a mass society.

For Stow Persons, writing the history of ideas transcended the pleasure of the enterprise. He believed in the individual and social importance of ideas in their historical careers. To cite a single but notable example, he took account of the relations between the Puritan covenant, the joint-stock company, the community, the voluntary society, and the modern corporation. Scrupulously concerned with achieving the greatest possible objectivity in discussing patterns of ideas or movements of thought with which he may have had less personal sympathy than others, he believed that all these displayed the creative capacity that earmarked human beings, that made civilization possible, and that explained much of the present. Such a conviction was the more notable since it testified to his belief in the lasting value if not the autonomy of certain ideas at a time when many in the profession felt that the so-called relativist position denigrated the importance and dignity of ideas. [4]

Many young scholars in American intellectual history now seem to doubt the condition and status of the field. To some its limitations and loss of standing in the profession stem from an inadequate pursuit and use of rigorous methods. [5] Thus it is appropriate to look at Persons's conceptualizations and methods in relation to his stated purposes.

First of all, his work shows great concern for clear, precise definition of familiar as well as less usual terms. Few criticized his writing for vague or ambiguous use of terms. A reviewer of his first book, *Free Religion: An American Faith,* did think that the title was unclear since it did not indicate whether the thesis of the book was free religion as one of many American faiths, or if it meant a characteristically American faith. [6] Whether the point was justified or not, a close reading of all his work indicates his attachment to and effective use of clear, precise definitions. A few examples must illustrate the point. Thus the statement "the ethic of individual responsibility was perhaps the major legacy of Puritanism to American civilization" becomes understandable thanks in part to the definitions of such terms as Special Providences, covenant, church, perfect and imperfect regeneration, Arminianism, and perfectionism. The careful definitions of intellect and piety in the analysis of their interrelations and of the terms associated with revivalism merit high marks if the criterion is understanding.

Sometimes the functional uses or consequences of an idea defined it in a meaningful way. Thus the ethic of individual responsibility provided "the psychological attitudes, the personal discipline, and the rationale out of which sprang a host of merchants, speculators, and industrialists who never dreamed of the antecedents of their outlook. More than two and a half centuries were to pass," Persons continued, "before the character of business enterprise would change to the degree that for many individuals the Puritan ethic no longer seemed relevant to the facts of economic life. The dawning realization of this discrepancy, at the end of the nineteenth century, with the consequent disintegration of practical values that followed, was one of the chief causes of the moral and intellectual confusion of the twentieth century.''

When one turns to the discussions of democracy, the clarity of definitions and the functional uses of what the term stood for is likewise illuminated. Modern students who found the roots of American democracy in such radical sectarians as the Antinominians, Roger Williams, or the Quakers, should not forget that while these rebels resisted the "totalitarian discipline of the Puritans, the social institutions with which they replaced it were not necessarily congenial to the modern democratic temperament," nor was this their objective. Much insight was evident in the defining statement that "the central innovation of nineteenth century democratic theory was the equation of citizenship with suffrage," especially when the results of widening the suffrage were assessed.

The importance Persons attached to clear definitions was also abundantly illustrated in discussions of successive social minds. Romanticism was defined as "a temper of mind" in which a central importance was attached to the intuitive and esthetic aspects of experience. The importance of definitions was no less evident in the discussion of the naturalist mind. In Persons's words "the naturalist mind was the first pattern of thought in America to reflect industrial conditions. It was not the product of industrialism alone, but its conceptions of man and society were inevitably colored by the impact of industrialism upon the human consciousness." The sense of rootlessness that the naturalist felt in response to the rapid tempo of the shift from a rural to an urban society also reflected the undermining of individual responsibility, community cooperation, and the validity of a firm if not an absolute conception of morality. In another context Persons, by pointing out the imprecise uses of the phrase Social Darwinism, corrected some of its widely accepted misunderstandings.

In all his work, though in varying degrees, emphasis was put on ideas rather than on the individuals expressing them. This is to say that with some notable exceptions, such as Francis Ellingwood Abbot, Francis Wayland, William Graham Sumner, and Walter Lippmann, biography is always subordinated to an analysis of ideas. Though on at least one occasion Persons recognized the role of temperament in influencing choices individuals made in holding one position rather than another, he took no stand on the claims of those who underlined the psychological characteristics and experiences of a writer as explanations of ideas held. He may have thought that precise knowledge of such personal experiences was too fragmentary and uncertain for use as explanation.

Since Persons recognized the importance of assumptions, both conscious and underlying, it is well to note how he handled them. The Enlightenment speculation about anthropology or the natural history of man was dominated by the assumption of a static creator at a definite moment in time. Jefferson no less than the biblical account of creation assumed that the world had always been pretty much as it was in the eighteenth century though some thinkers did speculate on the possibility of plural creations. Again, assumption played a major part in the identification of moral transformation with the organic cycle of change and of virtue with youth, America being the paramount example of the latter. Moving into the nineteenth century a basic assumption of democratic ideology was "the conviction that a political order based on universal and equal political privilege is an ethical good." The theory of republicanism assumed that, in spite of the mixture of good and bad impulses in human nature, man was free from subjection because he is rational by the law of nature. Again, one of the most striking examples of the explanatory use made of identifying assumptions occurs in the discussion of the naturalist mind. The naturalists, Persons wrote, tended to be unaware of the underlying assumptions as well as of their debt to the past in professing to prize verified fact as superior to speculation. This led to inconsistencies of outlook on many of the broader aspects of life. Elsewhere he pointed out that "the naturalistic mind with its biological presuppositions devoted much attention to racial problems and assigned an important place in its general social theory to presumed racial characteristics." In the discussion of Walter Lippmann's analysis of public opinion, of the influence of symbols and stereotypes in perception, Persons observed that seen in the light of the manipulability of feeling and behavior the "democratic assumption of a society composed of self-sufficient individuals was substantially false." Still another example shows the ways in which Stow Persons recognized and interpreted assumptions. He noted that at first the exponents of civil liberties implicitly assumed that "the prime threat to civil liberty was to be found in the potential exercise of arbitrary power by government. Whatever validity such an assumption may have had did not derive solely from the revolutionary struggle through which the American people had just passed. It was also an inevitable product of the assumptions of Republican political theory." Thus experience and theory combined "to make plausible the assumption that the principal threat to liberty was to be found in government." Tocqueville later pointed out other threats, the reality of which were only too evident in the manipulations practiced during the era of the neo-Democratic mind.

We pass by examples of Persons's noting of ironies and paradoxes in assumptions and ideas, a procedure that has often been overworked by later scholars in American intellectual history. His use of these examples never pushed the point he was making beyond the limits of ready understanding though his intellectual sophistication made him fully aware of the subtleties of such contradictions and paradoxes.

As we have seen, in *The Decline of American Gentility,* Persons took on the task of explaining the reasons why a set of values—those associated with the social elites that followed the breakup of the colonial gentry during and after the Revolution—were influenced by changes in society. These changes, reaching everywhere in the emerging mass society, ended a long chapter in the history of a fairly well-defined code of values and conduct. In addition to the emphasis on the causal factors of change, the author carried further than he had in his earlier work the use of literary and sociological concepts. The book had the same concern with clarity as his former work. It also had more grace and elegance, explicable perhaps in the nature of the materials. One might add that it also differed from *American Minds* in presenting clearly and sharply an explicit thesis in the technical sense of the term.

These examples of the scope and methods that characterized Stow Persons's writings indicate why he is a major figure in the scholarship of American intellectual history and of what his distinctive contributions have consisted. With this statement this essay might appropriately end, particularly because Stow Persons is still actively engaged in research on an issue related to one of his very early interests.

Yet the usefulness of this account may be enhanced if some attention is given to the reception of his major works by other scholars in the field.

His first book, *Free Religion,* was a detailed and factual study of a revolt against what its leaders regarded as the failure of Unitarianism in the midnineteenth century to come to terms with contemporary science and its method, and, on the part of some, a further failure to meet pressing social issues with constructive action. William W. Sweet, the dean at that time of academic historians of American religion, commended the thorough research and the overall interpretation. He agreed with the thesis that the Free Religious Association, though a minor eddy, undoubtedly liberalized the Unitarian fellowship or, "as the author states, dechristianized it, and played a part in lessening the dogmatism of liberal Protestantism generally."[7] A leading Unitarian, Duncan Howlitt, wrote that "we owe Professor Persons a debt of gratitude for this study. He has not only rescued a significant chapter of American religious history from oblivion, but he has presented it to this generation with competence, clarity, and imagination." At the same time Howlitt felt that the book seemed to be "shot through with an irrepres-

sible urge to pass judgments." Though Persons had certainly emphasized the liberalizing influence of free religion, this reviewer somehow
felt that the long-range significance of the movement had not been ade-
quately assessed.[8]

A reviewer of *American Minds* who regarded it "on the whole a
first-rate book and probably the best 'introduction to the history of
American thought' yet written" nevertheless felt that the method used
had resulted in a static rather than a dynamic view of history. He also
commented that to describe the cluster of ideas "that gave a society
whatever uniqueness or individuality it may have in the history of
thought" was by definition a commitment to bridge the gap between
the elite and the popular mind.[9] Persons might have replied that he had
himself recognized and clearly stated this limitation, and that it was
impossible in one volume to achieve the immense and perhaps impossible task of showing the relation between basic systems of thought
among intellectual elites and the aspects of these systems that came to
be shared by other people. Another reviewer praised the book for its
freshness, high order of intellectual sophistication, and systematic analysis, but wished that the chronology had been less blurred and that the
relation between social minds and institutions other than religious ones
might have been explored—for instance, the educational establishment.[10] Howard Mumford Jones commended the author for his "gal-
lant attempt" to write a one volume introduction to the history of
American thought and for doing what he did very well indeed. He
noted, as others were to, the virtual omission of Southerners in the discussion of any of the five social minds. His chief regret was the omission
of themes he regarded as of great importance in American thought and
values such as the application of science to industry, the support of
higher education by industrialists and the rationale for this, Hegelian
idealism, the esthetic theories of the pre-Raphaelites, and the restriction
of the sources to formal writing in books. Actually Professor Jones was
suggesting work to be done if the objective understanding of "American Minds" was to be approximated.[11] In comprehensive accounts of
scholarship in American intellectual history, John Higham, in contrast
with some, commended Persons for his major effort in defining periods
in the history of ideas.[12] *American Minds* came nearer, in the view of
Arthur A. Ekirch, Jr., than any comparable synthesis to being "an in-
tensive history of ideas as against a more externalized type of traditional
intellectual history."[13]

The reception of *The Decline of American Gentility* was somewhat
mixed. In spite of the perception of some reviewers as an impressionistic
and even disjointed collection of essays, the book had a definite thesis.

It maintained that the American Revolution broke the influence and prestige of the American gentry as a social type, to be replaced by a series of functional elites. These made adjustments to changing social conditions and values, finally giving way altogether against the pressures of a mass society. The thesis, which derived in part from Tocqueville and which found support in many contemporary writers on mass society, European and American, drew its illustrations from such writers as James Fenimore Cooper, William Dean Howells, E. L. Godkin, Charles Eliot Norton, and Walter Lippmann. Consideration was given to the lady and her career, functions, and fate.

Some reviews claimed that the breakup of the gentry by the American Revolution was argued rather than documented and several regretted the slight attention given to the gentry of the Middle Atlantic states and especially the South. It does not seem quite fair to say, as some critics did, that the author never identified what he was talking about and that any such gentry as he seemed to have in mind probably never existed in the United States. Though Henry May called the book "a subtle, intelligent essay on an important topic by a justly respected writer on intellectual history," he thought that at times the subtlety turned into fuzziness and that the author did not always write from "inside the assumptions of this group as much as he seems to."[14] In May's view the author gave his readers much of value; but he felt the book would have been more effective if its limits had been more clearly defined.

Two reviews of competent scholars differed so markedly in their assessment of the book that one might well lose confidence in the judgments of experts. David D. Hall charged that categories were undefined, that the sociology was inadequate if not erroneous, and that sweeping assertions sometimes rested on the statement of a single writer. Though Hall commended the book for demolishing Richard Hofstadter's theory of gentry suicide in the Jacksonian period, he concluded that Persons, perhaps because of his misunderstanding of the nuclear family and social structure, had given inadequate attention to the interaction between these and belief.[15] On the other hand, Russell B. Nye spoke of the book as an enlightening and important one for literary and cultural historians. It provided essential material for studying men and movements hitherto lacking or hard to assemble and organize. It made recent social theory available to the critic and teacher in a useful, relevant way. In short, the publisher was quite right in describing the book as "wonderfully lucid" and "full of insight for the discerning reader."[16]

No one of course reviewed the reviews Stow Persons wrote—and he wrote a good many—of books by fellow workers in the field of his special interest. It is a pleasure to report that, as one might expect, they indicate a close reading of the book in hand, fairness, judicious judgments, alternative interpretations, and the correction of misstatements or dubious ones. Persons's reviews also offered insights and made useful suggestions for further research. At the same time many of these reviews illuminated his own conceptions of method, scope of inquiry, and plausibility of explanation.

Persons's articles and the prefaces in texts that he edited also enlarged the horizons of American intellectual history and showed the inadequacy of long-accepted interpretations. An example was the point Persons made about the light on the idea of progress revealed by an examination of the American aspects of the Enlightenment in relation to the Christian story of human redemption in time.[17] His analysis, to quote Cushing Strout, "significantly revises [Carl] Becker's influential image of the Enlightenment" in his highly regarded *Heavenly City of the Eighteenth Century Philosophers.*[18]

Probably no brief account, perhaps no account of any length, can do justice to Stow Persons's distinctive contributions to American intellectual history. Certainly this one has not done so. And it has necessarily left out altogether his influence through occasional conversations with other scholars who have profited from his acute and incisive thinking. These intangibles cannot be recorded with anything approaching adequate appreciation and indebtedness. Be it so. What he has done for the field he has so notably helped to develop is a permanent tribute that will not be lost to all those who continue to find interest and challenge in American intellectual history.

Ideas in America's Cultures

I

Religious Ideas in America's Cultures

C L E A R L Y religion has played a major role in American history from the seventeenth century to our own time. This has amounted to far more than the importance of religious beliefs and values to countless millions of Americans as individuals in the many groups and subcultures of the population. There have been larger effects as well. The separation of church and state, and the emergence of the denomination as the characteristic institution of worship in American society and culture, must be ranked as among the more important contributions of American civilization to the civilization of the West. These developments reflected and legitimated the religious pluralism of the peoples of America. The authors in Part I have taken for granted the fact of religious pluralism. They have also emphasized a common theme. In the myriad cultures of American civilization, religious thought and expression have often been directed toward socially useful ends, the chief of which has been the attempt to create a shared, public moral philosophy as a sure guide to public belief and action. One of the remarkable characteristics of many religious figures in America has been their commitment to the improvement of society and culture from their own perspectives, theological and moral, rather than to the elaboration of a rich, complex, and sophisticated theological tradition. Accepting the assumptions that the religious cultures of American civilization have been different, and that religious beliefs and values have always been important to millions of Americans throughout our history, each author has presented a case study of the larger phenomenon of the attempts of Americans to create a public moral philosophy from particularistic religious points of view.

According to Roger J. Fechner, the influential Presbyterian minister John Witherspoon is best understood as a bridge between the intellectual heritage of eighteenth-century Scotland and the emerging republican culture of late eighteenth-century America. If Witherspoon did not in the final analysis rank among the first order of American philosophes, and if one would be hard pressed to classify him as a truly original thinker, nevertheless we can learn much about the European and, in this particular instance, the Scottish influences upon the American Enlightenment by careful analysis of Witherspoon and men like him. Witherspoon was in his own time an important clergyman, college president, and leader of the revolutionary cause. Fechner presents persuasive evidence that the impact of Francis Hutcheson's moral philosophy was even more a decisive influence than orthodox Scottish Calvinistic theology upon Witherspoon, although admittedly it is difficult to disentangle the two in Witherspoon's thought. What is especially arresting about Fechner's analysis is the way in which Witherspoon, himself a very recent immigrant to America, fashioned a recognizably republican moral philosophy and political ideology from his Scottish intellectual heritage and the growing maelstrom of the imperial and revolutionary crises. If Fechner's major concern is with Witherspoon's ideas, nevertheless he does not ignore the larger cultural and political contexts in which Witherspoon was obliged to function. It is one of the strengths of his essay that he shows how Witherspoon developed as a revolutionary and a republican as the consequence of the intellectual commitments he carried with him from Scotland and those he acquired in his adopted land. Thus Fechner provides us with a valid case study of the genesis of eighteenth-century republican moral, religious, and political ideas, which also suggests a way to assess the impact of the European heritage on American thought.

As Howard A. Barnes reminds us, Horace Bushnell was a major thinker in nineteenth-century America. In a very real sense Bushnell attempted to create a moral philosophy for American public thought and action no less than Witherspoon, even though inevitably the historical contexts in which each thinker lived were different, and there were substantial differences in the sources and content of their ideas. If Bushnell has been subjected to more extensive scholarly analysis than Witherspoon, Barnes argues forcefully that the existing portrait of Bushnell must be seriously modified. Barnes presents solid evidence that the technical apprehension of Bushnell's ideas has been incomplete, not simply from a rigorous analysis of Bushnell's ideas, but also from a new interpretation of the social and political context in which Bushnell developed his ideas. Barnes's thesis is that Bushnell articulated his ideas as a response to the emergence of mass society and culture and to the severe difficulties mass society and culture created for the gentry class for which Barnes insists Bushnell attempted to speak. If Witherspoon was a major architect of republican thought in eighteenth-century America, Bushnell was, according to Barnes, a seminal representative of the gentry class in democratic, post-Revolutionary America, in sharply altered circumstances. The shifts in Bushnell's thought, as Barnes labels them, from naturalism to soft dualism, and finally to hard dualism, reflected the growing pessimism of the gentry class and of Bushnell as its spokesman about the possibilities of inventing and disseminating a moral philosophy for the democratic mass society of the nineteenth century. Bushnell's youthful optimism, and his pessimism as he grew older, reflected, Barnes concludes, the gentry class's increasingly disillusioned view of mass society. With Bushnell as with Witherspoon there was an attempt to create a public moral philosophy, grounded deeply in particularistic religious traditions, under strikingly different circumstances.

The effort to create a public moral philosophy on the basis of shared religious beliefs was not restricted to the efforts of single individuals or even to men of the cloth, as Carroll Engelhardt's valuable case study of formal religious and moral training in Iowa's public schools clearly demonstrates. Furthermore, Engelhardt argues, the existence of such efforts as an integral part of the professional actions of Iowa schoolmen over such a long period of time belies widely held assumptions about the separation of church and state and the concomitant secularization of American culture after the mid-nineteenth century. The emergence and coexistence of nonsectarian religious instruction and of civil religion in Iowa's schools, and the enthusiasm with which the vast majority of teachers and administrators pushed their campaign for moral education in the commonwealth's schools, have implications that transcend the particular geographical and temporal contexts of Engelhardt's study. More than has been true with other cultural institutions, public schools, because of the manner in which they have been governed and financed, have been unusually responsive to citizen pressures and lobbying. If the kind of moral education that Iowa's schoolmen publicly advocated had deeply offended the sensitivities and sensibilities of the taxpayers, probably those citizens would have protested vigorously. That their efforts at moral education went largely unchallenged is convincing evidence that they had at least grudging acceptance, and, more likely, hearty endorsement, from most Iowans. And, as Engelhardt points out, in a genuine sense Iowa was a microcosm of middle western rural and village culture. Unlike neighboring states to the north and east, Iowa did not experience the levels of urbanization and industrialization that northern Illinois or southern Wisconsin and Michigan did during these years; Iowa more resembled downstate Illinois, or central Missouri, or northern Minnesota than those states when the influence of their large urban centers is considered. At the very least, Engelhardt's study suggests that we reexamine the problem of the secularization of American culture from a more critical and particularistic perspective.

If Engelhardt informs us that religious and moral training persisted over many decades, Clifford Scott provides us with a similar interpretation of the perceptions of American Protestant missionaries about the indigenous peoples of sub-Sahara Africa in the first several decades of this century. About two decades ago Irwin G. Wyllie argued that social Darwinism was not the favored credo of American businessmen in the Gilded Age, contrary to the assumptions of some historians who had written about that ideological phenomenon. Rather, insisted Wyllie, the businessmen he studied continued to embrace traditional Christian beliefs and values.[1] One might think on first impression that the Protestant missionaries whose writings Scott has so carefully combed would have been even more inclined to ascribe the differences between themselves and their charges to evolutionary and racial causes, given the overwhelmingly racist atmosphere of the white culture in which these missionaries were reared and matured as adults. Yet the picture that emerges from Scott's authoritative account is far more complex. These individuals were culturally ethnocentric, to be sure, by the revealed wisdom of our own age; yet their refusal to employ the language, the social taxonomy, and the prevailing assumptions of evolutionary science suggests that cultural and intellectual historians must be wary of attributing to groups the views of the more famous and articulate elites. Moreover, another study of American missionaries among American Indians in the nineteenth century makes much the same point as does Scott.[2] The larger lesson that we may wish to draw from Scott's analysis is that the rise of secular culture—in this instance, popularized scientific culture—did not occur among all groups in the larger population and was not as influential in the culture as those cultural historians who have celebrated the rise of secular culture have assumed. Before we can make any grander statements, it is obviously necessary to understand far more about knowledge, belief, and context for the many subcultures of the population than we presently know.

H. C.

1

The Godly and Virtuous Republic of John Witherspoon

ROGER J. FECHNER

Besides in migrations and planting of colonies, in all ages,
we see evident traces of an original contract and consent
taken to the principles of union.

JOHN WITHERSPOON,
Lectures on Moral Philosophy, 1772

T H E distinguished historian of American literature, Moses Coit Tyler, writing at the end of the nineteenth century, made the following perceptive assessment of John Witherspoon's personality, character, and accomplishments during the American revolutionary era:

> Being perhaps equally apt for thought and for action, and having quite remarkable gifts as a preacher, debater, conversationist, politician, and man of affairs, happily he found himself, in the fulness of his ripened power, in a station of great dignity and prominence, near the centre of the new national life of America. . . .[1]

Tyler's judgment remains germane today, for Americans best remember the Reverend Dr. John Witherspoon (1723–1794) as president of the College of New Jersey (Princeton), as a signer of the Declaration of Independence, and as one of the founders of the American Presbyterian Church. But what Tyler did not emphasize is equally important; Witherspoon came to America in 1768 only after a long and distinguished career in Scotland as a minister, theologian, and ecclesiastical statesman in the Kirk. His public accomplishments as a Founding Father in church

ROGER J. FECHNER, Adrian College, Adrian, Michigan.

and state and his republican ideology during the American Revolution rested on the ethical and political ideas he adopted as a moral philosopher. The Scottish philosophical and theological underpinnings of Witherspoon's ethical and political thought are evident in his celebrated *Lectures on Moral Philosophy* (1772). His idea of America as a Godly and virtuous republic was formulated in his *Lectures* and was more fully developed in the sermons and speeches he delivered and in the political pamphlets and essays he wrote during the revolutionary era. An analysis of John Witherspoon's thought provides an excellent example of the international character of the Enlightenment and of the comparability of ideas on both sides of the Atlantic. Moreover, Witherspoon's works clearly delineate the intellectual linkage between Scotland and America as eighteenth-century cultural provinces of England. Finally, and most importantly, his moral philosophy lectures and revolutionary writings establish the strong connection between the republican ideology of American patriots and Scottish moral philosophy.[2]

President John Witherspoon delivered an annual series of lectures on moral philosophy to upper-class students as one of his several duties at the College of New Jersey. His lectures combined the two major components of his Scottish intellectual background, the ethical and political ideas of moral sense philosophy and the theological doctrines of Calvinism. Witherspoon's initiation into the ideas of the Scottish Enlightenment began at the University of Edinburgh, which he entered as an arts student in 1736. At Edinburgh Witherspoon studied physical science with Professor Colin McLaurin, Scotland's most famous Newtonian. He also studied Locke's empiricist epistemology under the tutelage of John Stevenson. In Professor John Pringle's moral philosophy course, Witherspoon read the moral and political works of the ancients, especially Aristotle and the Stoics, as well as the modern continental thinkers—Grotius, Pufendorf, and Heineccius—and the British theorists— Sidney, Harrington, and Molesworth. Most importantly, Witherspoon read Shaftesbury and Shaftesbury's most famous Scottish disciple, Francis Hutcheson.[3]

Francis Hutcheson (1694–1746), Presbyterian minister and University of Glasgow professor, was the leading moral philosopher and Real Whig political thinker in the early decades of the Scottish Enlightenment.[4] Hutcheson's intellectual influence was not limited to his homeland; his ideas were especially instrumental in shaping the philosophical and political thought of the American Enlightenment. His philosophy was critical in determining the direction of American philosophical development in the eighteenth century and beyond. Additionally, as a Jefferson scholar has recently shown, Hutcheson's moral and political ideas were central to the revolutionary thought of the author of the Declaration of Independence. And so it was with John Witherspoon, the leading academic Hutchesonian in the American Enlightenment and Revolution.[5]

Hutcheson was a social Newtonian. He sought to apply Sir Isaac Newton's scientific model to the analysis of man and society. His goal was to develop universal, empirical laws of individual and social behavior similar to Newton's laws of the physical universe. The historical record and the socioeconomic transformation of eighteenth-century Scotland furnished Hutcheson with the materials for his analysis. As a result of his intellectual endeavor, he and his fellow Scottish moral philosophers played a major role in establishing the theoretical foundations of the modern social sciences.[6]

Significantly for American thought and for John Witherspoon in particular, Hutcheson tried to make ethics an empirical inquiry. Building upon, but moving beyond Locke's epistemology and Shaftesbury's psychology, Hutcheson made moral science a field of social science. Although he did not believe the results of his empirical investigation of ethics would conflict with Christian doctrine but rather complement the teachings of Scripture and orthodox Calvinist theology, Hutcheson preferred to separate sacred and secular ethics. Accordingly, he divorced his study of moral philosophy from revelation and made it an empirical analysis of individual and social behavior. Hutcheson extended his inquiry beyond man to society and social institutions, including political institutions, and developed an empirical science of society. It was this rich and varied empirical style of analyzing moral and social ideas that he passed on to Witherspoon as well as other American and Scottish followers.[7]

Like Hutcheson, John Witherspoon's Scottish intellectual background was shaped by the reformed tradition in Protestant theology. Witherspoon began to formulate his religious beliefs as a child and boy under the direction of his father, the Reverend James Witherspoon. After completing his Arts degree in 1739, Witherspoon studied divinity at Edinburgh before entering the Kirk in 1743. He developed his theology in numerous sermons, treatises, and miscellaneous works during his Scottish ministry, which ended in 1768 when he left Scotland for America.

Witherspoon accepted the fundamental doctrines of John Calvin's *Institutes of the Christian Religion* (1536), as modified by the interpretations of the seventeenth-century covenant or federal theologians of

English and Scottish Calvinism, especially John Knox and Andrew
Melville, and as set forth in *The Westminster Confession of Faith*
(1647). In his sermons and in his two major treatises, *An Essay on
Justifieation* (1756) and *A Practical Treatise on Regeneration* (1764),
Witherspoon argued his version of orthodox reformed doctrines—the
absolute sovereignty of a righteous God controlling the universe, the
universal sin of mankind, the absolute necessity of Christ's suffering
and death as atonement for man's sin, regeneration through faith, and
the Westminster position on the dual covenants between God and man.
Reformed theologians had always emphasized the use of reason as an
aid to revelation in discovering God's purpose for man, and Witherspoon was typical of those eighteenth-century Scottish Evangelicals who
employed reason in defense of Christian revelation against the attacks of
philosophical skeptics. Witherspoon's theology was pragmatic in tone;
his writings stressed the moral applications of fundamental Calvinist
beliefs in the daily lives of his parishioners. Neither emotionalism, polite learning, nor elegant language characterized Witherspoon's sermons. Rather, he persuaded his listeners by the accuracy of his learning
and the force of his personal piety.

His staunch defense of theological orthodoxy and his forceful personality served Witherspoon well in ecclesiastical politics. Within a
short time after entering the ministry he became one of the leaders of
the Popular party, the orthodox faction of the Kirk. Their opponents,
the Moderates, espoused a theology that was basically in the Scottish
reformed tradition; they were the intellectual leaders of the new liberal
currents of thought that characterized the Scottish Enlightenment.
Hence their ministerial style was marked by polite learning and elegant
language in their sermons; by their participation in and support of the
arts, especially the theater; and by their social intercourse with the no-
bility. In the complex ecclesiastical politics that marked the eighteenth-
century history of the Church of Scotland, the Moderates allied
themselves socially and intellectually with the great patrons. Furthermore, the patrons—conservative, landed aristocrats—gained the power
in 1712 to chose candidates for church livings. The patronage law,
which reversed the revered tradition of Kirk government in which the
congregation chose their minister, was the major issue of contention between the Moderate and Popular parties in governance. Because of their
alliance with the patrons, the Moderates gained control of Kirk politics
in 1752 and dominated church government as well as the universities for
the remainder of the century. Except for Hutcheson, the Moderates
were Tories in their secular politics. They never accepted the principles
that justified the American Revolution—principles that Witherspoon

took directly from the Real Whig or Commonwealthman political tradition on through Hutcheson's moral philosophy.[8]

The Popular party, or High-Flyers as the Moderates derisively called them, fought vigorously against the Moderates' control of the Kirk. John Witherspoon and his fellow theological conservatives held fast to the traditional Scottish church governance system in which the entire congregation elected the clergy and elders, shared the authority over local Kirk affairs, and called the minister to a parish. Participation in such a mixed, representative system of church government—structured from the local Kirk session through the Presbytery and Synod to the General Assembly at the national level—afforded an excellent education in practical politics for Witherspoon, who was later to participate in the creation of a new, representative form of secular government across the Atlantic.

As the two clerical parties debated endlessly over doctrinal issues and ministerial appointments, Witherspoon served the Popular party with distinction in various church councils as an effective debater and author of stinging satires on the personal characteristics and theological beliefs of his moderate opponents. In his first and most effective satire, *Ecclesiastical Characteristics* (1753), he turned the elegant language and polite learning of the Moderates against them. Witherspoon characterized his foes as loose-living liberals who believed "All ecclesiastical persons, of whatever rank, whether principals of colleges, professors of divinity, ministers, or even probationers, that are suspected of heresy, are to be esteemed men of great genius, vast learning and uncommon worth; and are, by all means, to be supported and protected." Witherspoon also criticized his theologically liberal opponents for their desertion of orthodox doctrine, lack of personal piety, and open support of the stage.[9]

John Witherspoon's valiant defense of orthodox Calvinism by word and deed soon gained him numerous admirers at home and abroad. He received calls to several other parishes, all of which he refused. Finally after two years of difficult negotiations during which he rejected but then accepted a new and different call, the trustees of the College of New Jersey at Princeton elected Witherspoon their president. Although his Popular party was losing the struggle with the Moderates for control of the Kirk in the 1750s and 1760s, Witherspoon did not leave Scotland for America in 1768 because he was driven out by his enemies.[10] He went to New Jersey because he viewed the leadership of the Presbyterian college as an unparalleled opportunity to serve God and his fellowmen. Witherspoon's intellectual background in the moral and political ideas of the Scottish Enlightenment and in the theological doctrines of Scottish Calvinism were excellent preparation for his new challenges as college president and professor. His experience in ecclesiastical politics reinforced and gave meaning to the political philosophy he had learned from Francis Hutcheson. Thus it seems plausible to argue that the combination of Witherspoon's study of Scottish secular political theory and his involvement in Kirk politics led him not only to teach his Princeton students Hutcheson's version of Real Whig political thought, but it also inspired him to action as a republican ideologue and patriot during the American Revolution.

President John Witherspoon took up his new duties at the College of New Jersey with his accustomed energy. He raised funds, increased enrollment, and revised the curriculum along the lines of his Edinburgh training. Under his leadership Princeton prospered, and Witherspoon was soon recognized as one of the most respected college presidents in the colonies. His educational philosophy stressed the intimate union of piety and literature as the proper intellectual foundation for young gentlemen who were about to embark upon professional careers.[11]

Witherspoon lectured to Princetonians on a wide variety of topics including literature, eloquence, rhetoric, divinity, education, and history. But his most famous course of lectures was on moral philosophy. Like most eighteenth-century professors in colonial and revolutionary America, Witherspoon's moral philosophy was largely eclectic and derivative. It is not surprising that Witherspoon borrowed heavily from European and especially British moralists when composing his lectures; he had neither the experience in teaching nor the time for their preparation. But while Witherspoon took fragmentary bits of moral and political theory from a wide variety of thinkers, he owed a particular intellectual debt to Francis Hutcheson. A detailed comparison of the basic structure and key topics of Witherspoon's *Lectures on Moral Philosophy* and Hutcheson's major works, especially his *System of Moral Philosophy* (1755), reveals that Witherspoon organized his lectures on the same pattern and discussed the same issues as did Hutcheson. Upon closer inspection, it is clear that many of Witherspoon's writings are paraphrased or exact quotations of Hutcheson's language. Still, Witherspoon was not simply a slavish imitator of Hutcheson. For example, Witherspoon paid much more attention to Calvinist theological premises in his discussion of moral philosophy than did Hutcheson. He also allowed reason a much larger role in his analysis of the operation of the moral faculty or moral sense than did Hutcheson. Witherspoon's political theory laid greater stress on the social contract theory of the origins of society and government and on the consensual nature of the contractual relationships in domestic and civil society than did Hutcheson. Other differences in their thought will be considered in the following discussion.[12]

Lectures on Moral Philosophy lacks both originality and depth; it shows signs of having been hurriedly pieced together as a working text for Witherspoon's students. He realized all too well the rough and superficial character of the *Lectures*. Since his numerous college and public activities did not allow him time to revise them for publication, Witherspoon refused to permit their publication during his lifetime. Accordingly, the *Lectures* remained in student manuscript form until 1800, when they were first issued as part of his collected *Works*.[13] Still, the *Lectures* do have some positive attributes. They were carefully organized and brief enough for eighteenth-century undergraduates, boys in their teens, to absorb with relative ease. Moreover, Witherspoon wrote with a simple, clear style that commanded the reader's attention. Finally and significantly, the *Lectures on Moral Philosophy* conveyed the empirical flavor and methodology of Hutcheson's moral and political ideas in a form that could be readily understood by Princeton students. Given Witherspoon's forceful personality, his moral philosophy course must have made a deep impression on the intellectual growth of his students, many of whom became leaders in education, church, and state during the American Enlightenment, 1740–1815.

John Witherspoon's *Lectures on Moral Philosophy* were his attempt to synthesize the philosophical and theological ideas of his Scottish intellectual background into a comprehensive view of the relationships between God and man, man and society, ethics and politics. The *Lectures* made clear that Witherspoon relied more on his philosophy than he did on his theology. Witherspoon's moral philosophy revealed the fundamental tension between his philosophical and theological ideas, a tension that Witherspoon sought unsuccessfully to resolve. He usually followed the philosophical positions of Hutcheson, except when those positions conflicted with his orthodox Calvinist beliefs. In such instances Witherspoon either disregarded the conflict by simply asserting, not proving, that revealed knowledge agreed with reason or returned to Biblical precepts to prove his argument.[14]

In my analysis of Witherspoon's ethical thought, my primary focus will be on his major ideas—empiricism, man's nature, faculty psychology, the affections, moral sense or conscience, virtue, rights, and duties.

Witherspoon commenced his discussion of ethics by pointing out the supposed harmony between reason and revelation as the twin sources of man's knowledge. Employing the empirical model of New-

tonian physics, he followed Hutcheson's attempt to make ethics a
science of man. Thus he predicted: "Yet perhaps a time may come
when men, treating moral philosophy as Newton and his successors have
done natural, may arrive at greater precision." Since the principles of
moral duty and obligation were part of man's nature, Witherspoon held
that ethics was "that branch of Science which treats of the principles
and laws of Duty or Morals. It is called *Philosophy*, because it is an inquiry into the nature and grounds of moral obligation by reason, as
distinct from revelation." Witherspoon was critical of the attitude that
ethics should not be studied empirically, or that it should be grounded
only in revelation. For Witherspoon, Scripture and reason agreed on
what was true knowledge; hence religious belief had nothing to fear
from the inquiry of moral philosophy.[15]

In his search for the sources of moral duty, Witherspoon probed
human nature through observation and induction. Man was a com-
pound of body and soul or mind, and man's knowledge of the world
came from his external and internal senses. Witherspoon followed
Hutcheson's argument closely when he adopted his faculty theory of
psychology. Men ordered and interpreted their sensory experience with
certain fundamental operations or faculties of the mind that were basic
to all reasoning and common to all men. These faculties were the
understanding, the will, and the affections. Witherspoon concluded:
"These are not three qualities wholly distinct, as if they were three different beings, but different ways of exerting the same simple principle." Like his intellectual mentor, Witherspoon paid more attention to
evaluating the operations of the affections or emotions than he did to
the will or the understanding. He went beyond Hutcheson's discussion
of affections to include religious affections in his analysis.[16]

Witherspoon's consideration of internal sensation led him to conclude that man's noblest faculty was the moral sense. This was the
source of moral obligation or duty, for it enabled man to perceive the
nature of good and evil. For Witherspoon, the moral sense served to
harmonize his philosophical ideas with his theological beliefs. "The
moral sense is precisely the same thing with what, in scripture and common language we call conscience. It is the law which our Maker has written upon our hearts, and both intimates and enforces duty, previous to
all reasoning." The moral sense or conscience was the fundamental
principle of Witherspoon's moral theory as it had been for Hutcheson.
But for Witherspoon, unlike Hutcheson, reason played a role in
assisting the moral sense in determining moral truths. Furthermore,
Witherspoon's Calvinist assumptions led him to argue that even though
man's nature had been corrupted by sin, the moral sense allowed man

to lead a virtuous life. By treating the moral sense as a reflexive internal sense and as a faculty of the mind like conscience, Witherspoon created an intellectual bridge between his epistemological, psychological, and moral theories. And by appealing to God as the ultimate source of the moral sense or conscience, he believed he was establishing the complementary relationship between revelation and reason. The moral sense or conscience linked man directly to God in the moral dimension.[17]

Since the moral sense made man aware of virtue, Witherspoon examined several leading philosophical positions on the nature of virtue. He clearly favored Hutcheson's position and argued "that benevolence or public affection is virtue, and that a regard to the good of the whole is the standard of virtue. What is most remarkable about this scheme is, that it makes the sense of obligation in particular instances give way to supposed greater good." Witherspoon enumerated what he thought were the four basic positions on the foundation of virtue—the will of God, the reason and nature of things, the public interest, and the private good. Combining his empirical approach to ethics with reason and revelation, Witherspoon concluded:

> The result of the whole is, that we ought to take the rule of duty from conscience enlightened by reason, experience, and every way by which we can be supposed to learn the will of our Maker, and his intention in creating us as we are. And we ought to believe that it is as deeply founded as the nature of God himself, being a transcript of his moral excellence, and that it is productive of the greatest good.

He grouped the moral theories on the obligation of virtue into two kinds, interest and duty. Interest suggests that genuine felicity is achieved when men obey the obligation of virtue. Duty, however, requires that men obey a higher authority to whom they are responsible. Witherspoon chose the latter position. Moral sanctions, he argued, contained more than interest alone, "since it is plain that there is more in the obligation of virtue, than merely our greatest happiness. The moral sentiment itself implies that it is duty independent of happiness." Thus when man commits an evil deed, he has a powerful feeling of disapproval and penitence for his action. Not only is the individual responsible to himself in such a situation, but he is also responsible to his fellowman and to God.[18]

In his final four lectures on ethics, Witherspoon analyzed both sacred and secular virtues and elaborated upon the duties man owed God, his fellowmen, and himself. Since man had been the only earthly creature God had endowed with the powers of reason and moral sense, only man could discover and live by God's moral laws that governed the universe. God was the final source of morality, and man's specific social and self-regarding duties were derived from man's fundamental moral obligations to his Creator. Given his Calvinist presuppositions, Witherspoon could hardly have concluded otherwise. When he discussed the duties men owed God and their fellowmen, Witherspoon drew a direct connection between the two by making love its basic source. Love was divisible into four specific acts—esteem, gratitude, benevolence, and desire—and benevolence was the central motivation behind man's moral duty to his fellowmen. In his discussion of benevolence Witherspoon's reliance upon Hutcheson's ethics is clearly indicated by a basic distinction both moralists made between two kinds of benevolence: a "particular kind of affection" and a "calm and deliberate goodwill to all" that constituted the social dimension of benevolence. Like Hutcheson, Witherspoon concluded that the ultimate goal of the practice of benevolence was to promote the universal happiness of mankind; the utilitarian position of the greatest happiness for the greatest number.[19]

Witherspoon was concerned with how benevolence as a general virtue could be applied to man's specific obligations to others. Like Hutcheson, he agreed that rights played a crucial role in determining the moral relationships among men; duties and rights were the exact moral counterparts of each other. Unlike Hutcheson, who discussed rights only in terms of social and civil polity, John Witherspoon considered rights in both the ethics and politics sections of his *Lectures on Moral Philosophy*. Yet he did adopt the same categories as his Scottish mentor. The Princeton moralist held that rights could be divided into natural and acquired, perfect and imperfect, alienable and inalienable. Inalienable rights included man's rights to his ideas and opinions, to self-preservation, and to religious beliefs. And as a republican moralist of the American Enlightenment and Revolution, Witherspoon included liberty as an inalienable right.

In his last lecture on ethics, Witherspoon discussed the duties man owed himself. The self-regarding duties consisted of two types—self-government and self-interest. The duties of self-interest must not infringe on the rights of one's fellowmen. Witherspoon held that the truly virtuous citizen in a republican society would contribute to the public good by maintaining a just balance between his self-regarding duties and his duties to God and his fellowman.

His empirical exploration of man's nature not only led Witherspoon to posit ethics as a science of man, it brought him to the same conclusion espoused by moral philosophers from Aristotle to Hutcheson. Man was essentially a social animal; to realize his individual good, man must participate in the creation of the general good of society. Consequently, Witherspoon turned to the philosophical and practical issues of the science of society or politics in the second major section of his *Lectures on Moral Philosophy.*

After this extended discussion of ethics in nine moral philosophy lectures, John Witherspoon developed the fundamental principles of his republican political theory in three brief lectures on politics, domestic society, and civil society. The major topics he considered—the state of nature, the social contract, property, the power and forms of government, the right of revolution, and civil liberty—closely followed Hutcheson's earlier model, although there are critical junctures in his analysis where Witherspoon modified Hutcheson's ideas to conform to his own philosophical and theological assumptions. For Witherspoon, as it was for Hutcheson, the study of politics was simply the logical extension and application of individual moral rights and obligations to society. Witherspoon and Hutcheson defined politics broadly. Politics was not confined to a discussion of civil government; it included the widest possible range of social and political relationships. Furthermore, Witherspoon's discussion of politics was based upon his continuing attempt to synthesize philosophical and theological ideas. This was especially true of his identification of man's covenantal relationships with God and his fellowmen with the social contract theory of government.

Witherspoon's definition of politics assumed that the general laws or principles of society conformed to the moral law of the universe, and these laws or principles man could know through his moral sense or conscience. "Politics contain the principles of social union, and the rules of duty in a state of society. . . . Political law is the authority of any society stampt upon moral duty." Because he accepted a stronger version of the Calvinist premise of human depravity than did Hutcheson, Witherspoon was more of a political realist. Yet he was optimistic enough to believe that the moral sense—enlightened by reason, experience, and common sense—and assisted by God's grace would enable Americans to overcome the burden of original sin and create a Godly and virtuous republic.[20]

Typically, Witherspoon began his analysis of politics with the state of nature. He assumed a voluntaristic covenantal and contractual basis to society where men lived together on a consensual relationship. The voluntary consent of their association, according to Witherspoon, implied a state anterior to the social state, even though he acknowledged there were bitter controversies among political theorists on whether such a prior state had ever existed. Certainly there was no historical evidence of it. Witherspoon speculated that even if the state of nature had existed, it had not lasted long. His assumption that man was a social animal led him to conclude that man had always been in a social state. Witherspoon recognized a state of nature because "it is impossible to consider society as a voluntary union of particular persons without supposing those persons in a state somewhat different before this union took place—There are rights therefore belonging to the state of nature, different from those of a social state." It seemed to him that contemporary international relations between the states of Europe showed those nations were in a state of nature or natural liberty with one another.[21]

But was the state of nature a state of peace or a state of war? Witherspoon thought it a simple task to reconcile the opposing views of Hobbes and Hutcheson; they were both right. Hutcheson was right because "the principles of our nature lead to society . . . our happiness and the improvement of our powers are only to be had in society . . . is of the most undoubted certainty—and that in our nature, as it is the work of God, there is a real good-will and benevolence to others." Yet Witherspoon agreed with Hobbes's view of the state of nature as a state of war, but for different reasons. Unlike Hobbes, Witherspoon argued from his Calvinist presuppositions that mankind lived in the state of nature corrupted by Adam's fall. Man's corrupt nature led him to settle disputes by violence in the freedom and independence of the state of nature, uncontrolled by the moral law of God. Witherspoon believed that the only way man could guarantee his personal safety and security in such an environment was for man to create the social state by consent. "The inconveniences of the natural state are very many."[22]

Witherspoon reasoned that there were certain fundamental rights to life, liberty, and property that God granted man and that could not be taken from their original owner by force or given away through transfer. These natural, inalienable rights Witherspoon called perfect rights. These perfect rights, eight in number, were so much a part of natural liberty that man could resort to force to maintain them. Imperfect rights were rights that were the same in the state of natural liberty as they were in the social state. Such imperfect rights—gratitude, compassion, and mutual good offices—could not be secured by force, nor could man obtain them through law in a state of society. Presumably society conferred other rights, social or civil, upon its members.

Hutcheson had begun his analysis of society by a discussion of social institutions, but Witherspoon added an analysis of social contract theories. The social contract theory had a dual basis for him—the social compact ideas of John Locke and later British theorists and the federal or covenant ideas of Scottish Calvinism. "Society I would define to be an association or compact of any number of persons, to deliver up or abridge some part of their natural rights, in order to have the strength of the united body, to protect the remaining, and to bestow others." But how and where did society begin? Witherspoon contended that it began almost unnoticed with the family. But the individual eventually left the family and went out on his own. When these individuals established new societies, it was clear that they combined through a covenant or compact, either "an expressed or implied contract." Witherspoon was not bothered by the lack of historical evidence for such a contract; the origins of a social state evolved in imperceptible ways that were undetectable. He believed that when the members of a society decided that society was no longer protecting their rights, they were free to rebel or flee society altogether. This circumstance clearly showed that membership in society was based on voluntary consent. Accordingly, he concluded:

> From this view of society as a voluntary compact, results this principle, that men are originally and by nature equal, and consequently free. Liberty either cannot, or ought not to be given up in the social state—The end of the union should be the protection of liberty, as far as it is a blessing.

Reverting to his argument from reason, Witherspoon noted that "Reason teaches natural liberty." And he followed Hutcheson's utilitarian emphasis in ethics with the conclusion that "common utility recommends it."[23]

Witherspoon closed his discussion of society with a lengthy consideration of property rights and obligations. Man's right to property was created by God. History and revealed truth showed that God had made man the master of the lower animals and master of his own labors. Witherspoon defined private property as "every particular person's having a clear and exclusive right to a certain portion of the goods which serve for the support and conveniency of life." He thought that communal ownership of property existed only in imperfect societies. Furthermore, history showed that communal or subsistence property ownership had never worked in fully developed states except in ancient Sparta, which Witherspoon admitted had very unusual social arrangements. He thought communal ownership of property might work in small, voluntaristic societies based on religious principles, but it would last only ́as long as the morality of such societies was undefiled. Community property ownership was totally inappropriate for large, complex societies such as Great Britain or its American colonies. In such societies private property was absolutely necessary, because it was rooted in man's nature, established by reason, and essential to the public good. Witherspoon held that property arrangements in any society were a good measure of the society's morality. In a republican political society like America, a wide distribution of real property was necessary and essential for public utility because it promoted "industry . . . merit . . . charity, compassion, beneficience, &c."; and most importantly, it provided stimulus "to the active virtues, labor, ingenuity, bravery, patience, &c."—the self-regarding virtues of the Calvinist work ethic.[24]

Following Hutcheson's categories, Witherspoon examined the domestic social relationship of marriage, parents and children, and masters and servants. Throughout his discussion he emphasized the moral ties as well as the contractual rights and obligations that bound people together.

Witherspoon's final lecture on politics concerned civil society. Civil society was differentiated from domestic society as a voluntary association of a number of families in one state for their mutual benefit. Witherspoon's view of the origins of civil society was not an individualistic one. Rather, he emphasized the consensual basis of the family. Because Witherspoon failed to draw a careful distinction between the creation of society and the creation of civil society or government, his ideas on this critical issue are muddled. Still, the structuring of topics in his argument implied that he made this distinction. Once again he referred to the consensual basis of society in the social contract, which consisted of three major agreements:

> (1) The consent of every individual to live in, and be a member of that society. (2) A consent to some particular plan of government. (3) A mutual agreement between the subjects and rulers; of subjection on the one hand, of protection on the other—These are all implied in the union of every society, and they compleat the whole.

So powerful and binding was the social contract that Witherspoon could think of only one sound reason why the citizens of any society could break it. It was the moral right of people to resist bad government by overthrowing their government and creating a new civil society that would fulfill the original purpose of the social contract by guaranteeing them their natural rights. Such a crucial decision had to be approached with the greatest caution. Witherspoon's Calvinist assumptions about man's sinful nature were evident in his espousal of the right to revolution as were his experiences in the ecclesiastical politics of the eighteenth-century Kirk when he stated:

> But this is only when it becomes manifestly more advantageous to unsettle the government altogether, than to submit to tyranny. This resistance to the supreme power, however, is subverting society altogether, and is not to be attempted till the government is so corrupt as that anarchy and the uncertainty of a new settlement is preferable to the continuance as it is.

The right to resistance by members of society who were being denied justice was founded in the consensual nature of the civil compact. Who had the right to resistance, rebellion, and revolution? The mass of the people, the "large ignorant rabble" in Witherspoon's words.[25]

After dividing citizens into rulers and ruled, public officials and their subjects, Witherspoon enumerated the powers of government as legislation, taxation, jurisdiction, and representation. He then made a comparative analysis of the various forms of government. He considered the strengths and weaknesses, advantages and disadvantages of the classical forms—monarchy, aristocracy, and democracy. The fundamental problem, as he saw it, was to develop a governmental structure that was balanced; that would guarantee citizens protection of their rights while at the same time grant government the authority to rule. To achieve this end, Witherspoon would establish a government in which authority was divided, in other words, a mixed form of government like the Scottish Kirk—the kind Hutcheson recommended as the best form for a republican society. The role of government, an artificial creation, was to curb the selfish passions of man and to regulate the inevitable conflicts between men in society. Following the Newtonian model, Witherspoon supported a mixed form of representative government as the only form that would balance liberty and authority.

> Hence it appears that every good form of government must be complex, so that the one principle may check the other. It is of consequence to have as much virtue among the particular members of a community as possible; but it is folly to expect that a state should be upheld by integrity in all who have a share in managing it. They must be so balanced, that when every one draws to his own interest or inclination, there may be an over poise upon the whole.

To balance the contending forces in a mixed government, Witherspoon developed what he called a *"nexus imperii,"* a locus of authority to make the contending forces necessary to each other. To produce this *nexus imperii,* "some of the great essential rights of rulers must be divided and distributed among the different branches of the legislature." It is evident that when Witherspoon supported the *nexus imperii,* he rejected the British imperial system including the American colonies and replaced it with a republican system of balanced, mixed, and representative government. Other characteristics of this republican government included landed property in the hands of the rulers, a population that was not too large or too small, sovereign power lodged in the people, and dominion by consent.[26]

Witherspoon ended his discussion of politics with an analysis of the moral implications of his political ideas. Through a process of elimination, he sought an answer to the question: "What is the value and advantage of civil liberty?" He replied that civil liberty was not essential to virtuous conduct or personal liberty.

> What then is the advantage of civil liberty? I suppose it chiefly consists in its tendency to put in motion all the human powers. Therefore it promotes industry, and in this respect happiness— produces every latent quality, and improves the mind.—Liberty is the nurse of riches, literature and heroism.[27]

The significance of Witherspoon's lectures on politics was that they expressed the ideology of the British Commonwealth tradition for which Francis Hutcheson had been the most important eighteenth-century Scottish spokesman. It was this same political ideology that was circulating among American radicals in the political pamphlets of the revolutionary era.[28] Witherspoon's Calvinist belief in man's corruption—his political realism—combined with his optimism that man could be enlightened through the moral sense or conscience assisted by reason, experience, and common sense laid the moral foundations for his republicanism. And his analysis of the state of nature, the social contract, property, mixed government, the right of revolution, and the moral advantages of civil liberty summarized the political ideas of the American Enlightenment and Revolution.

John Witherspoon was not content to deal in abstractions. This practical bent led him to put his political theory into political practice. The moral and political ideas of his *Lectures on Moral Philosophy* were the basis for Witherspoon's participation in the American Revolution. Furthermore, his republican ideology—expressed in the pamphlets, sermons, and speeches he wrote during the revolutionary era—were extensions of his moral philosophy.

During the early 1770s the movement by the American colonies for independence gained strength with every passing year. Initially, John Witherspoon was hesitant about participating in secular politics because of his belief that ministers should not meddle in civil affairs.[29] But several developments in his life and thought led him to join the revolutionary struggle. His belief that George III and his ministers were trampling on the rights of Americans as British citizens was strongly reminiscent of his battle in Scotland to guarantee congregations the right to choose their own pastors. His travels about the American countryside soon after his arrival in Princeton also played a role in his Americanization, as did the growing patriotism of the students at Nassau Hall. But most importantly, his adherence to the moral and political ideas of the Scottish Enlightenment and the theological doctrines of Scottish Calvinism persuaded him that the American Revolution was intellectually and morally right. Thus his belief that useful service to God and to one's fellowmen was everyone's duty and his unbending opposition to tyranny in either church or state determined Witherspoon to become a patriot.

At first he was cautious about playing an active part in politics and did not participate in local politics until July, 1774, when he joined Somerset County's committee of correspondence. By mid-1776 he had become the leading New Jersey advocate for independence. In June he was instrumental in the action of the New Jersey Provincial Congress that removed the royal governor, William Franklin, from office. Witherspoon was elected as a delegate to the Second Continental Congress and arrived in Philadelphia in time to vote for independence. During the war he served with distinction on important committees of the revolutionary government. Witherspoon left national politics in 1782, but later he served briefly in the New Jersey State Assembly and the New Jersey Convention that ratified the Federal Constitution of 1787. He was also instrumental in founding the American Presbyterian Church.

Witherspoon's participation in the American Revolution was not limited to political action. He applied the ethical and political ideas of his *Lectures on Moral Philosophy* to the revolutionary crisis. Witherspoon's development as a republican ideologue is clear in the numerous pamphlets, sermons, and speeches he wrote in the 1770s and 1780s. Witherspoon's synthesis of Calvinist theology and Scottish philosophy prompted his emphasis of several of the most significant republican ideas.[30] Revolutionary events clarified his political thought and heightened his fervor for the cause. Thus the development of his political ideology mirrored his increased political participation.

His political writings of the early 1770s drew a sharp contrast between British and American society. Initially, he thought the imperial crisis derived from British ignorance of America. As he observed Britain's actions, Witherspoon became convinced that British society was more corrupt than the virtuous American society. Although he praised Britain's constitutional arrangement, as did most American and European thinkers, Witherspoon contended that increased wealth had loosened bad passions and debased British society and government. Such corruption had encouraged Parliament's thirst for greed and power. By the summer of 1774 Witherspoon had come to the conclusion in his "Thoughts on American Liberty" that British suppression of the rights of Americans was a conspiracy against liberty.[31]

Witherspoon held that America had developed a new culture—a different society—a product of European ideas and the American environment. It was a republic whose fundamental characteristics were public-spiritedness, freedom, and happiness. The American provinces had governments founded on social compacts. And in America the people were the sovereign authority. Furthermore, history, experience, and reason all proved that only a virtuous society could be a free society. He prophesied that America would become a beacon light for liberty. "I look upon the cause of America at present to be a matter of truly inexpressible moment. The state of the human race through a great part of the globe for ages to come, depends upon it."[32]

By May of 1776 he concluded that Americans had to be freed from British imperial control before they too were corrupted. In his most famous political sermon of the revolution, "The Dominion of Providence Over the Passions of Men," Witherspoon applied his Calvinist assumptions to his republican ideology. American independence was the handiwork of a Providential God, watching over and rewarding His people for their piety and virtue. With God on their side, Americans would win their struggle with Britain. The key to success would be their ability to keep the "impetuous and disorderly passions . . . subject to the dominion of Jehovah."[33]

After the Declaration of Independence, as Americans fought their War of Independence and went about the business of founding republican state governments, John Witherspoon continued his emphasis on moral philosophy. As he had in his *Lectures,* he stressed the reciprocal relationship between government and citizens. Not only did a virtuous people make government good, but good government made people virtuous. Witherspoon continued to clarify the specific attributes he believed American republican governments should possess. Governments should be representative—mixed governments with checks and balances built into their structures so that one branch could not gain control over the others. Political power belonged in the hands of those citizens who owned real property, and since land was so widely held by Americans, Witherspoon envisioned a society in which the majority of the people would actively participate in public affairs. Although he required that a legislator be a person of high intellectual merit and social standing, Witherspoon warned that too much political power corrupted men. Accordingly, legislators should be limited to short terms of office and should be elected by secret ballot.

During the 1780s, with the state governments established as republics and the Confederation attempting to cope with the numerous problems of national government, Witherspoon's outlook about the future of the new nation was optimistic. Once again this Princeton moral philosopher reaffirmed the ethical qualities he believed would keep America a Godly and virtuous republic. The future greatness of America would be based upon the preservation of civil and religious liberty, freedom, and truth. Furthermore, America's material prosperity would be the reward of industry and sobriety. To the end of his life John Witherspoon was confident that despite man's depravity and uncontrolled passions, "He who makes a people *virtuous,* makes them *invincible.*" Thus Witherspoon concluded that God would continue to bless Americans with prosperity, civil liberty, and happiness if they would remain a Godly and virtuous people.[34]

After his retirement from national public life in 1782, John Witherspoon returned to his presidential duties at Princeton. Through his developing ideology and actions during the American Revolution, the Presbyterian minister, moral philosopher, and college president became a republican ideologue and radical patriot. It was a transformation wholly characteristic of the age. The ultimate significance of John Witherspoon's *Lectures on Moral Philosophy* and his revolutionary writings was that they summarized the ethical and political ideas of the American Enlightenment and vindicated the goals of the American Revolution. Witherspoon's America was truly a Godly and virtuous republic.

2

Horace Bushnell: Gentleman Theologian

HOWARD A. BARNES

ALTHOUGH Horace Bushnell (1802–1876), American theologian and intellectual, has not suffered from historical neglect, a satisfactory study of his life and thought has yet to be published. Several reasons account for this. Bushnell scholars have failed to present a realistic picture of the man because of personal bias, narrow focus, and the complex, changing nature of Bushnell's thought.[1] Most important of all is the lack of social theory to place him within his social milieu. This chapter is part of a study in progress that seeks to present a comprehensive view of Bushnell's career. The social dimension is provided by Professor Stow Persons's mass theory. This theory is most relevant to Bushnell's explicit social statements and allusions, but it also illuminates certain aspects of his theology, the topic of this chapter.

According to mass theory, colonial America was dominated by an upper gentry class that filled all major leadership roles. But during and after the Revolution the class system weakened because of popular demands for legal and social equality, high geographical mobility, and slow but steady social mobility.[2] By the age of Jacksonian Democracy the society was still stratified but the divisions were so porous and ambiguous that mass is a more accurate characterization than class. The exception to this generalization as always was the Negro slave who was the victim of a caste system. That the masses were coming into their own in the nineteenth century is implicitly affirmed by such terms as mass democracy, mass production, mass transportation, and the mass media,

HOWARD A. BARNES, Winston-Salem State University, Winston-Salem, North Carolina. The author wishes to express his appreciation to the Consortium for Research Training, Greensboro, North Carolina, for a grant that made an earlier version of this chapter possible.

which truckled to the ever more literate masses and their shifting tastes and fads.[3]

Because mass society families had fewer exclusive benefits to preserve and perpetuate for their members, the nuclear family gradually replaced the extended family that was so characteristic of class and caste societies. Set relatively free and equal, individuals might have experienced severe anxiety because failure was attributed to personal inadequacy, not the constraints of class and caste.[4]

Probably the best known nineteenth-century commentary on American mass society was by Alexis de Tocqueville who concluded in *Democracy in America* that general standards of religion and morality were the chief means of stability in a society that places sovereignty in the masses. He warned that popular sovereignty might lead to excessive conformity and the debasement of excellence, and pave the way for demagogues who would play on mass fears and prejudices.[5]

In mass societies leadership is provided not by a unified upper class but by separate elites.[6] Each social activity generates its own elite, the members of which must function, that is, perform in a superlative manner to retain elite status. For instance, a permanently injured member of the sports elite loses his status because he can no longer perform in a superlative manner. Like mountain peaks of varying visibility, elites rise above the anonymous masses. Of importance for this study are the nineteenth-century political elite, the economic elite (also called the socioeconomic elite because they were the style setters, or as their detractors often called them, fashionists), and the cultural-intellectual elite. The last not only provided artistic and intellectual leadership, but were committed to high ethical and moral standards—the gentility they had inherited from the old colonial gentry class. It should be emphasized that gentility, or as the gentry often called it, moral character, was the one common characteristic of elites, whose incomes, politics, and ideologies varied widely. Before the Civil War there was considerable overlapping of elites, and gentry individuals could be found among the political and economic elites. But as the nineteenth century progressed the overly refined sensibilities of the gentlemen gradually incapacitated them for leadership of America's masses, and from a growing sense of alienation and impotence they voiced their stern disapproval of the ungentlemanly political and economic elites. Early in the twentieth century the gentry elite disintegrated. While this represented something of a liberation, it also deprived the intellectual of a social bond with his community.[7]

From the perspective of mass theory Horace Bushnell distinctly appears as a member of the gentry elite. Clearly, his most fundamental values involved an ideal society of ladies and gentlemen of moral character. Special motifs included intense nationalism and an organic theory of the family, church, and state.[8] Social relations are not intimately related to abstract thought, but mass theory, together with an accent on development and change in Bushnell's thought, does throw his theology into higher relief. I contend that Bushnell passed through three phases: naturalism, soft dualism, and hard dualism. In the first he saw essentially good humans progressing under a benign God to ever higher levels of felicity. He stressed reason, nature, and the development of genteel moral character. In the second phase Bushnell completed a dualistic world view that rationalized his liberal comprehensive methodology. With increasing ill health, public criticism, the trauma of Civil War, and the decline of the gentry elite, Bushnell moved into a harder, more Calvinistic version of the dualism that qualified the natural development of a moral and religious character with supernatural intervention.

Bushnell's religious growth began in a western Connecticut farm home where formerly Methodist and Episcopalian parents took their six children to the nearby Congregational Church but at home softened the stern Calvinism with warm Christian nurture. Dotha Bushnell dedicated her first born, Horace, to the ministry, and he dutifully joined the church as a social thing. In 1823 he entered Yale College where his religious faith fell victim to a cold rationalism, and after graduation Bushnell briefly tried teaching and journalism before returning to Yale as a law student. He became a tutor, providing instruction, guidance, and discipline for underclassmen. Bushnell was eminently successful; his young charges literally sat at his feet. Then a revival swept the college and placed the young rationalist in a quandary. The revival preachers demanded conversion and most of Bushnell's followers waited to see what he would do. For some time he resisted the evangelicals. Finally he decided that his own moral character and the welfare of his students required conversion. Moreover, he enrolled in Yale Divinity School as his mother had urged all along.[9]

That Bushnell had accepted the norms of gentility is apparent in his farewell address to his students, whom he advised to aim for "perfection of character," which consisted of intelligence and "good manners, habits and principles." These attributes were essential because "there is a difference between a gentleman and an educated brute."

Bushnell admitted that his theology consisted only of a belief in "the immortality of the human mind" and "accountability." Although he had much to learn, he had intelligence and a gentleman's morality.[10]

While revivals fired the emotions of the masses, intellectuals struggled with theological intricacies. Bushnell's Yale professors and others looked for an intermediate position between orthodox Calvinists who stressed God's sovereignty and man's depravity and the schismatic Unitarians with their benign God and wholesome humanity. For instance, Yale professor Nathaniel W. Taylor declared that depravity was man's free choice of some object rather than God as his chief good, and it was man's nature that he would sin "in all appropriate circumstances." The New Haven school employed governmental terms, a prevailing interest of the day. God became a constitutional monarch ruling through established laws. Lyman Beecher defined moral government as *"the influence of law upon accountable creatures.* It includes a lawgiver, accountable subjects, and laws intelligibly revealed, and maintained by rewards and punishments." Thus individual moral character is in harmony with God's universe. Although committed to morality, Calvinistic conservatives could not compromise God's sovereignty, and icily polite letters, articles, pamphlets, and books agitated the theological environment. Gardner Spring, conservative (Old School) minister of the Brick Presbyterian Church in New York City, for example, wrote that infants were sinners from the very moment of their creation, and there was no recourse but to wait for the decision of an inscrutable God.[11]

Years later Bushnell averred that he had joined no theological school but had gradually developed a comprehensive method designed to incorporate the essentials of all sides. This proved useful at his first and only ministerial position, Hartford's North Church (Congregational) where in 1833 he found himself "daintily inserted between an acid and an alkali," meaning conservatives and liberals. An early sermon exemplified the comprehensive technique. The minister emphasized that humans possessed no natural ability to achieve holiness. "If we speak on natural ability to do good, a soul has no more natural ability to maintain the state of perfect goodness, than a tree to grow without light, or heat, or moisture." Like all natural things, man is dependent on God's will. Bushnell's version of regeneration is virtually synonymous with natural progress. The references to depravity serve as verbal tranquilizers for the orthodox. A few conservatives left North Church, and Deacon Seth Terry expostulated with his pastor, gravely informing him that he would tell a child "that he was all the time sinning and rebelling and that he must yield himself to God as a sacrifice, and that nothing short of that will avail." But the young minister's naturalistic orientation corresponded with the views of most of his members. Gaining confidence, he urged them to emulate God, who had worked with infinite "patience of detail" to set the universe moving under natural laws. "The importance of living to God in ordinary and small things is seen in the fact that character, which is the end of religion, is in its very nature a growth."[12]

During this early period Bushnell closely associated God, man, and nature. He saw man progressing under a benevolent God to ever higher levels of individual and social perfection. He would not say, with Leibnitz, that he lived in the "best of all possible worlds," but he did believe that the United States held God's special mandate to develop an organic society of ladies and gentlemen that would be a model for the world. The only times that Bushnell spoke distinctly of human depravity, he attacked the political and socioeconomic elites for their ungentlemanly behavior that hindered the development of individual character and endangered social stability and the Union itself.

The first of Bushnell's moral uses sermons appeared in the 1840s. Employing a lively imagination, he showed how God had designed nature to aid moral development. "The Great Time Keeper" had deliberately adjusted the cycles of the universe to impress each human with the necessity of constantly tending to his character. "The sun returns to his place, and says to all that live—I have given you now another year. The conscience hears his report, and says—what now have I done with this year?" God made the sea expressly to expediate human progress, and he sends stormy Sundays to invigorate and spur man on to greater things. In a more somber period Bushnell republished the sermon on the sea with some new essays as *Moral Uses of Dark Things.* But the early sermons on God's design in nature might appropriately be called "Moral Uses of Bright Things."[13]

Not surprisingly, Bushnell's liberal outlook included an ecumenical strain that was overshadowed by his somewhat aggressive personality. He frequently employed invective for effect and played upon popular prejudices. In 1843 Anglican Bishop Brownell of Connecticut delivered an address entitled "Errors of the Times," and Bushnell responded with an article that positioned him momentarily on the side of the revivalists, an awkward position for the gentleman. But he felt compelled to answer Brownell's allegations that the Congregational Church overemphasized individualism, denied infant baptism as a regenerating sacrament, and was outside apostolic succession. The last charge was quickly disposed of, and Bushnell's call for freedom of conscience falls in the tradition of John Milton and John Stuart Mill. On baptism,

Bushnell was forced to admit that the Bishop had "hit his mark," although he maintained that he personally would never neglect the nurture of children while waiting for God to move.[14]

Following his first signs of tuberculosis in 1845 Bushnell's church gave him an European vacation, and after visiting the Vatican the intrepid minister published a letter to Pope Gregory XVI in which he variously appeared indignant, satirical, sanctimonious, and munificent. He charged that Italian religious-civil government, with its "ambitious and greedy priesthood," retarded material progress, weakened the family institution, and ruined individual character. A promiscuous mix of anti-Catholic cliches masked the general thrust of the argument which was toward reason, truth, and freedom. Bushnell admitted that Protestantism was less than perfect, but with intellectual freedom truth would soon triumph.

> If it be uncomfortable to us all, still let it go on. If in this universal interfusion Protestantism is dissolved by Romanism, and this again by Protestantism, then, if it please God, let them dissolve, and it may be they will crystallize together. I will dare to trust anything to truth.[15]

Never much of a joiner, Bushnell did throw himself into organizing and promoting the Protestant League, which became the Christian Alliance. He envisioned a great coalescing of Protestants and liberal Catholics in Europe and America that would force Rome to modify its authoritarianism. He lectured, wrote letters, and issued public statements, but it came to nothing. In America conservative Congregationalists and Presbyterians were unhappy rubbing shoulders with Unitarians. Episcopalians and Dissenters in England looked askance at each other, and the Papacy refused to collapse (although Bushnell claimed it was weaker in Rome than Cincinnati).[16]

Bushnell drew his first serious criticism when he delivered an oration entitled, "A Discourse on the Moral Tendencies and Results of Human History," before the Yale Alumni Association. A scholarly audience provided him with an opportunity to delineate his monistic world view, an example of nineteenth-century natural progress with Hegelian overtones. Few persons can have helped noticing, he said, a universal law which is simply, "What is physical first, what is moral afterward." Through human language, which is based on natural things and actions, "the physical world takes a second and higher existence . . . in the empire of thought." Even religion begins with physical demonstrations like sacrifices, priesthoods, and idols, "but in the later ages God is a spirit; religion takes a character of intellectual simplicity and enthrones itself in the summits of the reason.'' With a nod to the conservatives, Bushnell denied that his was a philosophy of ''mere natural progress,'' because it included ''the world with all God's supernatural working, that of his Providence, that of his Spirit, all Christianity in fact included in it.'' He rhapsodized about the future when liberty and equality would come into their own; politics, ceasing to be synonymous with cunning, would become rational and moral; and war would be no more. Like Emerson, he asserted that no one was ''ever inspired through his memory. The eye of genius is not behind.'' Implacable conservatives are like ''owls flying toward the dawn and screaming, with dazzled eyes, that light should invade their prescriptive and congenial darkness.''[17]

This was too much for Benet Tyler of the conservative Theological Institute of Connecticut who, under the pseudonym of Catholicus, pounced upon Bushnell's address as full of ''Rationalistic, Socinian and Infidel'' tendencies. Tyler charged that it smacked dangerously of the ideas of David Hume, Ralph Waldo Emerson, and Theodore Parker. (Bushnell had, in fact, recently spent an evening going ''over the whole ground of theology'' with Parker.) Tyler complained bitterly about Bushnell's romance with naturalism, philosophy, and progress, and also about his flippant attitude toward the Holy Scriptures. He inquired if Bushnell preached to his flock thusly: ''Have you a double character, a Christian Teacher, and an infidel Philosopher?'' In a crisp reply to Tyler in the *Religious Herald* on December 20, 1843, Bushnell commented that he was not frightened because one of the ''ecclesiastical owls'' had lighted upon him.[18]

Bushnell did not have a split personality, but he was greatly interested in the formation of character. The series of articles that culminated in his famous *Christian Nurture* began in 1838 when the still not solidly established minister cautiously dissented from revivalism. He criticized the dualism that pictured the comings and goings of a ''desultory'' God. The proper view was the ''simple doctrine of God's omnipresence.'' Not that God's spiritual agency was always uniform, for like the weather and seasons, ''God's works and agencies necessarily involve variety and change,'' designed to ''produce character'' in His people. The gentleman objected to ''the artificial firework, the extraordinary, combined jump and stir'' of revivals, and asserted that religion ''must come to pass naturally, or emerge as a natural crisis of the ordinary if it is to have any consequence.[19]

In 1844 Bushnell presented his organic theory of the family, church, and state. Greatly impressed with the physical and social mobility, the rapid expansion, flux, and change of America's burgeoning mass society, with its corresponding individualism, he felt compelled to redress the balance. He considered excessive social ferment, including the excitement of revivals, as detrimental to individual character and conducive to a dangerous centrifugality that could tear asunder the nation.

To the family belonged the primary responsibility for producing stable citizens of moral character. He commented:

> . . . if we narrowly examine the relation of parent and child, we shall not fail to discover something like a law of organic connection as makes it easy to believe, and natural to expect, that the faith of the one will be propagated in the other. Perhaps I should rather say, such a connection as induces the conviction that the character of one is actually included in that of the other, as a seed is formed in the capsule; and being there matured, by a nutriment derived from the stem, is gradually separated from it.[20]

The child begins life with a tabula rasa conscience—as a "mere passive lump"—and Bushnell affirms that God includes infants "in the womb of parental culture, and pledges himself to them and their parents, in such a way, as to offer the presumption, that they may grow up in love with all goodness, and remember no definite time when they became subjects of Christian Principle."[21]

Some members of Bushnell's ministerial association requested that he discuss the topic with them, whereupon he delivered two discourses that were published by the Massachusetts Sabbath Society. Then Bushnell's old nemesis, Benet Tyler, struck again, publishing a letter in East Windsor Hill that caused the society's immediate suppression of the book. Undaunted, Bushnell added his two earlier articles and two new sermons as well as a long "Argument" to the discourse and published them as *Views of Christian Nurture and of Subjects Adjacent Thereto* (1847).

Bushnell clearly had shifted the responsibility for the salvation of coming generations from God to the American home. God still reigned, but the gentleman had transformed His lightning bolt into a benevolent glow. And Benet Tyler knew it. Again, as in 1843, he was concerned with tendencies that he considered dangerous to the souls of men. Tyler had little objection to Bushnell's practical Christian nurture; the theory was what bothered him. Parents should love and care for their children to the best of their abilities, but they must never presume that God will do anything in return. A blithe assumption that justification naturally accompanies nurture is a colossal error.

In his "Argument" Bushnell accused Tyler of fourteen years of harassment and dismissed his latest attack as being dependent "on a certain theory of depravity and regeneration that was debated . . . some fifteen years ago, and, as I believe, forever exploded." He refused to be intimidated by the charge that he was virtually a Unitarian and stated that it was his method "to reach after the most comprehensive form of truth possible; to see how far I can dissolve into unity, in views I present, the conflicting opinions by which men are divided."[22]

Almost all Bushnell scholars, taking their cue from his daughter's biography, have noted that 1848 was a pivotal year. He reached an intellectual and emotional peak that revolved around his search for a more satisfying world view that could be used to unify warring sects and, incidentally, make a greater name for himself.[23] Unity had always been a fundamental goal, whether it related to the family, church, or nation. He longed for a close-knit society of ladies and gentlemen.

Early in 1848 he published a philosophical yet practical guide to the formation of an enlightened character. It was to apply to adults as his Christian nurture work had applied to children. Taking Victor Cousin's three world views—fairly typical of nineteenth-century progress philosophy—as a key, Bushnell asserted that in a controvesy truth always lay between the extremes of "abstract infinity" and the "empirical finite." The third and middle view was neither complacent like liberalism nor vacuous like neutrality; rather it involved a positive search for the germ of truth in disparate human ideas and characteristics. Bushnell ran through a long list of polarities, including charity and censoriousness, faith and reason, and prudence and emotion. "The more numerous and repugnant the extremes of character, excepting those which are sinful, you are able to unite in one comprehensive and harmonious whole, the more finished and complete your character will be." The article indicates that Bushnell had adopted a dualistic methodology. However, ambiguity marked his metaphysics because it was not clear if he had retained his naturalistic monism or now saw the universe as divided into infinite-supernatural and finite-natural realms.[24]

The minister's feverish search climaxed one cold February night in 1848. In the morning when his wife asked what he had seen, he replied, "the gospel." He immediately delivered a sermon entitled "Christ the Form of the Soul." He began: "What form is to body, character is to spirit," and explained that the human soul shows its objective form in character. By analogy, Christ is the finite form of infinite God. Sin spoiled the human soul, alienating man from God, who revealed Him-

self in Christ so that those who believe may begin the regeneration process.[25]

This dualism balances spiritual and natural realms. The human
soul belongs with God in the spiritual half of the universe, while Man's
physical body is part of nature. The fall caused God to emanate Christ
the Savior to redeem lost souls. Ability balances depravity. Bushnell
clearly states that sin inevitably deforms souls, but human reason reveals
the path, through Christ, to salvation. The undertaking represents a
joint effort of God and man and provides a vital role for the God-man,
Christ.

As if by providence Bushnell received invitations to lecture at Harvard, Yale, and Andover. Although his daughter indicated this was
purely coincidental, Bushnell probably had a hand in making arrangements to be heard by leading Congregationalists and Unitarians. The
resulting discourses, with an introductory language theory, were published as *God in Christ* (1848). This book has long provided a lush field
for scholarly exegetes. Mary Bushnell Cheny asserted that it was the
"key . . . to the whole scheme of his thought," and Bushnell himself
later wrote that it was "the setoff, so to speak, of all that I have
done."[26]

The introductory language dissertation presents the framework of
the new dualism. Language arose, he wrote, when humans named
things and actions in the natural world. When they wanted to express
their subjective thoughts or emotions it was necessary to use these same
words, or their derivatives. Thus language has two spheres: a natural
one where words stand for things and actions, and an intellectual and
spiritual one where the same words are used as signs or analogies to carry
subjective thoughts and communicate them to others. Illustrations of
the dual use of words include: "spirit," which originally meant breath
or air in motion; "religion," from *re* and *ligo,* to bind back; "faith,"
from a tie or ligature; and "heart," of which the two meanings are ob-
vious.[27]

Since language was not entirely exact in the natural realm—words
refer only to categories, not individuals—how could it be exact in the
intellectual or spiritual derivative? This was the main point: language
was a nebulous and untrustworthy means of ascertaining and imparting
spiritual truths. Words, imperfect carriers of ideas, cannot literally con-
vey a thought from one mind to another, but are merely hints, images,
analogies for communication. Not only are words inexact, but

> they always affirm something which is false, or contrary to the
> truth intended. They impute *form* to that which is really out of
> form. They are related to the truth, only as form to spirit—earthen

vessels in which the truth is borne, but always offering their mere pottery as being the truth itself.[28]

Thus far the theory smacks of naturalism or epiphenomenalism. If religious ideas are based on words that are only natural, are the ideas only natural too? Bushnell avoids this by positing a "Divine Logos" that "weaves into nature types or images that have an inscrutable relation to mind and thought." Theologians must engage in a semiinstitutional search through all language—Biblical, traditional, and current—for the hidden truth or Logos. Bushnell held that a great deal of strife and confusion had resulted from failing to understand the nature of language. Literalists render themselves miserable, quarrelsome, and unproductive. By contrast, those like Coleridge and Goethe successfully mine nature's spiritual gold. "Poets, then, are the true metaphysicians, and if there be any complete science of man to come, they must bring it." As statements of absolute truth, creeds are worthless. However, as a sly dig at the Unitarians, Bushnell remarked that he could not see why they held creeds in such repugnance; personally, he could accept about as many as came his way, melt them down, and extract their elements of truth.[29]

Bushnell did not suddenly discover the language theory; he had been interested in it and its mystical, romantic ramifications since his college days. But in 1848 it became the foundation of his system, as a theory of knowledge and, more particularly, as it pertained to the Trinity concept and the role of Christ. Bushnell argued that Christ was truly divine, different in kind from man, while at the same time the finite expression of infinite God. The Godhead is a unity (three interior persons mock the reason) that emanates three forms—the Logos of the language theory. God the Father, Son, and Holy Spirit are forms of God, absolutely essential for human salvation. Bushnell hoped to please the orthodox with his argument for the divinity of Christ and the Unitarians by insisting on the oneness of God. He failed to maintain a balance because the logic of the language theory tended to reduce Christ to nature. Words, based on natural things, carry spiritual meanings. Just so, Christ is the natural vehicle for divine truth. To preserve Christ's holiness, Bushnell abandoned logic (a characteristic of his when reason proved inadequate) and produced an effusion of colorful, emotional rhetoric, praising imagination while disparaging speculation about the person of Jesus. He wanted Christians simply to accept Christ, the Father, and the Holy Spirit as supreme expressions of God.

Thus we have three persons, or impersonations, all existing under finite conditions or conceptions. They are relatives, and, in that view are not infinites; for relative infinites are impossible. And yet, taken representatively, they are each and all, infinites; because they stand for, and express the Infinite, Absolute Jehovah.[30]

He called his concept an instrumental Trinity because of its effectiveness in making an infinite God understandable without any reduction in His majesty.

Turning to Christ's Atonement on the cross Bushnell again attempted to mollify conservatives by acknowledging the absolute necessity of God in Christ on the cross. "Reason as we may about human depravity, apologize for men, or justify them as we may, they certainly do not justify themselves." Bushnell classified the Old Testament institution of sacrifice and related words like curse, blood, and wrath, so dear to conservatives, with the objective or ritualistic side of Christianity. These altar forms, like other natural things, are the vehicles for subjective spiritual verities. Without these natural, but Logos-carrying, acts and words, humans would have had no way of comprehending and expressing the spiritual meaning of the Atonement—the ultimate expression of God's love and law. "Thus, instead of a religion before the eyes, we now have one set up in language before the mind's eye."[31]

The language dissertation and the first two discourses are complex and uneven. The explanation given here reveals little more than the dualistic skeleton that rationalized a genteel mysticism while attempting to combine conservative and liberal views of the Trinity and Atonement. Bushnell began the third and concluding discourse with a long harangue against mere natural reason, speculation, philosophy, theology, logic, and other terms associated with ratiocination. He employed a variation of the dualism to balance objective, natural reason with a subjective faith side. According to the language theory, spiritual truths arose only from natural things, but Bushnell circumvented nature's Logos-carrying forms with direct inspirations. He celebrated the inner light, religion of the heart, and other visions. He even espoused a kind of antinomianism: those truly in the spirit could judge those not similarly blessed. But the gentleman still had little use for the "rawness and passion" of revivals.[32]

Bushnell frequently misled readers through overemphasis. In this instance he merely wanted to negate dogmatic theology and balance reason with inspiration. Jonathan Edwards had explained over one hundred years earlier:

> There is a difference between having an opinion that God is holy and gracious, and having a sense of the liveliness and beauty of

that holiness and grace. There is a difference between having a rational judgment that honey is sweet, and having a sense of its sweetness.[33]

Bushnell also used poor judgment in closing his book with an attack on the Calvinists who held the "penal substitution" view of the Atonement, making Christ a "paymaster," who suffered God's wrath in man's stead. He charged that the conservatives also exaggerated human depravity. "They come before God in confessions of sin, so extravagant . . . that if a fellow man were to charge upon them what they confess, they would be mortally offended."[34]

God in Christ raised quite a storm in Congregationalism. Although Bushnell was not without supporters, the conservatives seized the initiative. One charged:

> He mixes up in his volume the most incongruous materials. He is rationalist, mystic, pantheist, Christian, by turns, just as the emergency demands. He is extravagant to the extreme of paradox. He adopts, on all the subjects he discusses, long exploded heresies of former centuries, and endeavors to cover them all with the gaudy mantle of the new philosophy.[35]

Bushnell's theory of the Trinity was called Unitarian or Sabellian; he was accused of denying that Christ's person contained both divine and human elements. It was alleged that he had subverted the truth of the Atonement as a propitiation of God. These points, and a general charge of having controverted scriptural authority and credal confessions, became the basis of a heresy campaign.[36]

Because of Congregational decentralization, the difficulty of defining orthodoxy, and the ambiguity of Bushnell's book, he escaped a heresy trial. Obviously he was not orthodox; his system was related to nineteenth-century philosophical idealism and American transcendentalism. The language theory was based on a soft supernatural-natural dualism, with the Logos concept giving the impression of pantheism. The Calvinists were understandably distressed with what appeared to be an Emersonian "transparent eyeball" in their very midst. What they actually were witnessing was a unity-minded gentleman attempting to forge a system that would satisfy all reasonable men.

Philosophical dualism had provided Bushnell, as it had Immanuel Kant and Samuel Taylor Coleridge, an escape from naturalism. Bushnell admitted that Coleridge had influenced him more than any other

nonscriptural writer.[37] His new system balanced natural and supernatural realms and provided a role for Christ as the saviour of sinful
man. Although the two spheres were distinct, nature contained signs or
analogies of the supernatural; although man was a fallen creature he was
not radically depraved, and salvation was a rather benign process.

In the 1850s a harsher note began to appear in Bushnell's thought.
According to the version of mass theory presented here, the gentry elite
gradually found itself the loser in the competition for the mass mind.
As the brash political and socioeconomic elites coalesced before and
after the Civil War the gentlemen vented their frustrations in ways appropriate to their individual personalities. In Bushnell's theology it appeared as a more otherworldly orientation coupled with an accent on
sin. Other factors contributing to the growth of Bushnell's hard dualism
included the heresy controversy that showed how spiteful even ministers
of God could be; his increased suffering from tuberculosis, the disease
that eventually claimed his life; and the Civil War, which he saw as a
"bloody baptism" for sinful men.[38]

By 1854 Bushnell was criticizing both Unitarians and "pantheists"
(transcendentalists) and presenting a more orthodox version of the
Trinity. God expresses himself in three ways, which is "as truly inherent
in him, as if it were the form of his divine substance itself." He asserted
that with Unitarians

> There is . . . discovered an almost irresistible tendency to
> naturalism, and so to a loss or dying out of all that distinctively
> constitutes the gospel. God is the king of nature, and nature is the
> inclusive name of all that constitutes his dominion. There is, in
> fact, no legitimate place for anything but nature. Sin is softened,
> depravity ignored.[39]

He mocked the "new kind of gospel" that "preaches not so much a
faith in God's salvation as a faith in human nature; an attenuated,
moralizing gospel that proposes development, not regeneration."[40]
Bushnell remained a Christian gentleman to the end, but in his last
years he became convinced that character was not enough. Supernatural
intervention was the necessary correlate of his growing otherworldliness
and disenchantment with the natural goodness of man.

The minister bluntly told his church members, most of whom were
probably ladies and gentlemen according to the standards of gentility,
that they were highly susceptible to "respectable sin," which was only
different in degree from the vice and crime occurring outside their
polite circles of character and decency. Virtue is not necessarily sinless,

he said, if it means merely abstaining from what society calls evil, oblivious to the spirit and love of God.[41] When forced by ill health to resign his pastorate, Bushnell delivered a farewell sermon in which he noted that the North Church had greatly increased in numbers and wealth. However, he regretted what he now saw as his overly rational approach to religion, and he warned his congregation to resist the encroachment of a "destructive and vapid liberalism."

> Assert, above all, and stand by the assertation of, a supernatural gospel; for there is, in fact, no other, and whoever scorns or only disowns such a gospel, let him be to you as a heathen man and a publican—deist, pantheist, pagan, but no Christian.[42]

Yet Bushnell was an incurable rationalist. He praised intuition and celebrated direct inspirations, but always within the context of a logical system. In the 1850s his concern that naturalism would dissolve the supernatural realm resulted in *Nature and the Supernatural* (1855), a long and complex book. Bushnell argued that there was a supernatural realm, separate from nature, but intimately associated with it. He defined nature as the realm of cause and effect, an absolutely lawful succession of events determined from within the system. By definition, the supernatural was that which impinged upon nature from without. There was no need to look for the supernatural in ghostly apparitions, for it could be seen in man's conscious freewill acts, by which he entered into nature as an uncaused force and produced new combinations and results. Man first used his freedom sinfully, spoiling his soul and reducing nature to a state of unnature. Only God's intervention in the form of Christ and other manifestations could regenerate both the human soul and nature.[43]

The argument rests on the assertion of human free will and sin. If it can be shown that humans, as uncaused powers, impinge on nature, the existence of the supernatural is established; and if it can be shown that they act sinfully, ruining their souls and unnaturing nature, it should not seem incredible that God would intervene to rectify the damage. Bushnell needed to free man from both God and nature. In the former instance he used the traditional explanation that God wanted man to be a power capable of good and evil instead of a mere natural thing. It is interesting that he contradicted Jonathan Edwards who had defended the sovereignty of God by denying human free will. In the fullness of nineteenth-century naturalism Bushnell needed to establish man's freedom to save God Himself. The argument is circular: God made a free supernatural creature capable of consciously meddling with nature and this proves that God's supernatural realm exists.

Acutely aware of the naturalism inherent in evolutionary development theories, Bushnell argued that the seeds of life could never have sprung spontaneously from the earth, and no transitional forms that could prove the mutability of species had ever been discovered. He relied mainly on Louis Agassiz in arguing that a vast gulf separated man from the highest animals and that each form of life had been implanted by God.[44]

Consciousness, the linchpin of the argument, tells the story. Whatever logic or science may indicate, man is conscious of himself as a free agent. "Find what the consciousness testifies and that, all tricks or argument apart, is the truth." But is he a sinner, standing in absolute need of salvation? Bushnell answers with an emphatic yes. His first illustration of a human supernatural act is of a murderer who "is hung for what is rightly called his unnatural deed." Say what you will about the environment. Speak of poor families, bad education, and deprivations of all sorts. Excuse and rationalize sin. But remember that "we are all conscious of acting from ourselves, uncaused in our action. The murderer knows within himself that he did the deed, and that nothing else did it through him. . . . The sentence of consciousness is final."[45]

There is much else in *Nature and the Supernatural,* some of it extremely archaic sounding, like Bushnell's use of his language theory to show how God filled the world with repulsive "analogies" of the sin in man's soul. The gentleman, looking at the world in a realistic, dualistic manner, is now in no danger of melding man, nature, and God in a pantheistic "transparent eyeball." Bushnell's landscape contains a fallen race despoiling nature, and nature in turn reflects in its many dark and dreadful aspects the ruined state of the human soul. And only God's intervention can right the wrong.[46]

Paradoxically, at about this time Bushnell began preparing an expanded version of his naturalistic *Views of Christian Nurture.* In addition to the original chapters, virtually unchanged, it contained a great deal of new self-culturing material. The explanation involved Bushnell's persistent concern for the family as the prime inculcator of character. He never ceased to advocate loving care for children with their innocent failings as compared to his harsh attitude toward old confirmed sins. He hoped that readers would comprehensively balance his soft theology with the late harder material.[47]

Although he complained about being "pelted all round" by both liberal and conservative reviewers, he returned with undiminished concentration to the Atonement theory in his last major works, *The Vicarious Sacrifice* (1866) and *Forgiveness and Law* (1874), the latter being republished by his heirs as *The Vicarious Sacrifice,* volume two. In the early parts of the 1866 work Bushnell presented a moral view of the Atonement that associated Christ on the cross with such superlative humans as Socrates and Lincoln. The treatment is remarkably soft. Love is the theme. Man is so little sunk in sin that superior individuals can approach divine goodness, and the average human is saved through a beautiful act of love. But the tone grows harsh. Bushnell employs his dualism to distinguish between the law before government and law by government. The former, sometimes called the law of right and love, is related to ideal absolutes like time, space, and number, existing even before God's will. When man sinned, spoiling his soul and loosening confusion in the world (the state of unnature of *Nature and the Supernatural*), God instituted government by law. In its various manifestations, it trains recalcitrant humans in loyalty to the absolute law before government; namely, the Old Testament institutions and language forms rising from them like Atonement, propitiation, and expiation, which should be interpreted as cleansing "lustral" symbols, presaging Christ's supreme act on the cross. Bushnell asserted that he wanted no picture of Christ

> offering only sweets for motivities, and bathing in soft odors and oily promises the obstinacy of sin. No! The Christ of the old gospel, he of eternal punishment, he of the judgement-day—the more I think of him, and of man, and the kind of Saviour man requires to get hold of him, and rouse him out of his death-torpor in sin, the more clear it is that he, the terrible Christ, is the Christ we want.[48]

Concerning eternal punishment and annihilation of souls, the stern gentleman remarked that he was aware of the disappointment he might "inflict on certain progressives, or disciples of the new gospel, but after much struggle he has concluded that these are fundamental to the Christian religion." Bushnell seemed to have a deadly fascination for the topic, for he held it, examined it from every angle and in every light, like a child who has picked up a shell on the beach. He rejected annihilation of the wicked, almost accepted it, then resolved the problem mathematically through an analogy of the asymptote line that inexorably approaches a curve but never reaches it. He suggested the possibility that incurably bad souls may spin through eternity on the asymptote line, neither saved nor extinguished.[49]

As before, conservatives declined to play the old heretic's game. One critic remarked that Bushnell "runs with the hare and chases with the hounds." Younger liberals regarded him as sui generis and appropriated those elements congenial to their views while disregarding the rest. Meanwhile, slowed by deteriorating health but inspired by "new light," Bushnell continued work on the Atonement theory. Earlier he had associated man with God through consciousness (*Nature and the Supernatural*) and the ideal law of right and love (*The Vicarious Sacrifice*). Now, in his last book, he used propitiation as a characteristic common to man and God. Just as a man initially feels "disgusts, indignations, revulsions," toward an enemy, then, when propitiated or reconciled, suffers inwardly for him, God does the same. Christ's life and sacrifice reveals God's propitiation of Himself through His suffering identification with sinful mortals. Bushnell shifts the content of his dualism. Whereas earlier he had divided God's law into the supernatural law before government and the natural law by government, now he speaks only of the law as part of nature's harsh discipline. Christ's commandments, directed to man's feeling and conscience rather than rational expedience, fill the subjective realm. They are to faith as law is to works. This was the gentleman's last summary statement. He combined the love of God with severe discipline for sinful humans; thus ministers could preach in a soft or hard vein as the occasion required.[50]

No story can ever be told in its entirety, but through sympathetic understanding and conscious hypotheses historians can move toward the truth. Bushnell's thought reflected his particular genius and the social and intellectual milieux within which he moved. Clearly, some of his most fundamental values stemmed from the moral character ideal that unified the nineteenth-century gentry elite. Bushnell always stressed gentility, but after about 1848 he balanced correct behavior and morality with a subjective, otherworldly strain. Although a shift from piety to morality characterized New England theology in the eighteenth and nineteenth centuries, Bushnell reversed the process in his own life.

His theology reflected his social position and such intellectual currents as naturalism, progress, Transcendentalism, and Calvinism. It is not wrong to refer to Bushnell as a liberal precursor of the social gospel, if one also notes the Calvinism in his later thought. If Bushnell "Transcendentalized" Calvinism, he qualified his mystical, pantheistic tendencies with a more orthodox dualism. Perhaps the most accurate characterization of Bushnell would be as a unity-minded gentleman who attempted to provide religious, moral, and intellectual leadership for America's burgeoning mass society.[51]

3

Religion, Morality, and Citizenship in the Public Schools: Iowa, 1858-1930

CARROLL ENGELHARDT

SPEAKING to the Iowa State Teachers Association as its new President in 1878, Clinton Superintendent Henry Sabin declared, ". . . this is in name a Christian nation. . . . If our government has any stability it is a stability rooted and grounded in the heart of a Christian people." It is clear, Sabin concluded, that the state has a vital interest in the moral training of its citizens and that educators "cannot safely exalt talent above virtue, education above rectitude, knowledge above religion. . . ."[1] As a leading Iowa educator, Sabin continued to stress moral and religious training in public schools as a requisite for good citizenship and social order during his four terms as State Superintendent of Public Instruction (1888–1892, 1894–1898) and as editor (1899–1901) of the state's preeminent educational journal, *Midland Schools*. Sabin's views were typical of those held by most Iowa and American educators from the mid-nineteenth through the early twentieth century. This is not surprising. From their founding, Americans charged the public schools with promoting social stability by inculcating basic American values and training good citizens. As implied in Henry Sabin's address, educators insisted that good citizenship rested on sound morality, and that true morality required instruction in the Christian religion. In other states—Oregon, Kansas, Illinois, and Wisconsin—a religious atmosphere, a kind of Protestant middle ground between sectarianism and secularism, existed in the common schools.[2] That the state educational establishment in Iowa was committed to a similar Protestant ambience and to some kind of religous training was

CARROLL ENGELHARDT, Concordia College, Moorhead, Minnesota.

reflected in the many publications of the state superintendents of public instruction, the proceedings of the Iowa State Teachers Association, the activities of the Iowa State Normal School, the actions of the county superintendents of public instruction, and the textbooks used by children. In a very real sense religion and state were not separated; religious concerns were more than pious rhetoric, and Iowa educators seriously attempted to base moral and civic teaching on Christian values.

Although it is difficult to define this religious atmosphere with precision, an analysis of Iowa educational literature between 1858 and 1930 reveals two manifestations of religious values in public education. The first followed Horace Mann's doctrine of nonsectarian religious instruction that he considered compatible with religious freedom if it did not favor any sect and taught only agreed upon elements of Christianity. Instruction in the common elements took the form of inculcating the moral virtues of honesty, fairness, truth, and reading from the Bible without comment. In this way religious freedom was protected, yet moral training retained its necessary foundation in religion.[3] Mann's views on Bible reading were incorporated into an 1858 Iowa law that stated: "the Bible shall not be excluded from any school . . . nor shall any pupil be required to read it contrary to the wishes of parent or guardian." The Iowa Supreme Court in an unanimous decision, *Moore v. Monroe* (1884), upheld the law's constitutionality.[4] The second manifestation Robert Bellah has called civil religion; it derives from Christianity and is implicitly Christian in its emphasis on America as a special nation under the guidance and judgment of God.[5] Considered essential foundations of morality and citizenship by educators, both types coexisted for most of these years. Eventually nonsectarian religious instruction evaporated and left as a residue the civil religion to be taught in all school activities and to be observed in the rituals of patriotic holidays.

The persistence of nonsectarian Christianity and its transformation into civil religion refutes the thesis that after 1850 public schools were quickly purged of everything sectarian and that their dominant aim became civil rather than religious.[6] Historians have erred in assuming a clear demarcation between the religious and civic realms, a dichotomy that did not exist in the minds of most educators. And they have overestimated the degree and rapidity of secularization after 1850, as the example of Iowa schools makes clear. Unlike other state studies of this phenomenon, this one shows that the Protestant middle ground of nonsectarian Christianity gradually evolved into civil religion, another version of the lowest common denominator. There were two major reasons for this evolution: first, civil religion, being implicitly rather than explicitly Christian, provided a way to avoid the charge of sectarian religious instruction frequently leveled against public schools by Catholics, Lutherans, and other religious groups; second, civil religion still provided a way for educators to ground moral and civic training in transcendent, now unspecified but presumably Christian values. A compromise, the civil religion enabled educators to continue what they considered the traditional function of public education which was to articulate and inculcate a set of common beliefs in all children.

Throughout the period under study Iowa remained primarily an agricultural state with no great cities, with a slow rate of population growth well below the national average, and with urban population not exceeding rural until 1956. Iowa's rurality helps to explain the persistence in the schools of religious values so long associated with village America. Moreover, this concern for the presence of religious-moral-civic instruction to maintain the social order was a constant interest of Iowa educators which did not fluctuate with the changing ethnic and religious composition of Iowa's population. Although the percentage of foreign born in Iowa increased from 12.3 percent (1850) to 20.7 percent (1870) and then steadily declined to 9.4 percent (1920), the fear of immigrants expressed in Iowa educational literature did not vary with the increased or decreased number of foreign immigrants. Perhaps this was because the vast majority of immigrants came from northwestern Europe and thus were judged acceptable. Perhaps too it was because the Protestant majority were not greatly threatened by a Catholic minority of only 8.6 percent in 1890, and only 9.4 percent in 1906, notwithstanding the founding in 1887 of the anti-Catholic American Protective Association by Clinton lawyer Henry Bowers.[7] More likely, expressed fears of immigrants were symbolic, as Joseph Gusfield has applied that term to the prohibition movement. Iowa educators were alarmed by anyone who did not fit their norm of citizenship. Therefore the poor, the ignorant, the criminal, the radical, and the immigrant were all symbols of an alien culture to the middle-class educators of a rural state who, despite their fears, remained confident that the schools could transform a heterogeneous population into one united people. Iowans were helped in their confidence by the fact that their fears were raised more in response to national events than to specific problems with labor, immigrants, or radicalism in Iowa.[8]

Yet in another sense the state's rural character hindered efforts to transmit a set of shared values in the schools. In the late nineteenth century the average country schoolhouse was by modern standards an unattractive place, and parents permitted their children to attend school only when there was no work for them on the farm. In 1875, for example, Iowa schoolhouses were valued at only $8.6 million and apparatus at just $119,591. Libraries totaled about 13,000 volumes—a woefully small number for a state with a school population of 533,571. Only 407 institutions were graded; over 9,000 were ungraded. The average academic year was just 6.8 months. With no compulsory education law, only 60 percent of the children between 7 and 16 attended. Almost 40 percent of the teachers were teaching with less than one year of experience. Preparation for teaching consisted of a common school education and possibly three weeks at a summer normal institute. Very few teachers had seen the inside of a high school and fewer still had attended college. They received teaching certificates solely on the basis of examinations administered by county superintendents who were often political appointees.[9]

Beginning in the late nineteenth century, Iowa schools, as did those in neighboring states, underwent a modernization based on the corporate-bureaucratic model developed for the reform of urban schools and now applied to rural education. Consolidation, higher taxes, compulsory attendance, state certification with higher professional standards for teachers, and greater professional control of the schools were all instituted with considerable impact on the quality of education. By 1920, for example, the value of schoolhouses had increased to over $54 million, the value of apparatus to over $2.9 million, and the number of volumes in libraries to over 780,000. More than 50 percent of Iowa's 23,343 schoolrooms were graded, the average academic year was 8.7 months, and 87 percent of those between 7 and 16 attended. Only 18 percent of the teachers were teaching with less than one year of experience and 33 percent held state or normal training certificates with the remainder being certified on the basis of state examinations. The state's 191 normal training high schools produced 2,500 graduates annually and summer sessions at Iowa colleges had replaced normal training institutes as a means of preparing teachers.[10] Such reforms did not change the central function of public education as perceived by educators, nor did reforms change the values they wanted to transmit. Modernization was advocated and accepted because it made the schools more efficient instruments for inculcating the basic religious-moral-civic beliefs educators saw as essential for creating good American citizens and for maintaining social order.

Textbooks presented these values most directly. Throughout the nineteenth century school readers were filled with explicit and implicit moral and religious lessons. Given the poor training and limited education of most Iowa teachers, it was fortunate that such books were available. Through the prevailing method of rote memorization at least some moral and religious beliefs would be imparted to students. The famous McGuffey readers, widely used in American and Iowa institutions, illustrate the nature of this material. In addition to several selections from the Bible, the McGuffey series contained many moralistic essays and stories—"Respect for the Sabbath Rewarded," "Religion the Only Basis of Society," "The Bible the Best of the Classics," "The Righteous Never Forsaken," and "The Necessity of Education." Pointed questions followed each selection: "What would be the effect of the removal of religion upon the whole fabric of virtue?" (Disaster!!!) "Can the Nation continue free without the influence of education and religion?" (No!!!) "Why may we trust that God will not abandon our nation to ruin?" (The American people's belief in God and their virtue!!!) It is clear that these books perpetuated the notion that religion was essential for morality and that morality was necessary for good citizenship. Although explicit Christian content tended to disappear from textbooks during the late nineteenth century, the implicit Christian values of the civil religion continued to be emphasized until 1930 and later. As patriotic stories, literature, and nature study replaced religious materials, it was still expected that children would come to acknowledge God and learn the same moral lessons as before. Like American Protestantism, in the nineteenth century schoolbooks discarded theological doctrines and concepts for a religion of ethics, but that did not make them any less religious in the Christian or civil sense.[11]

Paralleling the rise of civil religion in textbooks of the late nineteenth century were innovations with the American flag and national holidays designed to inculcate patriotism in the schools. In 1895 State Superintendent Henry Sabin reported that he had twice sent county superintendents prepared programs "calculated to arouse and quicken love of country in the minds of pupils." Sabin also encouraged each institution to acquire a flag in order to teach children "to respect and honor it, because it is in accordance with the prompting of that patriotic instinct which the Creator has implanted in every heart. . . ." Sabin's ideas were eventually adopted. By 1913 Iowa law required each school to raise the flag over the building every day the weather permitted. In 1901 a manual for "special day exercises" was published by the Department of Public Instruction, issued biennially for the next decade, and used for many years thereafter. Consisting of programs of readings, recitations, and songs for Washington's Birthday ("flagday"), Memorial Day ("the solemn Sabbath of the Nation"), and Thanksgiving ("for God's and nature's bounty"), these manuals were part of a national movement, dating from the 1880s, which enshrined the symbolism of the civil religion in the ritual observances of American schools.[12]

The increased observance of civil religion in the 1890s did not mean the end of nonsectarian Christianity in Iowa schools. The recurring idea of the Christian teacher in educational literature is evidence that Iowa educators remained sympathetic to this kind of religion. Educators considered the Christian teacher an effective force for religious instruction, and they constantly invoked this image to prove that public education was not Godless. They frequently specified what the teacher's moral qualifications ought to be and how morality should be firmly grounded in Christianity. As Dubuque principal William Shoup said, "the teacher's moral character, to be genuine, must spring from faith in God and reverence for His established institutions." It was entirely proper, Shoup declared, to expect teachers "to recognize the hand of Providence; to have reverence for sacred things; to use pure and chaste language; and to be sober, honest, and industrious." Since the teacher's character served as a model, it was especially important that teachers possess the highest moral qualifications. For these reasons, another educator insisted, school boards should take as much care in securing teachers of "irreproachable character, healthful moral influence, and good habits, as was exercised in selecting pastors for churches."[13]

That these sentiments were reinforced by Iowa school law, which specified that applicants for teaching positions must possess good moral character, should come as no surprise. County superintendents were instructed to ascertain teachers' characters before certifying them to teach. The case, *Nora Oelke v. R. C. Spencer,* heard by the state superintendent of public instruction in 1899, indicates that county superintendents sometimes acted on their legal authority. The case arose from Spencer's refusal to grant Oelke a teaching certificate and to enroll her in the County Normal Institute. The state superintendent affirmed Spencer's decision, holding that it was the county superintendent's duty to exclude the morally unfit from the institute and the schoolroom. Spencer's charges were based solely on personal observation and he had repeatedly warned Miss Oelke and her father against her indiscretions, which had become a matter of public gossip. He had not received a satisfactory explanation nor did the defense offer any evidence of Miss Oelke's good moral character to disprove his claims.[14]

Excluding agnostic teachers from the classroom was the obverse of requiring teachers to be genuinely Christian. One incident reported in the 1890s involved a man identified only as Drew, a skeptic, who had been too free in expressing his agnosticism to pupils. Drew informed a school board member that he "believed in Tom Paine and doing right." The board member told Drew to keep his views from the students. Another episode concerned the hiring of a teacher. It was made clear that "if Lorenz leans in any way to agnosticism I would not for anything be guilty of putting him in a position where he could influence young people."[15]

The religious atmosphere which existed at Iowa State Normal School, soon to become Teachers College, provided further evidence that public school teachers were Christian. As President Homer Seerley observed in 1901, "state schools aren't necessarily Godless." The personality of Seerley, a deeply religious man, had much to do with the strong religious spirit of the college. He never missed an opportunity to impress upon students the importance of spirituality. At daily chapel exercises—consisting of hymn singing, Bible reading, and prayer— Seerley often gave short talks dealing with the importance of conduct and character. In his Baccalaureate addresses, taking Bible passages as maxims, Seerley repeatedly stressed that without cultivation of the spirit there could be no education. In 1918 Seerley made chapel attendance virtually mandatory. Under the new plan, students were furnished with cards for recording their attendance. If their attendance was unsatisfactory, the student could not expect recommendations or other favors from the college. In addition, Sunday Bible study classes, evangelistic meetings, prayer meetings, and nonsectarian afternoon services were all well attended. No wonder Seerley was very pleased with the religious life of the school and could estimate in 1901 that 75 percent of the students were church members, and that 95 percent attended religious services.[16]

Teachers did conform to the Christian behavior expected of them. As late as 1924 many public school teachers still attended local churches, taught or participated in Sunday school classes, attended young people's societies, and sang in church choirs. A questionnaire circulated in that year shows that almost 91 percent (1669 out of 1838 replies) of Iowa teachers in towns under 5,000 population claimed church membership.[17]

The prevalence of Christian teachers, the rituals of civil religion, and the persistence of religious values in schoolbooks were insufficient religious education for many Americans. Consequently the Religious Education Association was formed in 1903 for the purpose of modernizing the Sunday school by applying the methods and standards of secular education. This movement produced a renewed demand for more systematic religious instruction in the public schools and shortly thereafter the National Education Association offered a prize for the best essay on

"Instruction in Religion in Public Schools." A variety of Bible study plans appeared—Colorado (1911), North Dakota (1912), Kansas (1914), Gary (1915)—and were endorsed by the respective state teachers' associations. A number of colleges, including state institutions like Iowa State Teachers College (ISTC) and the State University of Iowa (SUI), introduced courses in Bible study, Bible ethics, or related subjects. In 1915, as a part of this general movement, the Iowa State Teachers Association (ISTA) formed a Committee on Bible Study in the Schools.[18]

As could be expected, the Bible study movement in Iowa rested on traditional American assumptions concerning the relationship of religion, morality, and citizenship. Speaking to the ISTA in 1915, State Superintendent A. M. Deyoe asserted that "religious instruction is fundamental to citizenship. There could be no better basis for moral instruction in the school than an accepted code of ethics founded on the Bible." Deyoe recommended that "credit for Bible study be accepted by our public schools on the same basis as other non-resident work in our high schools and colleges." Another schoolman maintained that "to make the teaching of citizenship in our schools function properly the Bible must have a prominent place in the education of the child." Such teaching, if nonsectarian, "can only make for a better citizenship by training the heart and conscience of the learner." The link between Iowa Bible study and moral and civic training is also seen in *Bible Ethics for School and Home,* a textbook designed for high school Bible study by D. Sands Wright of ISTC and published in 1926. Through a series of lessons on each of the Ten Commandments, Wright attempted to teach the traditional moral virtues of Protestant America. His effort illustrated the tendency of religious instruction in public schools to become training in a code of morality on which all sects would supposedly agree and showed how nonsectarian Christianity evolved into civil religion. The lessons on the Fourth, Fifth, and Eighth Commandments were typical. "Work is a fundamental necessity in human existence," Wright declared, because "evil, unjust, dishonest, impure thoughts easily inject themselves into the soul of one whose hands are idle." The Fifth Commandment required more than honoring one's parents; corollaries were "respect of the pupil for the teacher, and of the citizen for those in authority." Wright's discussion of the Eighth Commandment stressed property rights. Alienation of property by illegal or unethical means constituted theft and thus was always a sin in God's eyes.[19]

Appropriately enough, Wright concluded with a section on civic duties that clearly showed the Christian basis of the civil religion. "Love of country," Wright asserted, "is a beautiful and all but universal sentiment, God-implanted in the human heart.'' Furthermore, ''every man who lives a righteous and worthy life adds to his country's dignity and glory; while he who lives unrighteously and unworthily, degrades his nation and pollutes his flag.'' In addition to these religious obligations of loyalty and righteous living, Wright said every citizen had a moral duty to attend caucuses, to belong to a political party, and to vote in all elections.[20] It is evident that Wright retained the traditional assumptions about religion as the basis of morality, and morality as the foundation of citizenship, and that he believed religious and moral sanctions were helpful in compelling Americans to perform their civic tasks.

The ISTA Bible Study Committee—Wright of ISTC, Starbuck of SUI, Stuart (a Catholic) of Dubuque—agreed that the Bible was inherently related to citizenship and maintained that the Bible ought to be studied ''because its ideals and spirit were the basis of social, moral, and spiritual welfare.'' The committee accordingly drew up a syllabus for Bible history and literature which, approved by the Iowa Board of Secondary School Relations, was then offered to the secondary schools, the Bible schools, and the churches of the state. Under this plan, regularly organized secondary institutions could give at least two semester credits and Sunday schools and churches might offer Bible study for high school credit, but only if they met accreditation standards. As a capstone to the system, colleges promised to accept Bible study grades given in accordance with the proposal. Through this arrangement, Bible study became an optional subject in the curriculum for those students who desired it.[21]

In 1919 the ISTA passed a resolution urging Iowa school authorities to introduce Bible study for credit. During the academic year 1919–1920, 20 institutions started Bible study programs. By the end of 1920 the number had risen to 40. Growth of interest was steady and by 1921 nearly 100 high schools were offering the course. The program was greatly aided by the interest of State Superintendent P. E. McClenahan, who in 1921 published and distributed the *Bible Study Syllabus* at public expense. Through the efforts of the ISTA committee the number continued to increase, and by 1924 nearly one-fifth of Iowa high schools had adopted Bible study. Out of a total enrollment of 13,923, daily Bible classes were maintained for 2,228 students. The Iowa Bible study movement reached its peak in 1927 when 132 high schools gave credit to a total of 4,394 students. In most the subject was taught by the superintendent, principal, or some other faculty member, rather than by clergy. Only a few institutions dismissed students one period a week to attend their respective churches for Bible instruction. These students did not receive academic credit for their work.[22]

Given their assumptions about the interrelatedness of religion, morality, and citizenship, it seems that educators should have developed some program of formal religious instruction for the elementary grades. Recognizing this deficiency, in 1924 the ISTA enlarged the committee's function to include the elementary school. The committee did not formulate a systematic plan of formal religious training but merely summarized ways the spirit of religion might be encouraged. The committee recommended the story (or Jesus) method as one way for teachers to carry out their duty of fostering religion. Bible stories, ennobling literature, stories teaching moral lessons, and biographies of great men were all part of the story method of moral training. Religious art and music were suggested to train the student's moral sense. The physical surroundings and organization of the school, according to the committee, should inculcate desirable moral virtues. Teachers could actively encourage Sunday school attendance and participation in young people's associations. Institutions could further contribute to the moral uplift of children through weekday religious instruction. Under this plan students were released one hour a week, subject to school supervision, to receive religious training at their particular church.[23]

In 1927 the Bible Study Committee, for reasons that remain unclear, made its final report to the ISTA. Without its promotional work the number of Bible courses steadily declined from its peak of 132 until by 1944 only 12 Bible teachers remained in Iowa's 877 state-approved secondary and junior high schools. Although there was no reported opposition and the Catholic Church was credited with loyal cooperation, the committee's final report complained of the general indifference to the need for formal training in Christian citizenship and righteous living. The key word here was *formal*. Religious pluralism—combined with constitutional safeguards for religious freedom—made it extremely difficult for Iowa and American educators to agree upon the content for nonsectarian Christian teaching. As a consequence formal public school religious training—and faith in the power of such training—declined in Iowa as evidenced by the fate of the Bible Study movement after 1927. Many years before its demise, Homer Seerley had already pinpointed the difficulties on which Bible study would eventually founder when he said, "it is simply not practicable in America . . . to introduce any system of religious instruction into our schools of a formal nature or character, because of the peculiar constitutional conditions under which they are organized." Religious instruction was not possible "unless there can be some agreement on the question of fundamental propositions," and Seerley did not think that was likely in a pluralistic society since even single churches had difficulty reaching agreement.[24]

As formal instruction in nonsectarian Christianity as the basis of morality and citizenship faded from the schools, educators were left with the civil religion as they adopted the more modern methods of moral and civic education advocated by the Character Education Movement and exemplified by the prize-winning Iowa Plan of 1922. The first comprehensive plan for character education, the Iowa Plan, authored by a committee chaired by Edwin Starbuck of SUI, a member of the ISTA's Bible Study Committee, was widely circulated and influenced the creation and implementation of character education programs across the country. The plan was modern in that it combined progressive education's emphasis on learning by doing and the school as a model community with the emerging science of testing and measurement. Despite its modern features, the Iowa Plan retained the traditional emphasis on morality and citizenship rooted in transcendent values as the central goals of public education. For instance, in the area of civic relations the plan recommended that all activities throughout all twelve grades be directed toward citizenship preparation which would include the formal study of civics; the appreciation of patriotic music, drama, literature, biography, and pictures; visits and excursions; and participation in projects, clubs, and societies. It was also hoped that student awareness of the school as community with its attendant sense of participation, responsibility, and loyalty would naturally transfer into loyalty to the American state as students became adults. A final section on reverence and worship sought to make students aware that personal and civic morality rested on unspecified transcendent values.[25] In all these ways the Iowa Plan taught civil religion. Loyalty to state and nation was important and thought to rest on transcendent, presumably Christian, values. As it was becoming more difficult by the 1920s to make these Christian values explicit in the schools, educators had to be content with instruction in the civil religion and its implicit Christian foundations. That this shift toward civil religion was compatible with and a logical extension of earlier efforts at religious instruction is in a sense personified by Edwin Starbuck's participation in both the Bible study and character education movements.

To be sure, nonsectarian Christianity did not completely disappear from the schools and where it persisted it continued to coexist with civil religion. Iowa law still permitted Bible reading without comment and the limited number, from the more than 12,600 public schools in the state, responding to a questionnaire circulated by the Bible Study Committee in 1927 indicated that religious exercises of scripture reading, hymn singing, and prayer were conducted daily in 158 schools. Fifty-two offered weekday religious instruction to the intermediate grades. Supplementary reading books, ethical or religious in tone, were used in

104 institutions. Although it is not known what kinds of religious activities were occurring in the vast majority that did not respond to the questionnaire, two other pieces of evidence suggest the fading of nonsectarian Christian instruction leaving civil religion as the primary religion practiced in Iowa schools. Opening exercises, a traditional vehicle for devotional religious activity, were completely secularized in the Iowa Course of Study published in 1928. Speeches about pets, vacation experiences, excursions, musical exercises, oral stories, memory poems, jokes, anecdotes, and riddles were suggested to open the elementary school day. A questionnaire sent by the ISTA Character Education Committee in 1929 reveals something of the influence of the Iowa Plan and the kind of moral training conducted in some rural schools. Children formulated and memorized moral creeds, codes, and slogans. Concrete moral case materials and desirable trait actions were discussed in class groups—most frequently in language, literature, history, civics—and in opening exercises. Biographies and other literary materials were read aloud. Citizenship situations were dramatized, special days observed, and flag drills held. Significantly, nonsectarian Christian instruction is not listed among these many activities but there is considerable teaching and observance of the principles and rituals of the civil religion.[26]

By 1930 Iowa educators still perceived civic education in traditional terms: citizenship must be grounded in morality, and morality must be based on religion. Because religion was fundamental educators naturally sought to preserve it in the schools. The two types of religion coexisted throughout the period because they were in no sense incompatible. The civil religion was another version of the lowest common denominator of Christianity, which developed when the earlier version, Mann's nonsectarian Christianity, appeared sectarian to many religious groups. When nonsectarian Christianity proved unacceptable educators adopted civil religion as a compromise. It had the dual advantage of being nonsectarian and still providing transcendent values on which to base moral and civic training. Thus civil religion evolved out of nonsectarian Christianity and is a residue of it.

Both types of religion performed an Americanization function, enabling Iowa educators through the schools to inculcate a common set of values and create a unified culture and united people, which would maintain the social order and guarantee opportunity for all. While Iowa's rurality made it easier for educators to perpetuate the traditional religious values of village America, there is evidence that urban educators attempted to perpetuate similar values for a long time as well. Nor was Iowa fundamentalist in religion. Two popular fundamentalist issues of the 1920s, the Ku Klux Klan and the teaching of evolution, had little impact on Iowa politics and education.[27]

Although nonsectarian Christian instruction was declining and new methods of character education represented by the Iowa plan were being employed by 1930, Iowa teachers, as evidenced by the presence of civil religion in the schools, were as firm in their commitment to the disciplined, moral citizen as the necessary and proper goal of public education as Horace Mann and Henry Sabin had been seventy and fifty years before.[28] What had changed is that religious pluralism and the constitutional guarantees for religious freedom now prevented educators from making explicit any longer the Christian doctrines on which moral and civic training were to be based. But such doctrines were implicit in civil religion, which was still widely taught and practiced in the public schools.

4

American Missionaries
in Darkest Africa, 1890–1940

CLIFFORD H. SCOTT

F E W American college graduates of the past quarter century have escaped classroom exposure to a discussion of the application of Darwinian evolution to race and society in the late nineteenth and early twentieth centuries. Most students might well have concluded that the influence of evolutionary naturalism, especially under the rubric of social Darwinism, was widespread through the American public and that its particular application to race theory, scientific racism, was nearly universal in a white supremacist society. Revision of that perception has suggested the limited following for even popularized evolutionary views among American business figures and the continuing attraction of contrary democratic assumptions among broad reaches of the public. Recent scholars have pointed out the brief reign of social Darwinism among biological and social scientists who moved from one naturalistic stance to another in the twentieth century, spurred by new experimental methodologies and evidence concerning the nature of man, as well as by professional rivalries and discipline-building conflicts. Investigation of other American social groups, particularly those whose intellectual sources of authority did not rest with the empirical sciences, should reveal additional dissenters from naturalistic conclusions on matters of race. In that context, this study of the evaluation of black Africans by white American Protestant missionaries in Sub-Sahara Africa, 1890–1940, is useful in understanding the pluralism of American thought, the tenacity of traditional ideas in an age of modernization, and the circumscribed impact of social Darwinism on the American public.[1]

CLIFFORD H. SCOTT, Indiana University–Purdue University, Fort Wayne, Indiana.

To be sure, by the late nineteenth century evolutionary naturalism was a powerful new authority in American intellectual life, and Darwin was its prophet. To study man as a part of the natural biological world, to accept scientific fact as ultimate knowledge, to open up a new range of analogies and metaphors from nature for analyzing society, and to accept the deterministic power of biological and cultural inheritance as a basis for predicting human behavior were exhilarating ideas for young social theorists in an age of rapid demographic and economic change. The resulting search for authority in scientific knowledge and for social control from that knowledge was a cultural inheritance of the first order for twentieth century Americans.

Earlier scientific theories had similarly been utilized to explain the several major human groupings in America and to justify or to attack the dominant social relations among those groups. Especially prominent in the nineteenth century were theories that attributed major power to climate and geography in producing biological change. The theory of Jean Baptiste Lamarck, in a variation of environmentalism, was especially attractive to American democratic reformers who found confidence in the belief that exertion by an organism in response to its environment could produce permanent, progressive change to the species and might explain the variation that underlay Darwin's conception of natural selection. The internal development of biological knowledge, however, soon dashed that appealing theory as August Weismann's research into the mechanisms of biological inheritance found no evidence that somatic change influenced the germ or reproductive cells.[2] The factors of biological inheritance seemed fixed in family lines as Hugo de Vries and a new generation of geneticists at the turn of the century returned to Gregor Mendel's experiments in inheritance.

From Weismann and de Vries the naturalistic study of man branched out to study the discrete elements of reproduction in genetics, the measurement and change of morphological structure in anatomy and physical anthropology, and the physiological basis for psychic and intellectual phenomenon in psychology. Each field split into subfields as eugenics temporarily eclipsed genetics and as early psychologists sought explanation for some permanent element in human nature from instincts, intelligence testing, and reductionist experiments with rats. Cultural anthropologists, led by Franz Boas, allied themselves with sociologists to carve out the concept of human culture as a separate and distinct force from biological inheritance in explaining the social differences among humankind. Through parallel developments by the 1930s, based on experimental evidence, the several biological and social sciences established an uneasy division of labor and tenuous harmony, each admitting the interaction of individual biological characteristics with social cultural forces as well as the interworking of environment and genes in the expression of any biological characteristic.

Each turn in the course of developing knowledge in the human sciences had an impact upon the understanding of race in America and the appropriate social policy deduced for a multiracial society. For a period of perhaps half a century, from the 1870s to the 1920s, many social scientists argued on the basis of contemporary scientific conclusions that scientific racism most accurately described the nature of and reasons for racial differences. The argument persistently shifted, roughly following the course of scientific findings from analogies of racial hierarchies with biological species, to anatomical distinctions centering especially on the head and brain, to intelligence testing, to unilinear stages of cultural evolution, and to statistical studies of deviant cultural behavior. Yet central to all formulations of scientific racism were the assumptions that heredity acted independently of environmental influences, that cultural characteristics were the consequence of biological inheritance, and that distinct biological races that could be placed in a hierarchial order of capability determined the cultural attributes of all race members. Needless to recount, scientific racism provided an authoritative rationale for both traditional white supremacy and its more recent formulation of segregation. By the late 1910s and early 1920s scientific racism came under attack from cultural anthropologists, geneticists, and psychologists destroying each of the major elements in the racist position with new experimental evidence. It is unnecessary here to trace the course of the decline in the intellectual respectability of racism, but by the 1930s the theory no longer possessed scientific respectability for those who based their social theory on empirical evidence.[3]

In the changing social and political circumstances following World War II, the idea of racism, shorn of its recent naturalistic meaning, was applied to any practice or attitude that supported racial prejudice or discrimination; and such is its general current usage. While scientific racism lost the support of nearly all scientists, many in the American public continued to employ the naturalistic concept for years and even generations later. Concurrent with scientific racism and following its decline, still earlier theories of race superiority based on alternate sources of authority—such as the supposed curse on Ham's descendants recorded in Genesis—continued to be expressed by those Americans emotionally committed to a white supremacist position.

Against this background of the rise and fall of scientific racism, evangelistic Protestant foreign missionaries moved out of southern, midwestern, and New England small towns and rural areas to carry Protestant theology and an idealized version of American culture to areas of the non-Western world newly opened to Europeans and North Americans. One of their prominent mission fields was Sub-Sahara Africa, an area that brought white Americans into contact with black Africans of many different physical and cultural backgrounds.[4] How these white American missionaries reacted to black Africans and the reservoir of ideas and assumptions they used to understand their African encounter is the task of this chapter, and is based principally on the public expression of missionaries to their American supporters in the interdenominational missionary journals—*Missionary Review of the World,* which published material from nearly all of the mainline American Protestant bodies (Presbyterian, Baptist, Methodist, and Episcopal) as well as smaller groups (Mennonites, Church of the Brethren, Free Methodists, Missionary Alliance, and cooperative bodies such as the Inland Missions); the American Board's *Missionary Herald;* the more general *World Outlook;* and various missionary memoirs. What is particularly striking in the descriptions and analyses missionaries employed while attempting to shape Africa to their own image is the absence of ideas or assumptions borrowed from scientific racism in what was undoubtedly a major effort at cultural imperialism. Benevolent paternalism, an earlier cultural tradition in white attitudes toward blacks, paved the way for missionaries' optimistic stance in matters of cultural change more in keeping with their idealistic religious and social reform ventures and less dependent on the secular theories of contemporary science.[5]

Of course missionaries were not ordinarily systematic theorists, nor were they writing for intellectually sophisticated audiences. Yet even their strong ethnocentrism and paternalism were cast in terms of a traditional religious cosmology moderated by contemporary theological debate and the exigencies of colonial circumstances. When the major shifts in missionary evaluations of African cultures appeared in the 1920s, the major causes appear to have been the rapid historical transformation of Africa by European economic imperialists and the loss of home support, not the concurrent social science and genetic critique of scientific racism.

The presence of American Protestant missionaries in Africa predated the rise of evolutionary naturalism, though not of race conflict or theories of race in America. All of the major Protestant bodies—Baptist, Methodist, Presbyterian, and Protestant Episcopal—sent white and black missionaries to Liberia in the 1830s to support the colonization of free blacks from the states and to evangelize the indigenous population. Few missionaries survived tropical diseases and even fewer Africans were converted, but an American missionary presence continued. In the same

decade the American Board of Commissioners for Foreign Missions sent
a handful of New England missionaries to follow the contacts of New
England shippers in South Africa. Almost immediately the American
Board personnel in Zululand and Natal became embroiled in political
conflicts between Africans (Zulus) and colonial whites (Boers), a circumstance repeated many times during the next century.[6]

By the outbreak of the Civil War the American Board had slightly
increased its activity in South Africa and had established a mission post
on the West African coast in Gabon where the Presbyterians also located; yet the total American presence in the Sub-Sahara was well under
fifty missionaries. Northern Presbyterians branched out from Gabon
into the nearby Cameroons in the 1870s, and Baptists and Methodists in
small numbers advanced from Liberia into the Congo just before Leopold II of Belgium took control in 1885. Southern Presbyterians and
Disciples of Christ soon followed. The American Board's success in
Natal led to the establishment of mission stations in Portuguese East
Africa and Angola in the 1880s; Northern Methodists followed shortly
thereafter.

In the early 1890s the revival of evangelism in American Protestantism, led in part by Dwight L. Moody's mobilization of denominational college students, organized in the Student Volunteer Movement
(1891), and the flow of new wealth into missionary boards produced
high hopes for "the evangelization of the world in this generation."
Yet the number of missionaries sent to Africa was misleading; of 86
Methodists sent in 1896, for example, 11 died and 51 returned home
within a year. By 1910 there were 596 United States missionaries in Africa; the American Board was most visible in South Africa, Presbyterians
in Gabon and the Cameroons, Methodists in Angola and the Congo,
and Baptists in the Congo and along the West Coast. Still, American
Protestants were only a small minority of missionaries in Africa since the
ruling European colonial powers also dominated missionary ranks;
Americans constituted only 14 percent of all Protestant missionaries and
but 6 percent of all Christian missions when Roman Catholic missionaries were included in the total.[7]

By 1917 American efforts were near their peak with about 1,050
missionaries in Africa. The major change since 1910 was the dynamic
growth of Seventh-Day Adventists in Africa and the growing ecumenical efforts of the International Missionary Council to coordinate missionary activity.[8] Schools and medical facilities highlighted American
missions and provided opportunities for religious evangelism. By the
mid-1920s American numbers began to shrink as a result of reduced
benevolence contributions in the home churches, factional infighting in

American denominations over theological and social issues, and external and internal attacks upon the whole missionary enterprise. The Great Depression only quickened a process already under way as American missionaries increasingly turned over religious control to Christian Africans in the 1930s.

Throughout the era of American missionary efforts in Africa, the missionaries' descriptions of black Africans dwelled on a unified African type and culture which they defined according to religious criteria. Tribal differences were minimized, particularly in the missionary journals prior to World War I, since the important distinctions presented to readers were always those between Christian and pagan Africans. By the mid-1920s and 1930s attention was eventually given to a second basic division based upon the contrast between Africans of traditional culture and those partially assimilated into European culture. Significantly, by that later date, no close relationship was found between Christian culture and that based on European economic models. Moral criteria still predominated as missionaries worried about the moral and social consequences of modernization that did not fulfill their earlier dreams for Africa.

In virtually all of the early discussions and in a majority of instances following World War I, missionary attention centered on pagan social customs and the extent to which Christian Africans were acquiring the general culture of the West—in moral dress, housing, sanitation, and marital relations.[9] One is struck by the paucity of references to heaven and hell or the life of the soul in missionary discussions of their African work since the more significant emphasis by fundamentalist, orthodox evangelical, and social gospeler alike was the prospect of creating a Christian society in Africa.

In these discussions missionaries assumed the historical power of ideas to mold behavior and institutions—not the power of blood, genes, or physical environment. The root of each deprecated African custom, they contended, was found in false and demeaning religious ideas. What was necessary to create a new Christian society were Christian ideas. This sense of possessing liberating ideas and a superior culture quite easily led to strong religious ethnocentrism and paternalism in viewing the cultural life of Africans, but it did not necessarily lead to scientific racism. In virtually all their writings, American missionaries assumed that African values and behavior could be reoriented within one to two generations; there were no insurmountable instinctual, genetic, or intelligence roadblocks.[10]

The harshest judgments against Africans, accordingly, were applied to their religious beliefs. Witch doctors, as competing theologians and cultural leaders, were accused of personifying the evil and misleading ideas behind African culture. They were, said Walter Williams, a Methodist in Liberia, "full of all evil, murder, adultery, theft, and hatred." Missionaries painted highly exotic pictures of what they viewed as the repulsive fetishes employed by witch doctors, the cruel legal procedure of trial by ordeal, useless and barbarous medical practices, and offered a host of criticisms centering on polygyny and sexual life.[11] The dual criticism of all such customs was that they were first of all, immoral, and second, ineffective in achieving results.

The fascinated disgust expressed by missionaries was particularly strong when they wrote home to solicit volunteers and money. Robert Milligan, an orthodox Presbyterian missionary executive with field work in West Africa, declared that African customs were "horribly heathenish but mighty interesting." Tales of poison ordeals, child brides, and cannibalism were also useful to the missionary to offset mounting criticism of missionary work. Tantalizingly vague references to "lewd societies," lascivious dances, and sexual customs "too immoral to describe" dotted their descriptions of African life. The marriage system was excoriated in particular for encouraging infidelity, producing a low idea of womanhood, and promoting immodesty and sexual intrigue.[12] An older Christian theory of race, based on the association of immoral practices with the spiritually unregenerate, rather than a social Darwinian theory posited upon physical inheritance of cultural characteristics, emerges in such discussions. Also evident is a traditional white cultural view of blacks as romantic primitivists.

Less moralistic censure of traditional African society by the 1920s centered on charges that Africans suffered from low technological skills, inflexible attitudes and philosophies, and social stagnation. The more moralistic judgments, however, continued into the 1930s by orthodox evangelicals, such as the Presbyterians, and fundamentalist groups, including Southern Baptists and Seventh-Day Adventists. Where contemporary conditions did not warrant such criticisms, historical articles dealt with the earlier years when cannibalism and martyrdom were in fashion. Such articles by the late twenties and early thirties were a direct reply to American critics of missions and an appeal to the tightening purse strings of the faithful at home.[13]

Although missionaries described Africans in blatantly condescending ways, from their own ethnocentric biases, a comparison with other writings by American anthropologists, natural scientists, travelers, and fiction writers in Africa from 1900 to 1935 finds most missionaries far more optimistic in matters of race. Thus one of the most prolific American writers on African anthropology, Wilfred Dyson Hambly, an associate curator of Chicago's Field Museum, repeatedly accounted for differences of African culture by reference to exterior bloodlines, created stereotypic ideal-type "Negroes," and talked of "Negro languages."[14] Jerome Dowd, an academic sociologist with a Ph.D. from the University of Chicago, likewise criticized American missionaries in Africa in naturalistic terms for moving too swiftly with ideas of racial equality, literary education, and political suffrage without first having Africans pass through generational stages of economic development. American natural scientists in Africa appealed to even harsher naturalistic bromides. For example, William Gregory and Henry Raven, curators of comparative anatomy at New York's American Museum of Natural History, consistently compared Africans' physiology with that of anthropoid apes. Americans who wrote about their adventures in Africa employed a variety of racial perspectives on Africans; but the travel account with the largest circulation was Theodore Roosevelt's, which used a framework of biological evolution to describe different tribes ("races") as representing the various cultural stages in humankind's unilinear evolution.[15]

In contrast, the missionaries' society-building orientation led them—especially in their journals—to classify Africans not by tribes or cultural regions, as naturalists might, but by their religious affiliation. In their commitment to the creation of a new society, missionaries emphasized the relative ease of such an undertaking and a surprising lack of interest in contemporary racist theories. The missionaries' intellectual interpretation of cultural change justified their presence in Africa, their understanding of history, and the validity of their religious beliefs. From this perspective they described Africans in diametrically opposed images of the corrupted wrong-thinking pagan and the virtuous right-thinking Christian convert.[16] Moreover, their faith in the power of Christian ideas to transform African culture justified support from American churchmen. This ideological position supported by both religious faith and economic interest had considerable staying power.

American Protestant missionaries in Africa were driven, ironically, by the Protestant churches' lack of success in influencing American society and in reconciling the growing theological divisions between orthodox evangelicals and newer socially oriented Protestant Christians. While American missionaries appeared self-confident, the tone they employed in the 1900s and their explicit statements in the 1910s betrayed their fear that the Protestant churches in America could not compete with the material secularism of urban industrial civilization. This fear underlay their need to find an unformed, unsophisticated society that could be used as a laboratory to prove the effectiveness of

Christianity and thus invigorate struggling American Protestantism. To them Africa was still a pristine continent, not yet corrupted by urbanization, industrialization, and corrosive secular values; it provided an ideal testing ground to determine if a modern Christian society could be developed that escaped the evils of contemporary America. Thus, for the missionaries, scientific racism was not a useful or appropriate lens with which to view black Africans. The missionaries were logically obligated by their roles as American Protestant missionaries to perceive Africans as potentially able human beings who could be molded into modernized yet Christian beings.[17]

The missionaries' fears that Protestantism would fail to preserve American morality helps explain the many favorable comparisons they made of Africa with America, the sharp criticisms they penned of European and American traders and exploiters of natural resources, and the complimentary evaluations they drew of African Christians. Samuel Verner, a rural Southern Presbyterian, described New York City in the early 1900s as "more dark and wretched" than the lowest African village; Africans were more trustworthy, friendly, and better behaved than New Yorkers. Even more reflective of the rural missionaries' alienation from urban American life and their expatriate life in Africa was Verner's scorn for the "nauseating practices of civilized life [in America.]"[18] Similar criticisms of American life demonstrate that missionary strictures were clearly not limited to indigenous African culture.

Throughout these fifty years an articulate minority of missionaries consistently criticized European commercial and industrial interests in Africa. These missionaries denounced European interference in the missionary dream of creating a Protestant Christian society, as did, for example, the brutal activities of King Leopold II of Belgium in the Congo. Exploiting Africans and developing materialistic values in a once spiritual—if animistic—land made the missionary task more difficult, they agreed. The two leading missionary journals prior to World War I, *Missionary Review* and *Missionary Herald*, attacked European nations that "cooly proceed to 'develop' Africa by manuring the soil with Africans" and a South African government "more interested in making the black man do the white man's work than in giving the black man a chance in life." These missionaries' criticisms of the European colonials reflected both the contrast between their preachments about a Christian Western Civilization and European behavior and their virtual impotence to shape events in lands that the European powers controlled. Missionaries' suspicions and accusations abounded also about the advantages provided by colonial administrators for their own national missionaries, especially support of Roman Catholic missions by Belgium,

France, and Portugal. Even Great Britain, usually viewed as least hostile
to American missionary interests, was not above criticism by American
misionaries.[19]

Most other American missionaries agreed, if more quietly, that the
overall effect of European commerce on Africans was harmful. Robert
Nassau, an early Presbyterian in the Cameroons, commented that the
British and the French were often as bloody and violent as the Belgians.
This Pennsylvania cleric insisted that more virgins were sacrificed to
traders than had ever been devoured by crocodiles. The Europeans introduced rum and shoddy goods to the natives and were indifferent to
the natives' beliefs, thus threatening the morality and economy of traditional African society. Missionaries did mute their criticisms of colonial
administrations in order to gain favor for their evangelical and educational enterprises from the Europeans. But missionaries could not sup-
press all their feelings. John Springer, for instance, a Methodist friendly
with certain European mining investors, wrote that Angolese hatred of
whites was fully provoked by the Portuguese brutal system of inden-
tured labor.[20]

Gertrude Hance, for many years a Congregationalist missionary in
South Africa, concluded by World War I that "the real source of an-
tipathy towards missions are to be found in the appalling ungodliness,
class prejudice, ignorance, and selfishness of the dominant powers." By
then many American missionaries began to equate European secular
paganism with animistic paganism as the twin evils missionaries had to
overcome. By the 1930s better educated and more social reform oriented missionaries expressed greater concern over the corruption of
traditional African values and the advance of modern materialism than
with primitive animism. Africa revealed "the most disgraceful exhibi-
tion of greed, injustice, and murderous brutality, on the part of the
white man, to be found in the annals of our selfish race," concluded
Cornelius Patton, a spokesman for the interdenominational Missionary
Education Movement in South Africa.[21]

In the early 1900s and 1910s American missionaries made the major assumption that African society could be redeemed. Otherwise there
was little reason for them to labor and risk death in the bush. Their
commitment to redeem African society through their missionary efforts
made it difficult for them to view their potential converts as members of
inferior races. Racist interpretations of culture, based on inherent
biological determinants of culture and cultural potential, were incon-
sistent with the missionaries' assumptions. Consequently, missionaries
attributed the backwardness of African society not to race, as other
Americans presumably would have, but instead to the natives' unfor-

tunate animistic religious beliefs. Such supernaturalistic, pagan beliefs, they argued, made creative thought and the development of institutions grounded in cause-and-effect logic difficult for Africans. The natives' religious glorification of ancestral spirits hindered changes in their customs and their fear of witchcraft accusations deterred innovative ideas and behavior; it was only necessary for the natives to embrace modern Protestantism to be saved.[22]

By the 1920s and 1930s the missionaries became more pessimistic as they increasingly attributed the nonprogressiveness of Africa to material causes over which they had less control. Among these alternate explanations were the debilitating effects of the climate in the coastal lowlands and the geographic isolation of Africa from the currents of ideas and movements that had swept Europe. Medical missionaries pointed out that chronic disease sapped the natives' energy and made them fatalistic about life. Women missionaries argued that native women, presumably the carriers of culture in any society, were so overburdened with work in Africa that they could not perform their cultural function well.[23] Yet no missionaries attributed the cause of Africa's underdeveloped or static culture to race, nor did they repudiate their earlier assumption that only one generation was required to reorient the society.

While missionaries did not use scientific racism as an important focus for understanding Africans, they sometimes did employ black stereotypes—a predisposition for song and dance, volatile passions, and extravagant funerals—borrowed from American folklore. This was especially true of the southern fundamentalists, although other groups of missionaries occasionally employed these verbal pictures. To a certain extent, the medium shaped the message. In missionary journals, the necessary limits of space and of holding readers' attention encouraged writers to use stereotypes and to emphasize the exotic aspects of native life. When missionaries wrote longer accounts, such as memoirs and reminiscences, they did not use stereotypes nearly as often. These authors had usually spent more time in the field as well, and consequently they had more tolerance and understanding of Africans and their culture.[24]

Contradictions sometimes existed in the writing of individual missionaries on the nature of Africans—suggesting a certain amount of ambivalence in their attitudes. William Davis, a Presbyterian in the Congo, stated at one point that there were "subtle and inherent differences" in the thought processes of Africans, but he went on to say that any mental differences could be altered by changing the social environment. Julia Kellersberger, another Southern Presbyterian in the Congo, observed at nearly the same time that "the difference [between people] is not of race nor of color, but of character. . . . Those without Christ act as do those without Him at home." Yet Kellersberger too called on folk racial mythology in describing the "happy-heartedness" and "lovableness" of black Africans.[25]

Curiously enough, there were fewer examples of folk racial stereotypes in the writing of missionaries in the early twentieth century than in the 1930s. Robert Nassau, writing early in this century about his fifty years with West Africans, sounded like a field anthropologist of a later decade discussing the intricacies of traditional cultures.[26] Unlike missionaries who arrived later in Africa, Nassau declared that he did not believe it reasonable to disturb the cherished beliefs of Africans; he would first understand their way of life and then later incorporate Christian views where they were related to African beliefs. As might be expected from his broad-minded approach, Nassau quarreled constantly with more narrow-minded French colonial administrators over their treatment of Africans.

For at least some missionaries, folk racial stereotypes broke down after extended personal contact with the local culture. Samuel Verner, an orthodox Southern Presbyterian in the Congo, reported that at first all natives seemed alike in their savagery. But after close observation and learning the local language, he began to realize the similarity of Africans' nature to his own and the complexity and functional utility of cultural practices which at first had seemed immoral and irrational.[27]

Virtually without exception, missionaries spoke of the great unrealized religious, mental, and cultural potential of black Africans. DeWitt Snyder, a veteran Methodist missionary in Central Africa, wrote that Africans were cruel and unkind because they had never been *taught* how to love. In a metaphor based upon developmental assumptions he drew from his agrarian background, Snyder likened Africans to "a rich field of unbroken soil which needs but the intelligent hand of an honest and earnest cultivator to turn it into a rich and fertile farm." Thus the problem lay not in the nature of Africans but in their *nurture*. From West Africa sounded the same refrain from Melvin Fraser, an Illinois Presbyterian cultivator: "Every man is a liar, thief, murderer, adulterer, and every woman is a slave and a harlot *by compulsion of circumstances and customs*." Shifting metaphors, Fraser compared Africans to "diamonds in the rough" whose intrinsic qualities needed only the cutting and polishing supplied by Christian missionaries.[28]

Most missionaries favorably compared African students with white students in America in mental ability. Africans, they contended, as had Fraser, only needed teaching and the higher order of ideals provided by Christianity to develop their minds and their society. In character traits even the pre-Christian Africans were given high marks by seasoned missionaries. Speaking of a pagan chief and friend, Robert Nassau wrote that the man "never deceived me or took an unfair advantage of my needs. He was at least to me . . . true, honest, and just."[29]

Gertrude Hance, a veteran missionary in South Africa for the American Board, reported that the Boers were much more filthy, unprogressive and resistant to education than the Zulus. Zulus outside the contagion of western mine operators, she wrote, exhibited pride, courage, and intelligence. They were traditionally honest and trustworthy, but less so the more they came in contact with purveyors of what she considered European paganism. Albert Helser, a Church of the Brethren missionary in Nigeria, similarly reported that he had been favorably surprised by the Bura people: they were hospitable, industrious, and intelligent. The more he studied their language, he added, the greater he found its vocabulary and expressive power. Even in personal hygiene, he found that Bura babies he bounced on his knee smelled less offensive than infants back home in Indiana.[30]

It was Christian converts, however, to whom the missionaries gave an especially flattering description. The greater the original sin or the darker the original culture, the brighter was the redeemed subject. Glowing success reports clearly sanctified missionary effort as well as the missionaries and the funds necessary for their work. From the early 1900s on, the missionaries compared African Christians favorably with American Christians. Congo converts were now "industrious, clean, respectful, and whose honesty and virtuous lives make us ashamed of the horrible tales of vice and dishonesty which fill every day's paper in this [the United States] fair land." Perhaps to overcome suspected skepticism from American congregations, Arthur Pierson, an interdenominational missionary official, affirmed that African Christians were fully equal to whites in the virility and self-discipline of their new faith. In their enthusiasm for Christ evidenced by their sacrificial giving and courageous witness in hostile circumstances, he reported, they set a heroic example for all Christians.[31]

With such reports the reader wonders why the implication for Afro-Americans was not perceived. But it was an extremely rare missionary who was able or willing to see any connection between the potential of black Africans and black Americans. One who did, Samuel Verner, a Presbyterian from South Carolina, earlier in his career suggested that he was trying to repay blacks for wrongs suffered in the United States. Verner noted the irony of mission work: "These Luebo people had become as civilized and more Christianized than the colored people of my own Columbia in five years' time. Surely if the white people in America took as much interest in the welfare of the negro at their doors, as they did those in heathen Africa, a revolution in that race would ensue more profound than that caused by emancipation and enfranchisement."[32] The failure of other missionaries to draw similar conclusions suggests that the nature of American racial segregation and the ambivalent values of most white Christians made Africa a more favorable location for the expiation of guilt and the building of biracial reconciliation than southern or midwestern states. Indeed, expatriation to Africa by missionaries suggests an effort by some to escape the restrictive burden of American history and to start afresh in a presumably simpler society.

A noticeable emphasis in the reports on new African Christians was the attention paid to outward Western customs and behavior. The African Christian, missionaries reported, built his house sturdier than before, hung pictures on the wall, used bed linens, and held the chair for his wife. "The height of a man's front door in West Africa is a fair index as to his progress in Christian civilization," announced George Trull, a Presbyterian demonstrating his problem in distinguishing Christ from culture.[33] The close relationship between religion and general culture assumed by missionaries caused them numerous problems, especially in the twenties and thirties as secular Europeans supplied Western modernization without religious ideology. Exclusive missionary claims of cultural power diminished, and they became just another competing social agency. If missionaries were only one of several sources for cultural modernization, wherein lay their unique religious claims and their reason for being?

By the 1920s a new and more pessimistic tone began to appear in the missionaries' writings as a consequence of the rapid modernization in Africa and growing missionary apprehension. Earlier high enthusiasm for engineering a Christian civilization among "passive" Africans with an "undeveloped" culture waned considerably. The autonomy of African behavior and the interrelatedness of indigenous culture had been underestimated, missionaries concluded, and the power of Christian ideology as opposed to modern commercial interests had been overestimated. Outside criticism of missions by cultural relativists, inside criticism by liberal theologians, and the lack of success in creating a model Christian society led to substantial self-doubt and introspection. The missionaries continued their complimentary evaluation of individual Christians. But they either retreated into the bush in search of old-fashioned animistic pagans or in chastened tones began to speak of working together with Christian Africans in order to ameliorate the worst features of the new mining and urban centers. The earlier vis-

ion of an African Christian city "set upon a hill" had fallen victim to a
new reality—Africa's society was becoming as secularized as had America's.[34]

This painful reappraisal was voiced first by missionaries in mining
areas, such as John Springer in the Congo. In 1919 Springer, a midwestern Methodist, wrote that missions would never control events in Katanga; at best they could only mitigate the harmful effects of the mines.
Significantly, Springer now reported more favorably on indigenous culture than he had earlier; it no longer appeared as weak or as evil as it
had twenty years earlier. Missionaries belatedly recognized greater spiritual kinship with traditional African culture than with modern Africa.
They now perceived merit in native religion; they saw polygamy, dow-
ries, and secret societies, for example, as valuable means of social control
and stability. By the 1930s Springer was even more unhappy with the
cultural deterioration of mining districts. Bush culture was being transformed, he complained, but by natural resource entrepreneurs—not
missionaries. The recalcitrant American evils of alienation and secular
materialism had crossed the Atlantic to become the missionaries' devil
in Africa. Missionaries such as Springer now spoke of animism with nos-
talgia, even a certain fondness.[35]

To many missionaries labor strikes, alcoholism, prostitution, gam-
bling, and disintegration of old social institutions and authority were
altogether too reminiscent of urban problems in America. Faced with a
loss of support from home and growing personal doubts, fewer missionaries considered themselves as powerful Christian potters molding
African clay. "I may have exercised some slight influence," concluded a
tempered William Davis in the late thirties.[36] Race as a cause of the
problems of a new Africa was totally ignored in the missionary analysis,
nor was there any reference to the critique of racism going on in
America during the late twenties and thirties.

To avoid the perplexing problems of the coastal areas and mining
districts, a number of evangelical and fundamentalist missionaries traveled deeper into the bush where they could still battle a vulnerable animism of poison cups and child marriages. Other evangelicals in areas of
substantial European penetration fastened upon personal moral problems of westernized Africans as their new mission targets. African problems for these missionaries were still moralistic, only now the problems
were European beer, mining company prostitutes, and Sunday football.
One such American missionary, Julia Kellersberger, a Presbyterian from
Florida, revealed her loss of confidence in the evangelical mission when
she sadly admitted that "the mission cause can never compete with
material forces."[37]

Competition from secular agencies, declining missionary funds and volunteers, and the growing realization of rival values backed by economic imperialists led both liberal and orthodox missionaries to suggest the maturity of African Christians. Instead of pronouncements about the future work of African churchmen and the future autonomy of African churches, as had been given so often in the past, Americans now spoke of turning over major functions and power on the spot. African Christians were finally seen as capable of taking charge of evangelism and control of local churches. Through inherent ability and missionary training, Africans were now able to work alone with God without American help, wrote Herbert Smith, a fundamentalist from an interdenominational mission.[38]

The two major alternative approaches by missionaries to Africans in this new age were personified by Julia Kellersberger in the Congo and by Ray Phillips working among urbanized miners in South Africa. While both were Presbyterians, their responses varied considerably. Kellersberger's traditional program for a mission in the bush centered around the personal morality of prohibition, Sunday blue laws, purified sex relations, and the elimination of pagan morality.[39] On the other hand, Phillips, coming to South Africa at the close of World War I after corporate business experience in Chicago and a new theological degree from Yale, declared that the problems around Johannesburg were essentially the same as those in industrial America. Accepting the terms of such a situation, Phillips did not flee the city for an interior village, as did Kellersberger, but instead he attempted to apply his social interpretation of Christianity to the issues of employment, government, and housing.[40] Missionaries were dividing along the same theological and social lines as were Protestants in America.

Phillips, in this respect echoing Josiah Strong's views of America a half century earlier, argued that Africans were facing a critical period of transition between agrarianism and industrialism—the form of industrial civilization which developed would be decided within the current generation. Without the influence of Christianity to ameliorate conditions of labor and discriminatory South African legislation, he contended, South Africa would fall victim to those problems that ailed industrialism in the Western world. Phillips had little time for primitive animism since this was not the evil confronting the new Africans. Nor did Phillips spend time discussing such things as African ability or morality. From the beginning he assumed that these topics were irrelevant to the Christian imperative and to the very real African economic and social injustices, and that by improving housing, employment, and legal rights, mentality and character would take care of themselves.

Christians around the world, he urged, needed to work as one without thought of race or nationality against the common threat of materialistic heathenism. Racial segregation was no solution to African problems; agricultural training schools, labor unions, and cooperatives offered the only hope. Race was a false issue, according to Phillips; both black and white Africans needed a sound economy and society for the advantages a civilized life could provide. Phillips's critique of modern racism was striking in that there was no reference to any scientific analysis of race. Instead, his position was based on the moral injustice of social inequality and economic exploitation in light of Christian values.

Thus while most white American Protestant missionaries in Africa were heavily ethnocentric and at least superficially confident of the superior power of their ideas, they made little or no overt use of naturalistic racist assumptions or arguments. Compared to other American visitors in Africa, early-century missionaries were far more optimistic about the rapid assimilation of western culture into Africa and the development of an autonomous African society. The missionaries' image of Africans in the early 1900s rested on their idea of creating a model Christian society among potentially able people who had never previously been properly stimulated. Yet as Africa modernized during the teens and twenties, missionaries confronted their visible lack of success in fulfilling their objectives. Missionaries blamed corrupt foreign influences and industrialization, not the Africans, for this unexpected turn of events. A number of the more traditional evangelical missionaries followed their earlier dream deeper into the African bush where they believed themselves capable of coping with such problems there as the natives' belief in animism. Of those missionaries who remained in the growing European centers of Africa, one group kept primary focus on the personal moral ills of the new African work force, while the more socially conscious modernists asserted that African and American Christians, guided by culturally transcendent religious ideals, should work together to combat the values and inequities of an exploitive industrial order. In the continuing fluidity of ideas on race in America, missionaries consequently ranged from the cultural tradition of white paternalism through education and uplift to the more rare radical stance of racial equalitarianism through a fundamental religious critique of modern industrial society. Although they had never fully transcended popular eighteenth and nineteenth century racial folklore, their shared reluctance to employ Darwinian concepts in their religious analysis of society and their religious motives in creating a perfected Christian society in Africa within their own generation created yet another American social group little touched by social Darwinism.

II

Social Ideas in America's Cultures

F O R much of American history there has been a sense, shared by many Americans who belong to the diverse subcultures of American civilization, of conscious departure from or modification of prior cultural and social heritages imported into the new order and, in some instances, of fascinating innovations in the ordering of the social hierarchy and of social institutions. Many of the social institutions Americans take for granted, such as the denomination or mass political party, were, when they were founded, departures from established ways of organizing and directing human goals and energies, whether measured by the yardstick of American or European antecedents. For intellectual and cultural historians, the history of formal social theory has been a major, continuing interest. In recent decades this interest has often centered upon the social theories of intellectuals. It may well be that this will continue to occupy the attention of intellectual historians in the future. But in recent years some scholars have attempted to go beyond the traditional study of formal social theory and theorists to investigate and explain the ways in which groups and individuals not usually considered formal social theorists perceived and understood the social order in which they existed. This has produced some arresting and stimulating results. The assumption has been that ideas are the possessions of those people who are members of and participants in the many groups of the population, not merely of a social class of intellectuals.[1] Likely this focus implies not so much a denial as an enrichment and expansion of the research agenda of intellectual historians; it has been a central element of much of Persons's work, both in his lecture courses and in his more recent publications. Such a reorientation of focus can

lead to new perspectives and the broadening of the historical phenomena of intellectual history.

In a number of respects the essays in Part II follow this line of attack. Not surprisingly the authors have defined, as legitimate and appropriate research, problems that might also be of interest to the new
social historians. A decade or two ago many would not have been inclined to include literary domestics and Victorian women within a
sweeping panorama of the history of American social thought; nor
probably would they have focused on civic promoters and businessmen
or black sociologists. Another unifying thread running through all of
the studies is that in modern society and culture it is necessary for the
members of and participants in the various subcultures to work out the
social roles they play within the larger context of the social taxonomy of
classes. The essays also illustrate the differences between the social roles
of males and females, between public and private worlds; they suggest
that some social roles, notably race and gender, are perhaps more fundamental (or intractable) than others, such as occupation or profession.

The character of the social ideas and perceptions that women in
nineteenth century America acquired as the consequence of being
women is examined by Mary Kelley and Bruce and Joy Curtis.
Although there were important distinctions and differences between
the experiences of Kelley's literary domestics and the Curtis's Victorian
women, these talented women were in many respects prisoners of the
rigid sex roles society imposed upon them. There was, to be sure, some
element of chance and choice, but essentially among relatively circumscribed alternatives. As Kelley reminds us, the twelve literary domestics
were favored to be writers, not simply because of far-reaching changes in
the structure of the national and literary economies which made possible the emergence of a "novel" industry in which even women could
participate, but because of their particular talents and circumstances.
Much of Kelley's lively analysis focuses upon the genuine dilemma the
literary domestics faced between their almost secretive existence as female authors and their primary social identity as domestic beings first
and foremost. The literary domestics possessed such doubts about their
activities as writers that it must have taken remarkable courage and self-
confidence to carry on with their work. What made them different, presumably, from other women was that, by virtue of their work and the
unusual opportunities that beckoned to them, they were anomalies in
the social order and in the culture. What they could never escape, and
what insured that they could never become an autonomous functional
elite (as male authors could and did), was the fundamental identifica-

tion, which they accepted, of themselves as fulfilling a primarily domestic private social role.

Any independence and autonomy that Celeste Bush, Alice Sumner, Esther Sumner, Julia Elliott, and Sophie Raffalovich O'Brien were able to establish for themselves apart from their apparently primary social role as domestic beings was derived not simply from their individual shrewdness, energy, talent, and intelligence, but from their adoption of that quintessentially masculine social credo (at least so far as public behavior in the culture was concerned), the work ethic. And this in turn was a commitment not unlike the situation of the literary domestics that was in some sense made possible by impersonal market forces. It is one of the great virtues of the Curtises' analyses that they illustrate how five women whose life experiences were different were able to acquire a perception of the social order that enabled them to resolve their commitments to their domestic and public social roles in ways that were apparently enriching and broadening. Yet there seems little doubt that in many respects the contexts of the literary domestics and these Victorian women were not radically different. One had to play the game by society's rules and not challenge those pursuits clearly reserved for males, except anonymously or ambiguously so far as the public was concerned. Taken together, the two essays suggest much about how women of fame and of modest reknown struggled with the conflicts between their private and public social roles.

The last essays treat two issues central to America's public world, urban development and race relations. They also underline the importance of science as the heuristic guide and standard of judgment for that public world—which has been until very recent modern times, essentially a male cultural possession.[2] In Thomas J. Schlereth's authoritative account, Walter D. Moody was not a scientist; rather, he was a businessman and promoter who sought to use the language, rhetoric, and instruments of science as he understood them (however imperfectly) to promote what constituted a bold, daring, innovative plan of social engineering. He was confident that his plan would bring order and system to Chicago—and, by implication, to the nation's cities—through centralization, just as the work of the scientist made sense out of nature and centralized natural data into knowable laws of science which scientists would then bestow to the public's accumulating knowledge. Moody's methods of persuasion were borrowed quite openly from those two phenomenally successful applied social sciences and technologies of his day, advertising and progressive education, whose proponents sought to reshape society and culture with the laws of the emerging human sciences.

Moody's sense of centralization, of its appropriateness and naturalness, was matched by his sense of identity as a member of one of the new professional elites of the industrial order whose members were persuaded that they could offer peace, prosperity, and order through their expertise to all who desired their leadership. It was not incongruous for a member of one of the new professions to engage, as did Moody, in open, public, political activities. For basically the emerging professions of the new urban-industrial age were created by their members for expressly political purposes: to assist in the governance of the complex, hierarchial, modern industrial order by establishing the social authority of the professions. As Schlereth suggests, the ideology of men such as Moody was congenial to larger intellectual asssumptions shared by businessmen *and* progressive reformers.

Yet not all of the new professions that crystallized in industrial society possessed equal political and social authority. It was one thing to have linkages to the business community, but another matter entirely to identify with or belong to dispossessed or powerless groups. By the end of the 1920s the American scientific community had rejected the ideology of scientific racism. The reasons for this transformation were complex; certainly the demonstrations by geneticists and psychologists that it was difficult to make a plausible argument that races differed in cultural and moral potential for psychobiological reasons, and the aggressive theoretical challenges of the new social sciences to scientific racism such as the elaboration of the idea of culture by the anthropologist Franz Boas and his followers, played a role. Of course the specific repudiation of scientific racism dealt more with white immigrants and offspring of immigrants from southern and eastern Europe; with the closing of immigration by the restrictionist legislation of the twenties, the social reasons for the ideology of scientific racism largely evaporated.[3]

As the career of E. Franklin Frazier illustrates, the emergence of the cultural paradigm of racial equipotentiality within the scientific community may not have had large consequences for the objects of lay and scientific racism. In Dale R. Vlasek's portrait, Frazier emerges as an intellectual and social theorist of considerable consistency and complexity, devoted to the search for a scientific and political program for assimilation. Assimilation may have been an idea that flowed naturally from Frazier's family background, but as Vlasek shows, it was changed and enriched by his experiences and evolving work as a social scientist and intellectual. As a young man and neophyte scholar, Frazier advocated an economic program to create a black middle class, as similar to the white middle class as possible. In the late 1920s Frazier had become disillusioned with middle-class black businessmen, who seemed to treat their workers in ways too reminiscent of white employers. At the University of Chicago as a graduate student, and for more than two decades as a scholar, Frazier pinned his hopes for assimilation upon the new opportunities which the industrial city was apparently creating for peoples of varying backgrounds, believing that modernization would enhance assimilation. Eventually Frazier came to believe that even in the industrial city the black middle class would not and could not take a role of leadership in race relations and assimilation. In the third part of his career Frazier came to champion a new psychological and cultural strategy of fusion that emphasized the distinctive characteristics and heritage of black Americans as the only practical means of completing the task of assimilation. Obviously not all groups and their spokesmen could function or succeed equally well in a given historical context. In modern society and culture there were limits to the appeal and authority of science insofar as the hierarchial structure of the social order was concerned. For some, it was possible to use ideas and methods borrowed, however imprecisely, from modern knowledge and science to achieve long-range results of considerable consequence, as in the instance of Walter D. Moody. For individuals such as E. Franklin Frazier, it was, in Vlasek's able judgment, "ever changing and ever elusive." As the authors suggest in different ways, we must consider the public and private dimensions of human experience and perception and also the impact of modern culture, broadly defined, upon apparently enduring levels of the social order and culture.

H. C.

5

The Literary Domestics:
Private Women on a Public Stage

MARY KELLEY

NAY, fame never was a woman's Paradise, yet," Susan Warner wrote in her journal on August 2, 1851. Implicit in the confusion and ambiguity of Warner's words were several truths. Most immediate was that as a published writer Warner had been introduced to "fame." The female Warner had tasted it. At the time, her first novel, *The Wide, Wide World,* published in December 1850 when she was thirty-one, was an assured publishing success, although the full magnitude of its commercial success was as yet unrealized. At the very least she was well on her way to establishing herself as a popular writer. Over a month earlier she had completed a draft of *Queechy,* her second novel, which would prove to be another best-seller. Ever since she had been hard at work copying it by hand, putting it in presentable form for her publisher. She had yet to finish her task having done little else for weeks but rewrite the copy while neglecting other "duties." Three days before, she had noted in her journal that for "too long" she had not written in it. She had been too busy with her novel. Expending her last drops of energy in drops of ink, one per word, she had managed to put down, "One gets tired, and how then write journal?" Not that there was little to say. Much could be said about her recent public success. As Warner herself admitted, "I have had a world of things I might have written— praises from every quarter and multitudinous."[1] Obviously she was experiencing "fame." What was unusual was that Warner was a woman. She was a woman who had recognition beyond the home.

But what Warner acknowledged on other occasions was that the

MARY KELLEY, Dartmouth College, Hanover, New Hampshire.

praise apart from relatives or friends had come to "Elizabeth Wetherell," her literary public pseudonym, and not to Susan Warner, the domestic private woman. Herein was a paradox, namely that Susan Warner simultaneously was and was not "Elizabeth Wetherell." It suggested a dual, ambivalent identity. And it pointed to a larger historical paradox involving women and the world beyond the home. The development of a national publishing industry in the United States from 1820 to 1880 had the unlikely and unexpected result of providing a public platform for certain private domestic females and thereby engulfed them in an experience such as had never before befallen American women.

It was ironic that the traditionally male sectors of commerce and gentlemanly letters, transformed by economic growth, technological advancement, and demographic and political changes, would join together in an institutionalization of the nation's cultural and intellectual life and give these women the opportunity to broaden their own traditional sphere by becoming published, popular, commercially successful writers of novels, stories, and essays. That amounted to an extraordinary development. And considering what had been and what was the American woman's experience it was a development that would not have seemed likely. As Warner's words suggested, it was antithetical to what had been her historical experience, that is, "fame never was." Not surprisingly, although these women would achieve fame, they as private women would be uncomfortable in the public arena. At best they would feel ambivalent, at worst that they simply did not belong there. Again, taking a cue from Warner, their conflicted often adverse reactions to their status as writers amounted to a recognition that fame, in particular fame in the literary marketplace, was not and was not supposed to be "a woman's Paradise, yet." In a number of ways their words and actions suggested a profound sense of wonderment that they had arrived at the gates of paradise, guilt that they had passed through.

It is my proposal that these female writers be designated *literary domestics*. Previously, they have been dubbed by historians and critics as the sentimentalists.[2] But that term has a pejorative and ahistorical quality about it, calling into view maudlin, mindless celebrants of a cloyingly intimate and blissful home life; it raises the question whether such creatures of emotion could ever have written books, suggesting that somehow, out of a well of bathos, books appeared. *Literary domestics,* in contrast, directs attention to the historical process that made hybrids of these women; that when these females emerged in the literary marketplace as popular writers they appeared in nineteenth-century society as anomalous figures. The latter is implicit in the words of one of them, Mary Virginia Terhune, who declared, "It is my ambition to relieve literary domesticity from the odium that rests upon it."[3] Terhune's comment originally suggested to me the designation *literary domestic.*

The best-selling works of the literary domestics shared the subject of woman in and of the home. They focused upon the young female reared for and looking toward marriage; the adult woman as wife and mother; and the woman alone, whether unmarried, deserted, or widowed. Theirs was a prose of heroines with only a sprinkling of heroes; a prose mostly of women, whether married or single, who like themselves were portrayed as intimately involved with and deriving their identity from the domestic sphere. The writers themselves were the daughters and wives of the new American gentry identified by Stow Persons as one of a number of functional elites to emerge in the nineteenth century following a postrevolutionary dispersal of the powers held by the colonial gentry.[4] But these women came to have a status beyond their parental and marital connections with that elite. Indeed, the literary domestics constituted in unlikely fashion a functional elite peculiar to themselves. Their conflicted and contradictory response to their success as published, popular writers underlined that they were women of the home who came to assume simultaneously the male roles of public figure, wage earner, and creator of culture.

The massive expansion of the nation and economy, particularly from 1820 onward, set the stage. Having recovered from the disruption, chaos, and devastation of the Revolution, Americans enjoyed a fairly prosperous period from the 1790s until the panic of 1819. The first economic leap forward of an emergent market capitalism began in the 1820s and continued for approximately two decades with interruptions during recessions in the 1820s, 1834, and 1837, the last being the most severe and stretching into the early 1840s. Generally, however, metamorphosis and growth were tremendous and unabated. Together they made possible and provided the structure for the creation of a burgeoning publishing industry. Perhaps the most striking of the results were the commercialization and democratization of literature.

Literary economics paralleled the economic development of the nation. It was only in the 1820s that changes in the publishing world made it possible for a writer—male or female—to contemplate reaching a national audience. Little could be compared between what existed before and what came after. There had been neither a national publishing industry nor what legitimately could be called a profession of authorship in the United States before the third decade of the nineteenth century. Numerous factors had hindered the growth of American publishing before that time. A lack of capital typical for an underdeveloped country, high production costs, an inefficient system of distribution, poor transportation, and an absence of a predictable market were among the obstacles. But various developments combined to change that situation dramatically. The most important included a literal revolution in transportation with the construction and multiplication of roads, canals, steamboats, and railroads; a technological advance in printing greater than any since the fifteenth century; and an ensuing centralization in publishing itself, marked by the rise of Philadelphia, New York, and Boston as the dominant centers.[5]

Simultaneously, the audience for literature increased substantially. Beginning in 1790 when there were nearly four million people in the United States, the population doubled every twenty-five years into the twentieth century. The democratic goal of universal literacy in the new republic was translated into broadened opportunities for education with the result that approximately 90 percent of the adult white population, men and women, entered the literate category during the first part of the nineteenth century. By the 1840s America had the largest reading audience ever produced.[6]

In terms of both numbers of readers and dollars, a publishing world had been created for the writer where before there had been only a polyglot of provincial outlets. Previously forced to confine themselves to an audience restricted by locality and literacy, American writers by the middle of the century could command a geographically national and broadly based audience, and some could hope realistically to garner an adequate income for their efforts. Beginning in the twenties the rate of growth in American novels published in this country was phenomenal. From 1820 to 1829, 128 novels appeared; that was almost 40 more than had been published in the previous fifty years taken together. It was five times the number published in the previous decade. More than double that number, 290, appeared in the 1830s, and the total more than doubled again in the 1840s to nearly 800. That a mass market for books was being created can be seen in the dramatic increase in the production of reading matter as gross income derived from trade in books rose from $2,500,000 in 1820 to $12,500,000 by 1850.[7]

The literary domestics stepped into this public arena traditionally ruled by men and achieved a distinctive measure of success there. By the time they had exited the public stage, they knew they had been noticed. Beginning with Catharine Maria Sedgwick's first few efforts in the 1820s, followed by Caroline Howard Gilman and Caroline Lee Hentz in the 1830s, Maria McIntosh, E. D. E. N. Southworth, and Harriet Beecher Stowe in the 1840s, and by Maria Cummins, Mary Jane Holmes, Sara Parton, Mary Virginia Terhune, Susan Warner, and Augusta Evans Wilson in the 1850s, these twelve most commercially successful of the literary domestics came to dominate a substantial literary marketplace with their sales. They enjoyed their heyday in the fifties, sixties, and seventies, and some continued to write best-sellers and reap sales beyond 1880. The August 14, 1858, issue of the *American Publishers' Circular* listed seventeen works which it said were "among the greatest successes" in recent publishing. Seven of the titles represented the efforts of Cummins, Parton, Stowe, and Terhune. A table prepared by the *Boston Post* in 1860 listed "the most popular and widely circulated" authors. Warner's name was added to that list, which again included Cummins, Parton, Stowe, and Terhune. By 1871 nearly three-fourths of all the novels published that year came from the pens of women. If information supplied by the *Nation* and *Publisher's Weekly* in the next year was any indication, the literary domestics were still more than holding their own: the three authors whose works were said to be most in demand at public libraries were Southworth, Hentz, and Holmes, in that order.[8]

Rather than a historical development, the act of these creators of fantasy stepping upon a stage before a huge audience appeared a fantasy itself. The literary domestics responded as if they felt a time change had occurred and misplaced them in another world. What had happened did not seem real at all. In 1835, sixteen years prior to the day when Susan Warner would write in her journal of a "Paradise" that was not woman's, Catharine Maria Sedgwick, referring to a recent publication, noted in her journal that she had been met everywhere "with congratulations about my book." But to Sedgwick there was something odd about that, as if the plaudits had little relation to her own sense of female identity. Her "author's existence," she observed, had "always seemed something accidental." If Sedgwick's career as a writer had not begun accidentally, it certainly had been unplanned and what transpired had been unforeseen. Her first novel, *A New England Tale*, appeared in 1822 when she was already thirty-three years of age. She had begun it as a short religious tract for the Unitarians and had turned it into a novel at the strong urging of her brothers, Harry and Theodore Sedgwick. She needed such encouragement. A year before, probably when she was engaged in turning tract into novel or at least contemplating it, she wrote to a friend that "My dear brother Theodore makes a most extravagant estimate of my powers. It is one thing to write a spurt of a letter, and another to write a book."[9]

The success of the novel was a complete surprise. Shortly after its appearance, Harry wrote Catharine that Bliss and White, the publishers, had reported that "it was going off very rapidly, and much beyond their expectations, and would soon be entirely exhausted." In a few days, said Harry, bubbling with enthusiasm, he would send Catharine the draft of a preface for the second edition. Less than four months after the appearance of the first edition, the second edition was out. Sedgwick continued to write books. She had written eight by the time she dubbed her career an accident. Her volumes proved undoubted commercial successes and Sedgwick became a public figure. She, too, attained fame. But thirteen years of success notwithstanding, she would reflect in her journal that everything about her authorship still seemed somehow spurious, again, as if it should not have happened. All of that, she wrote, felt "extraneous and independent of my inner self."[10]

Sedgwick's response should not be surprising. That she or any of these twelve women came to have a public voice and role as a popular writer could hardly have been predicted. As women they were not supposed to participate in their society's public life. They were not trained or expected to become statesmen or politicians, judges or legislators, entrepreneurs or merchants, or in any way simply prominent public citizens. Sedgwick herself would publicly (and ironically) proclaim in the aptly titled *Means and Ends, or Self Training,* "I cannot believe that women should lead armies, harangue in the halls of legislation, bustle up to ballot boxes, or sit on judicial tribunals."[11] As gentry's daughters they were the heirs and beneficiaries of a cultural heritage. Under that aegis more education was provided them than many males in their society. They were prepared to be the cultured wives of gentlemen and the nurturing mothers of future citizens of the republic. It was even an education more than sufficient to enable them to become writers. But in no way were they consciously trained or educated to become published, income-earning writers.

Instead, these women were nurtured as private domestic beings, conditioned to live as private individuals, and directed to accept woman's private domestic role. As Caroline Howard Gilman wrote in *Recollections of a Southern Matron,* God and tradition prescribed that, for woman, "Home was her true sphere."[12] Assertions that woman should take her place beside man in the public arena, said Maria McIntosh in *Woman in America: Her Work and Her Reward,* are "contradicted alike by sacred and profane history." Instead, women and men should continue to be called to "*Different* offices and *different* powers—this is what we would assert of them.''[13] Woman's office was out of the way, in the background. Even as a moral figure in the guise of wife and mother she was to exercise nominal influence in an indirect, subtle, and symbolic fashion. Any voice was to be soft or subdued. In her society, woman's was to be a mostly invisible presence.

These women did not originally expect or plan to become professional published writers. That is suggested in part by their ages when their first volumes of fiction appeared. Nine of the twelve were thirty years or more. Three of those nine did not publish volumes until they were close to forty or older, and two others issued only one volume in their thirties, waiting until their forties and fifties, respectively, before another appeared. The only three of the twelve to publish volumes in their twenties, namely, Cummins, Terhune, and Wilson, significantly were the last of the group to publish, in the 1850s. The example had been set for them. They had the advantage and perhaps the motivation of knowing that some had gone before.

Regardless of the age at which these women began their professional careers or whether others had preceded them, there remained a psychological and social dilemma. To have the influence of a writer was to have an influence beyond the home, to have a role beyond the home. It was to leave woman's sphere for man's, to meddle in the public affairs of men. Familiar circumstances and attitudes facilitated the private becoming public. No doubt it helped that they could write behind closed doors in the privacy and secrecy of their homes. It helped, too, that they could write behind the shield of anonymity or a pseudonym. That provided a significant cover for women. In effect, they could *do it* and yet *deny it*. At the very least anonymity contributed to a sense of psychological security. In peculiar, contradictory fashion the literary domestics could write and, as it were, hide the act. Psychologically as well as physically they could write behind closed doors. They could write hesitantly for the world and try to stay at home.

The anonymous American lady author began to appear at the end of the eighteenth century. Lyle Wright's *American Fiction* counts thirty-two works of fiction by American women during the half century previous to 1820. All thirty-two appeared from 1793 onward, and the overwhelming majority were published anonymously. If one eliminates the seven novels of the British writer, Susannah Rowson, which Wright numbers among the thirty-two, the figures are even more striking. Three of the listings were those of Mrs. Caroline Matilda Thayer, Mrs. P. O. Manville, and, simply, a Mrs. Patterson, whose single effort amounted to twenty-seven pages. Two by Ann Eliza Bleecker appeared posthumously, ten and fourteen years after Bleecker's death, rendering them effectively anonymous. All of the remaining twenty were anonymous publications. It was a time when no one imagined that the emergence of a national publishing industry was only a few years in the future; when, as was the tradition, all or most of these publications were probably financed by the author or author's relatives rather than by the printer or bookseller; when publication was local, noticed only by a few, and sales were small; when, in short, *the lady* barely ruffled the dignified calm of her domestic anonymity with her single, mostly unnoticed fictional appearance. But if publication was a very different phenomenon and public attention practically nonexistent for these American women, to go down the list of publications and see once a year or once every few years the appearance of "By a Lady," "By a Lady of Philadelphia," or "By an American Lady" is still to sense the hesitant, timid, and apprehensive character of their acts. It is to detect their own reaction to the dictum that a woman was not supposed to be a published writer.[14]

The literary domestics provide evidence that the dictum remained in force. Ten of the twelve literary domestics resorted to anonymity at least at the initial stage of their careers. Sedgwick, again the pioneer among them, wrote anonymously throughout her career. Thirteen years after she began publishing in 1822, "Miss Sedgwick" appeared with *Tales and Sketches.* For fourteen years after that Sedgwick again wrote anonymously before an edition of her collected works bore her name on the title page. And there was no name issued with her last novel, published in 1857, when she concluded her career. Of the last three writers to appear in print in the 1850s, Cummins wrote all of her four novels anonymously before her death at thirty-eight; Terhune wrote under the pseudonym of "Marion Harland" throughout a career that lasted sixty-odd years into the twentieth century; and Wilson published her first and her third novels anonymously. Between the first and the last of these writers, Gilman resorted to the pseudonym of Mrs. Clarissa Packard; McIntosh published for six years before using her name; and Parton and Warner began and continued to write under the pseudonyms of Fanny Fern and Elizabeth Wetherell, respectively. Generally, Southworth and Stowe did write under their own names, but at the very least Southworth's first story appeared anonymously and Stowe also contributed anonymous pieces to periodicals before *Uncle Tom's Cabin* made her a controversial as well as a public figure. For example, when one of her first essays appeared in *The Western Magazine,* Stowe wrote a friend, "It is ascribed to Catherine, or I don't know that I should have let it go. I have no notion of appearing *in propria persona.*"[15]

While it is true that the literary domestics were practicing a well-worn tradition in publishing anonymously, one that went back at least to the practices of the British aristocracy, gender for them was far more significant in this regard than gentry status.[16] When gentlemen had demonstrated the learning of their letters for polite society, they wrote anonymously because it was considered vulgar to expose oneself to an inferior public. But for these women the psychological and social implications of maintaining anonymity went far beyond the desire to maintain a facade of gentility. Obviously, anonymity served as a partial means by which the dictum could be served. The writer was a woman, but the published work was not ascribed to her. Just as important, women could still consider themselves private domestic beings. They had not stepped beyond the doors of their homes—only their works had, and anonymously at that.

With the publication of her first novel, Catharine Maria Sedgwick recognized that her life had changed drastically and, in her opinion, for the worse. "I am more anxious than I can express to you to remain unknown," she wrote to a friend, "but that, I fear, is impossible now." As she phrased it, the problem was that by publishing she was "obtruding myself upon the notice of the world." It was a problem that would remain for Sedgwick. Five years later, while laboring over her third novel and in anticipation of its appearance, she wrote to her brother, Charles, that "to be the subject of public inquest is not agreeable to a woman of any womanly feeling." When Mary Virginia Terhune was twenty-four, her first novel, appropriately titled *Alone* and privately financed by her father, became an unexpected best-seller in 1854, thirty-two years after Sedgwick's first novel had appeared. It was then that Terhune committed herself to writing, but she had already gone "out in the world" as early as age fourteen with the decision to send a few essays to daily and weekly papers. They were submitted during the years before the publication of *Alone,* but always "under the shelter of a nom de plume." At sixteen she wrote an article titled "Marrying Through Prudential Motives," rewrote it at eighteen, and using the initials of her forenames submitted it to *Godey's Lady's Magazine* under the pseudonym of "Mary Vale—a veiled suggestion of my real name." Mislaid by the editor, the article was not published for six years.[17]

Prior to that, at age nineteen, the inevitable happened when a few friends discovered that Terhune was the author of a series of articles on religion which had appeared under the name of "Robert Remer," another of her early pseudonyms. With the disclosure, she wrote to a friend, "My surprise was only equalled by my mortification and wounded feeling." For Terhune it was not an inconsequential event as was illustrated by the substance and intensity of her response:

> Believe me, it is no laughing matter with me; I cannot, I do not ex-
> pect others to understand the feelings which induce me to keep
> this secret, but you may perhaps think they are weighty, when I
> tell you, that I would rather anything else that my bosom guards in
> silence should have been proclaimed.

Her final determination concerning her incognito was based upon the initials of her first and last names before marriage, and "Marion Harland" appeared as an author of a temperance story. It was, as she said again, "a hint of my name, so covert that it was not guessed at by readers in general." When she was over sixty years of age, in reply to a letter inquiring about her use of a pseudonym, Terhune explained that "My reason for choosing a 'pen-name' at all was the desire of a young writer to screen her personality from even her intimate friends." Terhune might just as well have attributed the desire to a young *woman,* or for that matter, to *woman,* as she never lost her sense of what it was to be a private female being in the nineteenth century.[18]

The frustration experienced by John S. Hart in his attempt to inform the reading public about the women behind the books revealed the literary domestics' determination to remain private beings. With so many women in print by mid-century, Hart among others compiled biographical volumes; his was titled *The Female Prose Writers of America* and was first published in 1852. Gilman, Hentz, McIntosh, Sedgwick, Stowe, and Warner were included. Noting in his preface that women were not readily disposed to provide information about themselves, Hart admitted that he had experienced "much difficulty" preparing the collection of sketches. "Few things," he said, "are more intangible and elusive than the biography of persons still living." (Readers of today would note the irony that when Hart referred to "persons" he meant *women.*) Anxious to emphasize that his volume contained "an unusual amount of authentic information," Hart practically undid himself when he stated that his information had been "difficult to obtain" and that his sketches were "as full and minute as circumstances would justify, or as the writers themselves would allow."[19]

The sketches would have been more detailed and complete had respondents like Caroline Howard Gilman been more forthcoming. She replied to Hart's request for information about her life by observing, "It seems to me, and I suppose at first thought, it seems to all a vain and awkward egotism to sit down and inform the world who you are." On the basis of such an opinion she had made her decision not to tell all: "I have purposely confined myself to my earlier recollections, believing that my writings will be the best exponents of my views and experiences." Susan Warner was even less cooperative. Unlike Gilman, she declined to have anything published about her. The reading public wanted to know " 'Who is Elizabeth Wetherell?' " Hart wrote, but that inquiry had resulted "so far in no disclosure beyond the fact that she is the author of the 'Wide, Wide World,'—and nothing more." In short, he concluded, "the authorship of these volumes is a secret and likely to be so kept for some time." Actually, Hart already knew who "Elizabeth Wetherell" was, and he had asked Warner more than once if he could let the public know. Somehow, he had discovered Warner's identity a year earlier and had written her to ask permission to print that information in *Sartain's Union Magazine*. She had refused him and let him know that she was upset that he possessed such knowledge: "I had no mind in the first place to have my real name known at all," she wrote Hart, "and though that is now beyond my control, I do certainly wish never to see it in print." As Warner's sister, Anna, who was also a writer, phrased it, "we had both wished to keep our names in hiding." Symbolically, the two sisters had reached back to two other invisible females, that is, to their grandmothers and borrowed their names: "I was going before the world as 'Amy Lothrop,' " Anna related, "while for a long time my sister was known chiefly as 'Elizabeth Wetherell.' " Not surprisingly, then, Warner informed Hart that regarding public acclaim, "I desire that Miss Wetherell take it all,—not I." She was pleased that the public appreciated her work, but otherwise her authorship was a private matter, a private experience. By 1855 Warner's authorship had become slightly less private when in a subsequent edition of his biographical sketches, Hart disclosed the "real name of Elizabeth Wetherell." Nevertheless, after identifying Warner, Hart added that "as she continues to use her *nom de plume* in all her publications," he would do the same in writing further of her.[20]

Warner might never have written for publication if her affluent New York lawyer father, Henry Whiting Warner, had not encountered a series of financial setbacks beginning with the panic of 1837. Directly as a result of the family's difficulties, Warner's aunt said to her one day, " 'Sue, I believe if you would try, you could write a story.' " Anna, who recalled the incident, was uncertain if her aunt had said specifically that Susan could write a book " 'that would sell,' " but, said Anna, "that was what she meant." By that time, the late 1840s, even women in the home were well aware of the existence of a substantial literary marketplace. Apparently, there were some publishers who had yet to take the measure of the popular appeal of literary domesticity. George Palmer

Putnam, the publisher of Warner's *The Wide, Wide World,* wrote her
four months after publication that "I certainly did not anticipate the
half of it." He would remain surprised: estimates are that the novel
eventually sold more than a half million copies in the United States
alone.[21]

Money played an important role in at least eight of the twelve literary domestics' careers. Some began writing for publication only after
they were in need of money, while financial exigencies significantly affected the productivity of others. As Stow Persons has noted, the gentry
were not necessarily people of wealth. And even for those who were, af-
fluence was not necessarily forever. As was the case with Warner, McIntosh, Parton, and Southworth might never have launched their careers
had they not needed the money. Unmarried and in her middle thirties,
Maria McIntosh did not look to writing for support until she had lost all
of her family inheritance in the financial crisis of 1837. Two decades
later a letter to Maria Cummins indicates that McIntosh was still dependent upon her pen. She was anxiously awaiting a payment from her
publisher John P. Jewett, she informed Cummins, "as enabling me to
meet some debts here." Bemoaning her situation, McIntosh added, "If
I were only not in debt, I should care for nothing—but that others
should lose by me—that I should be compelled to fail in my obligations
troubles me a little."[22] Sara Parton did not begin her career until she
was in her early forties and even then not until her first husband had
died and she found herself separated from her second husband and
faced with the support of herself and her children. She first attempted
more traditional means, starting a school and taking in sewing, and failing these she turned to writing for a living. Parton's third husband, the
biographer James Parton, would wonder after Sara's death, in that she
had demonstrated potential as a writer when a young woman, why she
had waited so long to write when her financial needs arose. As a social
commentator on his age, James Parton obviously had one blind spot at
least.[23] E. D. E. N. Southworth also began her career only after she was
separated from her husband and had to support herself and two children. She too became a teacher first and had reached thirty before her
first novel appeared.[24]

Financial need was a determining factor in enlarging the careers of
Caroline Lee Hentz and Harriet Beecher Stowe. Hentz was thirty-three
when her first novel was published in 1833. Thirteen years elapsed
before her next novel appeared in 1846. A few years later the in-
capacitating illness of her husband, the scientist and educator Nicholas
Hentz, made her the sole financial supporter of the family. For the last
seven years of her life, from 1850 to 1856, Hentz published the startling

total of nine novels and six collections of stories. Stowe, too, had published some stories before *Uncle Tom's Cabin* radically altered her literary career as well as her life. A volume of fictional sketches had appeared in 1843 when she was thirty-two. Her next volume did not appear until nine years later when *Uncle Tom's Cabin* burst upon the political as well as the literary horizon. Having received ten thousand dollars from the first nine months of sales alone, Stowe wrote to Eliza Cabot Follen that such had been "an agreeable surprise." After all, she said, "Having been poor all my life, and expecting to be poor to the end of it, the idea of making anything by a book, which I wrote just because I could not help it never occurred to me." Stowe was not being exactly truthful, however, and contradicted herself in the same letter.[25]

Although the novel's popularity and her remuneration were a surprise, Stowe was already well aware that she could garner income from her writing, however small the amount. And she revealed as well that whatever the amount of earnings derived from her writing in the past, it had always gone to meet the needs of her family. While as Stowe said, "The nursery and the kitchen were my principle fields of labor," it did not take her long to discover that "when a new carpet, or a mattress was going to be needed," she could make the purchase with a publication. Her efforts became imperative when financial stability was threatened and the "family accounts 'wouldn't add up'—then I used to say to my faithful friend and factotum, Anna . . . 'Now if you will keep the babies and attend to the things in the house for one day I'll write a piece, and then we shall be out of the scrape.' " That, said Stowe, was how "I became an authoress."[26] What she was actually saying was that she had begun as a sometime authoress while a full-time wife and mother. As the material needs of her family occurred and as Stowe realized more and more that she could meet some of those needs through her writing, she became more and more a writer while remaining a full-time housewife. The unexpected financial success of *Uncle Tom's Cabin* made her earnings a greater factor in her family's sustenance and significantly altered her literary career. A part-time writer before that success, she produced nine novels, a number of volumes of stories, and other miscellaneous writings in the next quarter century. All but one of her children who survived to adulthood continued to rely upon her for financial support and after her husband retired in 1864 he became fully dependent upon her.

The degree to which the material needs of their families played a role in the careers of Augusta Evans Wilson and Mary Virginia Terhune is not totally clear. But they did play a role. Wilson did not marry until she was thirty-two, and then she chose Colonel Lorenzo M. Wilson, a prosperous financier almost thirty years her senior. However, previous to that, sickness, financial disaster, and war reduced her once affluent parents to occasional poverty, and there is evidence that Wilson provided aid with income from her books. For example, with money from the sales of her second novel, *Beulah,* she purchased a home the family had been renting and registered the deed in her father's name. Terhune was both a prolific writer and a best-seller but in an autobiography of approximately five-hundred pages her long career gets short shrift. Terhune wrote and published two novels prior to her marriage. The unexpected success of the first novel that launched her career receives due treatment in her autobiography. But as if to suggest that she thought it improper to discuss such endeavors once she was married, little of the rest of her career is discussed including the success of her second novel, *The Hidden Path.* However, after more than 360 pages of the autobiography, there is one reference to her career that is revealing. Noting that she had three books in the hands of a failing publisher, all of which were " 'good sellers,' " Terhune added, "I had come to look upon royalties as my husband regarded his salary, as a sure and certain source of revenue." She also commented that until that time, "We had never known the pinch of financial 'difficulties.' " But, now, there was a difficulty as her clergyman husband, Edward Payson Terhune, was suffering from ill health and needed extended time away from the pulpit. Fortunately, in lieu of Terhune's royalties, her husband's congregation produced the necessary funds.[27]

Although Terhune came to rely upon the money from her books, her relative reticence about her career suggested that she felt uneasy in that role. It was the father or husband who was supposed to have the salary or income. Gentry females were neither expected to earn money nor was it thought proper for them to do so. The role, then, was not one in which the literary domestics were confident or to which they became fully accustomed. Wilson reportedly hoped that her parents' respect for literature would overcome any objections they had to her acceptance of money for her endeavors. Fourteen years after the publication of her first novel, Catharine Maria Sedgwick who had profited from her books would scoff at her brother Charles's references to her ability to make money, saying, "with characteristic confidence in another's ability and success you put me up to making money out of my poor brains— Depend upon it," she assured him, "this is a dream." Harriet Beecher Stowe clearly found it a novelty when her early tales and sketches brought her money. In 1838, fifteen years before her husband, Calvin, would tell her that "Money matters are entirely in your hands," she wrote to one of her sisters to tell her that she had received forty dollars for a "piece." "Mr. Stowe says he shall leave me to use [it] for my personal gratification," said Harriet, which was an idea she thought ludicrous—"as if a wife and mother had any gratification apart from her family interests."[28]

What Stowe was revealing was that she had the identity of a private domestic female. But her words also demonstrate that the very identity that barred woman from the role of family provider simultaneously motivated the female Stowe to increase her literary productivity and gave her the necessary rationalization for her efforts. For the literary domestics, "family interests" barred them from earning income while it paradoxically justified their endeavors to do so. That a number of these women became the sole providers of their families and still others supplied important supplementary income meant that, for whatever reason, no man in their family was totally fulfilling that male responsibility. It was a condition of their lives that made them distinctly uncomfortable. Given their socialization, they felt the need and were quick to rationalize their income on the basis that their families needed the support. To justify their pursuit of literary income simply as the right of any individual was neither easy nor likely for them. To have expected them to do so, or to do so without grave misgivings, would be to remove them from their historical context.

After she had begun to provide the entire support for her family, Caroline Lee Hentz in a series of letters to one of her publishers, Abraham Hart, tried to legitimate her attempt to gain more money for her fiction, not on the basis that she was a professional writer and thus had the right to do so, but because she needed money to support her family. In one letter, Hentz said to Hart that "so you may not think me dictated by mercenary motives," she wanted to explain why she desired more money for her novel, *Rena, or the Snowbird*. The reason was simple: her husband was sick. Were he able to fulfill his role as family provider, Hentz wrote, "I would think it a privilege to write for the mere pleasure and further reputation that I might acquire." But because her husband could not meet his responsibility to his family, she had to: "On me alone rests its support—Urged by this sacred duty I now write, not for *mere* pleasure or reputation, however dear the last may be."[29] *Rena* appeared in 1851 under the imprint of Hart's firm.

Toward the end of that year, Hentz was bargaining with Hart again, this time about compensation for *Marcus Warland; or, The Long Moss Spring*. But she had more leverage now. She had shown the novel to another publisher and received a higher bid than Hart offered. Before signing a contract she wrote to Hart to tell him of the other offer, hoping that he might raise his. Using exactly the same phrase, she assured him again that, "I am not actuated by mercenary motives." Instead her husband still suffered from ill health and thus, said Hentz, "I am compelled to turn my brains to gold and to sell them to the highest bidder." Hart was not enthralled and apparently claimed that she had already agreed to his offer and therefore had no right to solicit a higher bid from another publisher. Hentz responded by reiterating her justification for her actions, namely, that her husband's incapacity meant that "the whole support of the family devolves upon me." Given that circumstance, she asked, "is it strange that I should try to obtain the highest value for my productions?" At any rate, she concluded, how much was Hart willing to pay? Apparently enough, as *Marcus Warland* was published by A. Hart in 1852.[30]

It may be argued that Hentz was using her husband's illness as a ruse, that her plea of poverty was merely a false pretext for jacking up the price. But that seems unlikely. Nicholas Hentz was seriously ill for the last decade of his life, and she did have to support the family. And it should be noted again that in the two decades prior to her husband's illness she had published only two novels. After he became incapacitated, she produced fifteen volumes of fiction, novels and stories, in less than half the time. The change in her family's financial circumstances motivated her to increase her literary production and drastically altered her female life. Most significantly, it led to her adoption of the traditional male role of family provider. She was able to rationalize her act on the basis of family need, but it was a rationalization she needed. The same can be said about E. D. E. N. Southworth who also had to support herself and her children. Southworth bargained again and again over the years with Robert Bonner whose *New York Ledger* served as an installment outlet for her novels. She always sought to justify her requests on the basis of her family's material needs. Bonner did pay her liberally, and she constantly expressed her gratitude for his generosity in what she regarded as her difficult and abnormal circumstances. Southworth was, as she expressed it to Bonner in 1875, "a woman with the lifelong double burden of man and woman laid upon me."[31]

The literary domestics were proud that they as women were able to assume their double burden. But pride did not efface their defensive posture, a posture that reflected a sense of deviance. Family need was a necessary rationalization. Sara Parton was as prideful as any of these women. She was also as defensive as any of them as demonstrated by a fictional sketch in which she attempted to rebut those who looked askance at women as writers. The critical attitude in the story is voiced by Harry Seldon, the friend of one James Lee whose wife, Emma, is engaged in literary activity. " 'I understand he has the misfortune to have a bluestocking for a wife,' " says Harry, " 'and whenever I have thought of going there, a vision with inky fingers, frowzled hair, rumpled dress, and slip-shod shoes has come between me and my friend— not to mention thoughts of a disorderly house, smokey puddings, and dirty-faced children.' " Clearly, a woman who writes is not a woman at all or, at the very least, she is a woman who fails her true calling, who shirks her domestic duties. Harry concludes: " 'Defend me from a wife who spends her time dabbling in ink, and writing for the papers.' " A visit to the Lees disabuses Harry of these false notions. To his surprise, he discovers that the Lees' home is a model of cleanliness and neatness, their children loved and secure. Most important of all, Emma Lee, a paragon of traditional femininity, is a writer only because her financially distressed husband needs her aid.[32]

Inadvertently, Parton's sketch says that the wife is not legitimately a writer at all and Parton's use of the epithet "bluestocking," an eighteenth-century British term applied in pejorative fashion to a woman who had intellectual or literary interests, indicates her recognition that woman as a creator of culture also was perceived as an anomalous figure. Women could acquire culture, at least in limited fashion. They could be receptors of culture. But to apply their knowledge as creators of culture was to encroach in yet another way upon a traditionally male domain. Indeed, women were even suspect as intelligent, articulate beings. Catharine Maria Sedgwick was well aware of that long before she began her career as a writer. Her diary of 1811 records an encounter at a social gathering with "two young men of sense . . . who thought it worth their while to talk to me, as if I had an intellectual character in common with them and could comprehend something beyond the first lesson of infancy." It was an experience that was as unusual as it was pleasant. Augusta Evans Wilson also expressed her contempt for what she considered to be her society's demeaning regard of women as intelligent beings, writing to a friend that "to be 'feminine' is scarcely a synonym for weak-minded, idiotic, or frivolous."[33]

To be a creator of culture represented the more presumptuous act of all on the part of woman. As the literary domestics discovered, this more aggressive threat to man's claim to the exclusive rights of intellectual achievement was met with scorn and disdain. Wilson suggested what her experience was through the use of a fictional alter ego. In her

novel, *St. Elmo*, Edna Earl's intellectual ambitions and her efforts to
support herself as a writer meet with entrenched hostility. She learns
through a male friend of her society's judgment of a "bluestocking":

> A 'bluestocking,' my dear, is generally supposed to be a lady,
> neither young, pleasant, nor pretty (and in most instances unmar-
> ried); who is unamiable, ungraceful, and untidy; ignorant of all
> domestic accomplishments and truly feminine acquirements, and
> ambitious of appearing very learned; a woman whose fingers are
> more frequently adorned with ink-spots than thimble; who holds
> housekeeping in detestation, and talks loudly about politics, sci-
> ence, and philosophy; who is ugly, and learned, and cross; whose
> hair is never smooth and whose ruffles are never fluted.

The friend asks Edna if she understands the matter and is told that " 'I
do not understand why ladies have not as good a right to be learned and
wise as gentlemen.' " Edna encounters male condescension and hostility toward her intellectual and literary ambitions directly in the person of
Douglass Manning. A prominent figure in the literary world and the
editor of a national magazine for which she writes, Douglass has a low
estimate of female intellect and judges Edna's first, projected novel as
" 'beyond your capacity—no woman could successfully handle it.' " He
is not her only detractor. She hears constantly from those around her
that her ambitions are unnatural for a woman and certain to end in
failure. After a while, Edna wonders if "all women were browbeaten for
aspiring to literary honors?" Mary Virginia Terhune's Phemie Hart, in
Phemie's Temptation, meets with the same charges after she embarks
upon a literary career. She is told that her actions are unwomanly and
that she is transgressing her true domestic sphere. Her husband who says
of " 'literary women' " that " 'I detest the class,' " declares that " 'you
have unsexed yourself.' "[34]

Although Wilson's and Terhune's portrayals of the female writer
scorned represented counterattacks, theirs were not cases of simple
rebellion. Their defense of the position of the literary woman revealed
inadvertently that they accepted the basic premise underlying their
society's hostility, namely, that woman's place was in the home per-
forming her rightful role as wife and mother. The original reason for
Edna Earl's literary career is that as an orphan she has to support herself.
When she marries at the end of the novel, she stops writing. Phemie
Hart when unmarried begins her career in order to pay her sister's
medical expenses and after marriage continues to write to fund her
brother's private schooling. Once her husband leaves her, writing
becomes the means to support herself and their child.

As writers, Edna Earl and Phemie Hart cannot even be considered intellectual figures. They are moral figures. Just as woman is a moral servant to the family, so the literary domestic is a moral servant to the family of society. Wilson describes the writer Edna Earl as "an instrument of some good to her race. . . ." Earl wants her books to sell, to be popular, but, she says, " 'I desire it not as an end, but as a means to an end—usefulness to my fellow creatures.' " Terhune's Phemie Hart writes because she has an "earnest desire to do good." She is motivated by "her sympathy with the lowly and oppressed, and her charity for the erring." She is simply a woman, she says, who " 'longed to do my full work in the world.' " Rather than creators of culture, the literary domestics were mothers of morality.[35]

It was the ultimate rationalization. The roles were made one. Literary domesticity was an office with powers and purposes different from those of a male creator of culture. Perspective, even language, was different. There was little attempt to tout their books as significant intellectual or artistic productions. Instead, they were "my little books" (Wilson), "my simple tales" (Terhune), "my little enterprises" (Gilman), or "my humble literary labors" (Sedgwick).[36] But these women could proudly, and lovingly, speak of their literary efforts as "brain children" (Terhune), or of the female writer, herself, as "a mother who had a child" (Sedgwick).[37] Caroline Howard Gilman would tell John S. Hart that "I have never thought of myself as a poet, only a versifier." Or, speaking of her novels, she would admit to Hart that "My ambition has never been to write a novel." Of the so-called novels she had written, Gilman said, anyone could see that "the story is a mere hinge for facts." Instead, she would say, "My only pride is in my books for children," adding confidently that "I know that I have learned the way to youthful hearts. . . ."[38]

Branded by their society with a sense of intellectual inferiority and guilt that as writers they might be abandoning their prescribed female domestic role, these women in conflicted fashion questioned, derided, and dismissed their literary efforts while at the same time they defended, rationalized, and justified those efforts in such a manner that the literary and domestic became one or, rather, to such an extent that the domestic absorbed the literary. No matter what their success in the literary marketplace, they remained private domestic beings. That was their primary identity. In saying with regard to her literary tasks that "Domestic duties have never hampered me," Terhune was saying in essence that she had never abandoned her role within the home and never would.[39] When late in her career Parton's married daughter died leaving a child, Parton informally adopted the girl although that "involved a sacrifice of much literary work, or its unsatisfactory uncompleteness." But she did not regret her action. "*She* is my poem," said Parton of her granddaughter.[40] Fifteen years after Stowe had acquired national prominence with the publication of *Uncle Tom's Cabin,* the demands of her family still came first. Having temporarily ceased writing she said to her publisher's wife, Annie Adams Fields, that she had "not been able to write a word, except to my own children." One should understand, said Stowe, that the varying needs of her children required that she "write chapters which would otherwise go into my novel."[41] Four novels and eight years after Sedgwick had begun her career she would "confess" to a bank that she had no occupation. It was a confession, she said, that made her feel "inferior."[42] But what else could a woman have said who, as Sedgwick later wrote, thought of herself as "too exclusively a domestic creature to undertake to write anything beyond little essays for the bettering of humble life for which my experience fits me."[43] The simple fact was that the literary domestics were never able to separate their literary careers from their domestic vocations. They never became fully professionalized. Their fiction made them public figures, but they clung to their private selves. Although some became the primary or sole wage earners in their families, they considered themselves substitutes for males. Rather than writers of books, they were more naturally mothers of work. With little choice, the literary domestics lived domestic fantasies as they wrote them.

6

The Harder, Nobler Task:
Five Victorian Women and the Work Ethic

BRUCE CURTIS and JOY CURTIS

T H E five virtually unknown subjects of this chapter endured and to
some extent prevailed over the difficulties of being women in the late
Victorian era. Had they been men with the same talents, their opportunities, their careers, their entire lives would have been profoundly different. Celeste Bush, Alice Sumner, Esther Sumner, Julia Elliott, and
Sophie Raffalovich were conventional women who were born and bred
or aspired to become ladies at a time when the ideal of the lady was still
pervasive and had barely begun to be challenged by that of the New
Woman.[1] Despite the lady's widespread appeal, however, a combination of character and circumstance would not allow these five women to
be satisfied with the ornamental and passive aspects of a lady's role.
Rather they sought to be useful ladies and thus to achieve a measure of
self-realization and control over their own lives.

To be useful was to work—which might be for them an economic
necessity or a means of seeking independence, but which tended to
focus on their desire to engage in useful occupation, whether remunerative, volunteer, or domestic. Especially they believed that useful occupation was as necessary for a woman's fulfillment as for a man's and
that women as well as men might thereby contribute to the social good.
These five women, neither stereotypical passive ladies nor stereotypical
rebellious New Women, sought self-realization by adhering to an ethic
of work; they foreshadowed the future even as they clung to the past.

The ideal American lady's conflicting attributes seem too formida-
ble to rest upon the shoulders of any mortal woman. Older writers as

BRUCE CURTIS and JOY CURTIS, Michigan State University, East Lansing, Michigan.

diverse in their approach to the subject as Thorstein Veblen in *The Theory of the Leisure Class* (1899) and Emily James Putnam in *The Lady* (1910), as well as heightened contemporary interest in women's history, have enabled us to delineate her characteristics.[2] For aspiring lower-class women, the lady was a model of gentility and etiquette. For her husband, the gentleman or at least the hard-working urban businessman, she was an ornament who was dependent upon him for emotional fulfillment and financial support. Delicate and sensitive, moved by her romantic sensibilities to take up such diversions as novel reading and charities, chaste but dutifully willing to serve her husband's needs, often ailing—especially with varieties of nervous maladies that culminated in hysteria—one of the lady's outstanding traits was passivity.

But the ideal American lady was also at least secondarily a nurturant wife and mother to her husband's children, an industrious and economical manager of his household, the helpmeet who made him comfortable at home, entertained his guests, and encouraged him in his career. Another of the lady's salient characteristics, however, is that she did not "work." She might or might not have been able to perform the myriad tasks that managing a household entailed, but she certainly did not work for compensation outside the home.

The ideal New Woman, a product of late–nineteenth century ideological and economic forces, was from the beginning at war with the lady, even as she sometimes felt attracted to certain aspects of the enemy's role and style.[3] Consequently, like the lady, the New Woman was seldom fully realized in America. Both the lady and the New Woman were generally white and upper-middle- or middle-class in origin, but the New Woman exhibited characteristics diametrically opposed to those of the lady. By example, if not always by intent, she was a feminist. She was well educated and rational, practical and useful, healthy and hearty, and independent intellectually and economically. Rather than the lady's diversions or domestic tasks, the New Woman sought useful occupation outside the home. In her work the New Woman desired broadened career opportunities that would allow her to enter formerly male-dominated professions on terms equal to men rather than being automatically subordinate to them. And since the mores directed middle-class married women to work at home, the New Woman might regretfully forego a husband, sex, and children in exchange for her career. By contrast, the mass of lower-class women in factories, mistresses' kitchens, and other menial positions often tended to view paid work as an unfortunate and, they hoped, temporary necessity that was to be limited if possible, made endurable by gossip and banter with workmates, or escaped entirely by marrying.[4]

The subjects of this study were not New Women in that they did not challenge the rigid sex role system of their era; but in embracing the work ethic in their concern to act as useful ladies, they were at one with the New Woman. Students of the work ethic in Western society are generally agreed that in its origins the work ethic was Puritan, or Protestant, or at least religious in that adherents were "called" to glorify God in a particular occupation.[5] The ethic was gradually secularized, however, until work itself came to have a moral sanction and the individual adherent was free to seek, if not self-glorification, at least self-satisfaction in work. Furthermore, under the pressure of industrialization and the growth of an economy of plenty, the work ethic, traditionally a stimulus to productivity, had begun by the late nineteenth century to be challenged by an ethic of consumption. Indeed, the rise to prominence of the cult of the leisured lady—who played the role of consumer to her husband's producer—was symptomatic of that challenge. Nevertheless in reaffirming an ethic that was soon to be in decline if it were not already, the women of this study fastened upon a liberating ideology. For their allegiance to the work ethic had broad ramifications, as is apparent in their attitude that life was to be taken seriously, that the individual should throw herself energetically into useful occupations— whether remunerative employment, volunteer charity work, the creative arts, even recreation—and that useful occupation should have not merely a personal but a social dimension as well.[6] Such a vision of life is familiar to the student of the work ethic in Western society.

For the five women under discussion, the fortunate paradox is that adherence to the work ethic enabled them to meld certain characteristics of the traditional lady and the New Woman. It enabled them to retain the consciousness of being useful ladies even as it encouraged them to develop the rational, vigorous, and independent characteristics of the New Woman. Each woman under consideration here combined the characteristics of the lady and the New Woman to a varying and sometimes limited degree. Neither were they united in a conscious effort to better woman's lot when they stressed the importance of useful occupation; that fact may serve to reveal the increasingly pervasive belief that the salvation of woman lay in work.

Celeste Bush, the first woman in this discussion and the only one of the five who was employed for a lifetime, found satisfaction in doing useful work as a schoolteacher although she was impeded by an educational system that was controlled by men. She cannot be narrowly labeled as a lady—because she had to work for her living—or as a New Woman—because she accepted the subordinate female role.

Celeste Eduilla Bush was born into an East Lyme, Connecticut,

farm family in 1846, attended the common schools, had one term at a
private 'school, and began teaching in a district school for one dollar a
week and board when she was fifteen years old. She entered the profession that most women, facing extremely limited choices and aspiring to
a position preferable to the factory or the kitchen, inevitably chose. In
1871, at age twenty-five, she matriculated at the New Britain Normal
School for training teachers, graduated two years later, was made a
faculty member, and taught geography, history, and literature at the
school until the mid-1880s. Her record in 1880 indicated that she was a
"very successful" teacher. But a conflict with the State Board of Education over her teaching duties led to her resignation, and 1886 found her
teaching in the Farmville, Virginia, normal school for an annual salary
of $1,200 and board. In 1892 she was teaching at the Framingham,
Massachusetts, normal school. Late in the century, she returned to Connecticut to teach and later retire. She died in 1930 at the age of eighty-
four.[7]

Throughout her career, Celeste Bush wrote and spoke in support of
individuals and programs that she believed would strengthen public education. Significantly, she strongly and diplomatically defended the interests of other teachers, and her own, before the male Connecticut
Board of Education, but without permanently alienating its members.
In the mid-1880s, responding to the board's attempt to reassign her to a
model school, she argued that she could be most effective by staying in
her field of training and experience. Yet she insisted throughout this
and other controversies—which undoubtedly drew board members to
her even as she opposed them—that "Indeed, it is a kind of religion
with me to honor and obey those who are set over me in authority."
And yet she had the courage to remind the male board members of the
obligations of *"noblesse oblige:* your rank requires you to hear me when
I come to you in an honest cause" that concerned "the highest and
most sacred interests of an important public institution." Celeste Bush
resigned her position at the normal school, but only under pressure
from the board, for her tenure had been long and as an unmarried
woman she recognized that the school had "been to me what a home
and those things are to others."[8] Nevertheless she was resilient enough
to recover and go on to teach successfully elsewhere.

Celeste Bush managed to work successfully in an occupation controlled by men because she was sensitively aware of the sex characteristics that late Victorians assumed that men and women possessed. With
some of these assumptions she apparently agreed; others she seems to
have found not only false but amusing. And always she acted with a
pragmatic awareness that whether men were right or wrong, they were

in command and, if she were to accomplish anything, they should not be directly challenged or instructed. As an intellectually capable woman who exhibited what her era would have called a rational male cast of mind, Celeste Bush had little use for women who acted on the basis of misinformation and emotion. In 1899, for example, she sought to defend the secretary of the board of education against charges of immorality and loose living that were being fomented against him by the Woman's Christian Temperance Union (WCTU). Upon learning of the charges from "a lady who is deep in the counsels" of the WCTU, and that the women intended to do their duty by taking the allegations to the state legislature, she sought information with which to refute the charges. She wrote to William Graham Sumner, the well-known professor at Yale who was a member of the Connecticut State Board of Education, "You know what an organized body of excited, ill-informed women could do in such circumstances."[9]

Whatever Celeste Bush may have thought of the WCTU women, she did not generalize to herself. For she knew that she acted not only from principle but on the basis of sound evidence and logical argumentation. She was thus sometimes able to beat men in a battle of wits. In a letter to Sumner about her defense of a teacher before the board of education, she commented:

> I still think that I reached the only logical conclusion of the matter. . . . The ground from which I wish to recede is that whereon I must have seemed a little triumphant and amused. It delighted me to feel that a woman, and one who thinks rather small beer of her argumentative abilities, should have gotten such an incontrovertible sort of man as yourself into what seemed not wholly unlike a corner. It was like discomfiting an adversary at chess. But that is a small matter to divert one from the real principle involved.

Despite her minor triumph in this battle of the sexes, Celeste Bush was able to see clearly the major goal—the principles and the programs that had to be promoted. To do that, she was willing to accept the conventional sex characteristics and roles—to play the game by Victorian rules. For example, in 1901 she invited Sumner to attend a meeting of the State Federation of Women's Clubs at which she was to speak on reform of the public schools. "Personally," she wrote, "I shrink from seeming to imply that I can do anything to your edification." Nevertheless several women's groups, the federation, the American Collegiate Alumnae Association, and perhaps the WCTU

stand ready to cooperate in the effort to bring about greatly needed reforms. . . . But it is not seemly that women should take the
initiative in a matter that has so long been solely managed by men;
and therefore we want you, as the dean, in length of service, of the
State Board of Education to be present at this meeting and, if you
will consent to do so, to take part in the discussion.[10]

By judiciously using both her strength and her ability to compromise, Celeste Bush managed to live a productive and apparently satisfying life, even though required to carry on her occupation under male
domination. She was able in later years to view her forced resignation
from the New Britain Normal School, which might have been disas-
trous, as beneficial because it had forced her "to break new soil instead
of staying fast in the old . . . and I have reason to be grateful for such a
broadening out of my life." That broadening had continued, for the
same letter found her requesting information on "the outside classes at
Yale." Celeste Bush implicitly recognized a relationship between well-
being and occupation, for she wrote to Sumner in the same period, "I
have been well and generally busy since we last met." Similarly, when
in 1901 she invited him to hear her speak, she concluded with virtually a
testimony to the value of useful work: "I suppose the work of the world
is accomplished by doing everything we can and being willing even to
be a fool in a cause we would help on. And so, setting aside a sense of
unfitness, it would be a great gratification to me if you were present."[11]
Although Celeste Bush never became a New Woman who rebelled
against her assigned sex role, it is difficult to suppose that the men with
whom she associated thought she was a fool, especially in the ladylike,
principled, and effective way she went about advancing the useful work
in which she was engaged.

For Alice Sumner, the second woman in this study, work was both
a practical necessity and a moral imperative. Born into an immigrant,
working-class family, her socioeconomic position—similar to that of
Celeste Bush—and her parents' attitudes did not allow her to be trained
for the role of the ornamental lady. Rather, under parental guidance
and the pressure of circumstance, she came to understand that she must
take up, with an honest and disciplined adherence to duty, whatever
tasks came to her. Thus, her ideal inevitably became that of the useful
lady who developed her own potential by helping others and acting
responsibly in all things. Like Celeste Bush, Alice Sumner accepted the
constraints of the late Victorian social system even though—again like

Celeste Bush—certain of her characteristics as a useful lady were virtually synonymous with those of the New Woman.

Alice Sumner, born in 1861, was almost a generation younger than her half-brother, William Graham. In letters written in schoolgirl script to "Dear Brother Will," she repeatedly acknowledged his superior intellect and her awe of his status as a Yale professor. Yet her letters also show a spirited and independent girl intent on justifying her school marks and accomplishments. By the age of twelve, Alice had felt the fear and relief of successfully competing in school and of taking the competitive examinations required of those students who wished to enter the high school. To Sumner she confessed:

> It may seem very strange to you that I have not replied to your kind invitation, but I have been so troubled about entering the High School that I have not had time, and I felt that it would be very unpleasant for me to come to New Haven if I did not enter, but today we were told our average and . . . so I have entered and shall be very happy to come to New Haven. . . . You must excuse my bad writing as I feel very glad that I have entered.[12]

Alice learned from her immigrant father, an exemplar of the work ethic, the necessity of dependability and work. In a letter to "Dear Brother Will," she explained that her father had delayed another of her vacations to New Haven because her mother needed help: "Pa wishes me to tell you that he never thought of house cleaning until he saw Ma beginning to get ready for it Saturday morning. . . . When Pa did think he was quite 'worked up' about it. My vacation does last another week and Ma thinks we shall be through so that I can come if it will be convenient for you."[13] Alice vacationed after she helped her mother.

After graduating from high school at age seventeen in 1878, Alice left home because of her parents' difficult economic situation. She went to New Haven where she lived with Brother Will, helped rear the two Sumner boys, attended the New Haven Normal School where she became a teacher and then principal, and engaged in a wide range of social activities that included sailing and membership in an archery club. In caring for Graham and Eliot Sumner, while their mother, Jeannie, a classic Victorian ornamental lady, sought relief from nervous illnesses at health resorts, Alice showed herself to be reliable, loving, and able. Her letters to Brother Will are matter-of-fact and informative in their descriptions of her actions and of the boys' behavior and health. She adored her nephews and repeatedly reported their fine behavior and clever activities. She acted sensibly in crises as the following indicates:

Grae is not well and the doctor thinks he has the chicken pox! Yesterday morning he was very tired. His lips quivered and he seemed
used up. I went to school, but came home as early as I could. I
found him rather worse and observed spots in his face and neck. I
took him to Dr. C. at once. The doctor was out of town, and for an
instant I was dazed. Then I remembered that Dr. C. left his pa-
tients with Dr. Eliot when he went abroad, so I took Grae there.

After giving a detailed report of Grae's high fever, Alice added that she
should not miss another day of teaching and so had "telegraphed Mama
to be sure to come to-day." While Alice sensibly asked for help, the
general tone of her letters throughout this episode reflects confidence in
her own ability to care for the children.[14]

Other letters also indicate confidence that she could manage her
own affairs, even though at times she wanted help with such matters as
traveling trunks, especially in early letters when young Alice still ad-
dressed Sumner as "Dear Brother Will." Later he became "Dear Graham" to Alice, the name some of his male contemporaries used. In an
early letter, she wrote for Julia Elliott, Jeannie Sumner's older sister,
and herself that

Miss Julia and I found out all the possible ways of getting to N. H.
and I decided the safest way is to go to Hartford and from there to
N. H. and I think Miss Julia agrees with me. The other way is to go
to New York and take the afternoon boat, but I rather dread crossing the ferry and looking after my trunk all alone—though I would
do it of course if there was no other way. Then the New London
way is a little too expensive.

In another letter in which she outlined a trip for herself and the Sumner
boys, she wrote to Brother Will, "You have so much to think about and
arrange that I wish I could spare you any trouble about me. I shall not
be at all afraid. I suppose I shall have to look after my trunk at the ferry
won't I?"[15]

Alice did look after herself—and others—in the ten years between
her graduation from high school and her marriage. She concerned herself with the welfare of Jeannie, Julia, Sumner, the boys, and her
parents, while she rarely wrote of concern for herself. Under Brother
Will's stern eye she learned to manage her limited financial affairs, as
when she wrote to him concerning a loan, "About the money I feel
exactly as you do. I have always had the greatest horror of getting into
debt and it will be a very great relief to me when I can pay you. I will
surely try never again to let it happen." Again she wrote:

> I want to thank you for this money but I don't know how. I think
> with all your expenses and the ten dollars you gave me in the fall
> that this is a great deal too much. . . . I think that however large a
> load my "ship" brings in I shall never be able to half repay you for
> what you are doing for me—for us all in fact. I only wish there ap-
> peared to be a chance that some of us would get a ship load soon.[16]

But Alice did not sit and wait for good fortune; she continued to
work until her marriage, which she and Walter Camp, who was to become President of the New Haven Clock Company and Yale's unpaid
football "advisor," had to delay for two years because of their limited
financial means. Her father having died, she asked for her brother's
consent to marry but typically had already made her own sensible plans:

> You have heard from Mr. Camp, I trust, to the effect that with
> your consent I will engage myself to marry him some time. It can
> not be for a long time yet, as a sufficient income is first necessary. I
> have never cared for any other man. I am very sure of my affection
> for him and I am glad to go on with my school work until that
> time when I may become his wife.[17]

When Alice married in 1888, she had developed a considerable
number of useful skills—childrearing, teaching and school administration, the direction of a household—as well as the graces of the lady
through her long association with Jeannie, Julia, and their friends at
home and at various resorts. The life pattern that Alice Sumner chose,
given her limited financial resources, allowed her in ten years between
high school and marriage to experience various social roles and to meet
people from all classes. Her letters illustrate her growth from a young
girl to a confident and capable woman. One significant indicator of
Alice Sumner Camp's development is that as the wife of the "father of
American football" she developed a sophisticated understanding of the
game. For many years she regularly attended and took notes at Yale's
daytime football practices, while her husband was busy at the New
Haven Clock Company, and then briefed and advised him prior to his
evening and Sunday afternoon.meetings with the team. If Walter Camp
was the father, then it appears that Alice Sumner Camp was the mother
of American football.[18]

This working-class girl became a married lady, but hardly a leisured
lady. Like almost all young employed women of her era, she gave up her
career when she married, but not her work. By maintaining the discipline of her household and servants as strictly as she had her schoolroom
and her school, she demonstrated that she could fulfill the Victorian re-

quirement of acting as both her husband's ornament and his domestic helpmeet. This lady whom the British writer, Arnold Bennett, described as "one of the most brilliant women in America," and whom William Lyon Phelps, the Yale professor, referred to as a widely read, highly intelligent, and charming conversationalist of strong convictions, made the Camp home one of Yale's social centers, especially on football weekends, when she sometimes entertained hundreds. Nevertheless as Walter Camp's football advisor, Alice Sumner Camp dramatically extended her role beyond that of the traditional lady. Camp's confidence in his wife was such that he made her the executrix and sole heir of his estate of one-third of a million dollars, "deeming it better" that his children "trust entirely to their mother for their care and support."[19]

Esther Sumner, the third woman in this study who sought employment because of necessity, found that work offered her the hope of gaining control over her life, of achieving financial success or at least a measure of economic security, and of developing her talents. While her concern to realize her own potential was unremitting, whether as a shop girl or married woman, she aspired also to become a lady. Paradoxically, she complained openly about the Victorian constraints that the lady's role imposed even as she sought diligently to develop not only the manner but the cultured accomplishments of a lady. Thus as she worked to support herself and later enjoyed her relatively secure married life, she strove for success as a creative individual and for recognition as a lady.

Born in 1844, Esther, or Chet, as she always referred to herself, was for a long time under the shadow of men—her older brothers, Joe and especially William Graham, her father, and her various suitors. Understandably, the twin conflicting themes that emerged in Chet's life developed from her relationships with men.

The two themes were her desire for approval and her desire for independence. On the one hand, Chet wanted to be both socially accepted and popular. That meant she had to walk the classic fine line between acting in the ladylike manner that her father and brothers and certain suitors would approve and being charming and coquettish enough to attract the world of young men generally. Often she lost her balance—at least from the perspective of her brothers. Joe wrote critically from New Orleans, where during the Civil War he had gaily described the charms of Creole women, that his sister painted and dressed immodestly. Brother Will chastised her repeatedly for endangering her reputation by associating with men without a proper introduction or by allowing suitors to take liberties. Certainly, at age nine-

teen in 1863, Chet was fashion conscious and dazzled by her ability to
attract young men. Her letters detail, with sketches, how she cut and
sewed the most fashionable dresses and got at bargain prices hats, veils,
gloves, and jewelry to match. And her letters gloried in that "there are
never two evenings in the whole week" when she was not either called
on or escorted to "an entertainment," which ranged from the theater
and operas to dancing clubs, ice skating, sleighing, sailing, and "Pic-
Nics." Chet particularly enjoyed twitting socially proper Episcopalian
minister Brother Will about the Unity Club, a circle of young neighborhood ladies faddishly dedicated to sewing for Union soldiers. Chet
wrote that "We have gentlemen now to help us, so we get along nice, of
course (you will say). Well Will, no mistake the gentlemen are a help
anyway for attendance on the ladies' part if nothing more."[20]

Even when flippant, Chet also wanted very much to become a lady;
she modeled herself after such women as "Mrs. T—. I think she is so
very much like Mrs. Judd, so very ladylike. I am glad that I know her
and intend to keep up the acquaintance." To Brother Will, whom Chet
earnestly tried to impress with her good intentions and demeanor, she
protested in 1863:

> I resented very much your speaking of my being flattered by gen-
> tlemen. For that I am perfectly free from. There never was a young
> lady of my age that had more attention paid them by different
> gentlemen than I've had. . . . I flatter myself that I am as sensible
> and know how to carry myself as well as any young lady in any soci-
> ety.

Several years later, in 1867, when she was living alone in New York City
as a shopgirl of twenty-three, Chet still felt the need to convince Will of
her purity. She wrote that because of his mistrust of her

> This morning when I woke up I felt so lonely, and gloomy that I
> cried before I went out. You evidently can *hardly* trust me. Oh my
> Dear Brother, what have I done to give you so much anxiety. I go
> to the store like a lady and God knows I try to be one, and I find I
> am more modest and reserved than the large majority of *ladies.*

Chet's tone apparently caused Will to relent, at least temporarily, for in
her next letter she wrote that she had received his request that she for-
give any injustice he had done her, and that she had come "up to my
room and fell on my knees and thanked God that at last my Brother
whom I love so devotedly could trust me. . . . *I* have lost confidence in
the whole world and still I don't wish my parents or Brothers or friends

to lose confidence in me." As the preceding suggests, Chet not only tried to impress Will favorably and sometimes sought his advice about a suitor or proper course of action, but she also developed a guilty sense that she was a great deal of trouble to her already burdened brother, a feeling that made her amenable to his demands that she act in an appropriate ladylike way. To the impetus that guilt provided, Chet added her own awareness of the social and cultural advantages that being a lady promised. At such times, when Will's chiding strengthened her own determination, Chet could write a passage that would be entirely amusing if she had not been so serious: "I can be just as much a lady as anyone and enjoy it too. You will *see* if I cannot Will, if we both live long enough."[21]

Just as Chet deferred to Brother Will, so she tended to subordinate her judgment to that of suitors concerning important matters. In 1866, aware that her working-class father thought women should contribute to their keep, Chet went to work for a dressmaker, a demanding job that kept her busy from seven in the morning until at least six at night. Not wishing to have her steady company know she was working in a shop, Chet continued to go out or to entertain him at home every night, until "it did not seem as if I *could* sit up." But inevitably he learned the truth "and was very much displeased. He said he did not know but it was false pride but he said he had always said he never would marry a shop girl. When he married anyone it would be a lady. . . . He told me never to go again and I never shall."[22]

It would be misleading to suggest that Chet always suffered intensely from her dependence on and subordination to the will of men. At times, perhaps like Victorian ladies or like those who aspired to that status, Chet enjoyed the minor advantages of being treated as a lady. While rooming in New York City, Chet met and was introduced to "Captain Root of the 22nd Regiment," who paid her considerable attention for a time, particularly by escorting her to the boardinghouse when she worked late. And there was the "First Lieutenant of the Navy" who took her for an evening at "Steinways, the great Piano Forte makers," cousins of his; who also ran little errands and bought postage stamps for her; and who "gave me Whiskey one morning when I was sick."[23]

On a more serious level, Chet seems to have rather abruptly and without romantic illusions chosen to marry a Mr. Williams in 1868. Her rationale, which was noteworthy for its similarity to reasons that Brother Will often gave at that time for important decisions, was that "I consider it my *duty*. And trust to a higher power than my own. . . . He is a great deal older. . . . is large, and homely, has children, in fact *every-*

thing I said I never would marry I shall have. But I have made the decision and all I can do is to hope for the best and do as well as I can."[24] Despite her devotion to duty and trust in God, Chet's marriage lasted only a year or two, and she became a divorced woman. Nevertheless in 1877 she again married a widower with children, a pattern that her stepmother had established; this time Chet's marriage was happy.

Despite her occasional willingness in her younger years to subordinate herself to men, Chet sometimes expressed the urge to be perfectly free and independent of all restrictions, to travel, and find pleasures like a man. Once when out of work she wrote that if she managed to get anything to do, "I want to be the one that secured the situation. . . . I have heard of two places and without saying a word to any one have started off to see about them." Chet's concern to be independent inevitably related not only to men but to money. Particularly in her early adult years she suffered from respiratory ailments, especially in winter, that her doctor thought might lead to "consumption" or "the heart disease." The best solution seemed to be to go south for the winter and, as she had relatives in Cuba, Chet seized on the idea. But having worked only intermittently, she had no funds and had to turn to her father, who refused to provide the money, perhaps because he could not afford to do so. Frustrated, Chet could only complain against her father and assert that "There is not a man or woman in the world that would rather earn their own living than I. Oh, how I would like it to be perfectly independent of *everybody*. I have got ambition enough too. But what good does this do when I am not able to carry it out." In the period when Chet's health was precarious, she was often under the care of doctors who attempted to limit her activities and who prescribed medicines of the era that characteristically were heavily laced with alcohol or worse. Chet's discussions of dosing reveal much about medicine and more about her desire to be daring. One Sunday she wrote to Brother William that her friend, "Nellie was telling me about her medicine. It is the same as I had to take only in a different form. She was telling me how nice it was and said that she drank it for the fun of it. She went out and brought in two wine glasses full and we drank it. It was splendid. I tell you." One can therefore understand why on a later Sunday she wrote to William that "Dr. Jackson left some medicine which I have taken regularly and I would not miss it now for anything."[25]

Chet wanted to be daring, wanted to be independent. Money meant independence, and working outside the home was one way a young woman of Chet's class could get money. For a time Chet combined her interest in fashion, her skill as a seamstress, and her creative abilities in a New York City dress shop. There, through hard work and

long hours, she became head pattern maker and was gratified when returning customers sought her out. Even more gratifying were her creative efforts, about which she wrote in 1867, "And now Brother Will I
will tell you what your sister can do. I invented two dresses and an opera
cloak." She had been discovered by a man who had come into the shop
seeking original ideas, and so her creations would be featured in "flam-
ing colors" in the *Quarterly Review*. "I don't get anything by it," Chet
concluded. "This is all that I don't like." Work offered not only
esthetic satisfaction, it promised independence, and Chet began to plan
for the day when she would know the business well enough: "When I
learn to cut dresses perfectly I am going South."[26] But the dress
business declined in the fall of 1867, Chet was laid off, and to save
money she went home to Hartford and her father's disappointment that
she had lost her job. After she had considered trying to find a teaching
position, in the spring of 1868 she travelled through Vermont with a
woman companion attempting to sell subscriptions to a book. She married the homely Williams in the fall. But the story did not end happily
and Chet found work again in a shop. She continued to work for a time
even after marrying the widower Patterson in 1877. Surely the fact that
Chet made a thousand dollars a year to his eight-hundred and fifty
strengthened her position in their relationship. Two years after her marriage, Chet left her job to have a son; she had another son a few years
later.

The 1880s found Chet still happily married to "such a man you
have the privilege of meeting only once in a lifetime." They were living
in a flat but planning to build a house eventually, and Chet proudly
reported to Brother Will that he need not be "afraid of meeting more
poor relations," for "we add $60 (*at least*) a month to our bank ac-
count. Do not owe a dollar in the world. Have property in the North-
west increasing in value each year."[27] Perhaps even more impressive,
the often ill, young Chet Sumner had matured into the buoyant Chettie
Patterson who had not seen a doctor for two years and who hardly
weighed more than when she had been nineteen.

Finally, Chet had maintained her interest in cultural matters, still
attended concerts, and had taken up painting. Half-proudly, half-
defiantly, and perhaps still with a certain desire for approval, she sent
Brother Will a painting

> as a reminder that you still have a sister. When I took my painting
> exactly like it to Schans to have it framed, I asked him its value. He
> said if I would part with it for $60 he would like it. So you need
> not be afraid to hang it in your parlour. I presume you will be

amused and interested to know I never had a Master. I picked it up
for pastime like all my other art work. Bought books of instruction
and taught myself. I visit all art galleries and learn something new
each time. . . . Next winter I shall take lessons of the first Master
in New York.[28]

Chet Sumner's story is primarily that of the growth and maturation
of a socially mobile, upward striving, working-class woman. She may
not have found the perfect independence for which she had wished and
which distinguished the ideal New Woman. And she undoubtedly suffered from the disabilities that a working-class woman who yearned to
become a Victorian lady inevitably experienced. Nevertheless she managed to become successful and happy according to her own definition.

Julia Elliott, the fourth woman in this study, was born and remained a lady. Although her training prepared her for an ornamental
role, she eventually came to believe in the importance for herself of
useful activity. Since she never married and thus was unable to serve as a
nurturant wife and mother, she sought to express herself in religious
and occasional neighborhood charity work. For Julia, a traditional lady
with a trust income, such work was not an economic necessity but a necessary, even if limited, means of seeking both self-realization and the
social good.

By comparison with the preceding women discussed in this chapter, Julia Elliott's history developed from changing conditions of life
that began happily with her birth in 1837 into a protective, indulgent,
and well-to-do family where she learned the art of being a lady in a
house that is reputed to have had the first marble staircase in New York
City. But her businessman father died in 1868 and her sister Jeannie
married William Graham Sumner in 1871. Julia was forced almost in
midlife to depend increasingly upon herself and to seek meaning in her
own life and occupations rather than in those of a father, sister, or husband. To do so was extremely difficult. Julia wrote to Sumner before
the marriage that he had only "a dim idea of the attachment that can
exist between sisters." Julia had thought that neither sister needed another friend, for they had "been all in all to each other." They had
done everything together—sewing, reading, "outdoor pursuits"—and
had had the same interests. While Julia did not "for an instant wish"
Sumner "had not come to Jeannie," she admitted that she had become
very depressed after beginning to recognize how the marriage would affect herself:

The entire change it was producing in my life came upon me so suddenly last week that it almost broke my heart. It carried my thoughts back to Father, and I so longed for him in my loneliness, that it seemed to me that it would have been a mercy if I could have gone to him. It does seem so bright where he is and so dark here. The load is so heavy on my heart. You will help me, Will, won't you, to bear it, for my path through life seems so narrow and steep.[29]

According to her memory, Sumner had courted Julia as a future sister even while he had courted Jeannie as a future wife; in letters that mirrored Jeannie's in their loving and flattering tone, Julia expressed her intense desire to have him as a protective brother. She admitted to being exclusively interested in Sumner's church work, in his "intellectual culture," in her work in Hebrew under his tutorship, and in his impending union with her sister. In the same letter she wrote, "You are both so very interesting to me now, that it seems almost as if I were living each of your separate lives; and they are blending so beautifully together." Julia, the dependent onlooker, seemed desperately trying to live vicariously through the lives of her sister and brother-to-be. Her dependency appears as well in her use of childish terms, in admitting the naughty behavior of being distant during one of Sumner's recent visits: " 'I didn't mean to,' as the children say. It wasn't coldness in the heart, for my heart is just as warm as ever, but to tell the truth, it was a little shyness because I had confessed so much to you before. . . ."[30]

Perhaps Julia's reluctant willingness to relinquish Jeannie stemmed partly from her fear that she was inferior and useless. Only a few weeks before the marriage, Julia wrote pleadingly to Sumner:

> Don't joke so thoughtlessly by drawing unpleasant comparisons between Jeannie and me. Jeannie does play better than I, but why, because God has seen fit to give me a constitution which will not permit me to work, and improve myself, either in music or in any mental efforts. Thus Jeannie will always be more successful than I. Yet my desires to excel—to be useful in the world are very great. I do so long to be a useful and willing laborer in the vineyard of my Lord and Master, and my strength is totally unequal to my desires.[31]

Julia was ill occasionally during her life; yet visits to health resorts merely heightened her frustration over her inability to be useful in the world. Nevertheless she did not become a nervous invalid as did her sister; although she sometimes clung in a dependent way to others, she gradually became a stronger person. Two causes for this are important:

as a spinster she was thrown much upon her own resources, and she developed a sense of mission to be a guardian and witness for Christianity.

Significantly, Julia's later letters to her brother-in-law became assertive and direct. She was highly critical of his role as father and husband but especially of his failure to maintain a Christian home. In an 1889 letter she upbraided him by contrasting her childhood home and Sumner's. In her "father's home, God, our Heavenly Father, was *acknowledged openly* by daily *family* prayers. . . . A *real blessing* was asked at *every* meal, not a few hurried words which hardly seemed meant to ascend to the throne of grace. . . . In your *words* even, you are denying Him who *died to save you,* when you *rejoice* to escape from *prayers* to *Him* at the college."[32] In numerous letters that followed confrontations with Sumner about his slovenly religious behavior, such as his habit of working on Sunday instead of attending church, Julia did not appear to be in awe of him or even apologetic. Yet she could be understanding and sympathetic in discussing his problems as a family head with a nervous invalid wife.

Thirty years after Julia first wrote to Sumner of her personal need to be useful in the service of God, she confided to him in 1900 her concern for Jeannie:

> I am praying so earnestly that God will restore her to health, that she may be a blessing to you, and to us all, and also that she may be able to take up some useful work which will interest her, such as the day nursery, and make her contented at home and well there. It is useful occupations that we need, as you well know in your own experience, to make us well and happy. . . . She and I cannot do much, but we can do a little, if it is only the sewing of a garment for some poor child.

Only a few days earlier she had written to Jeannie with virtually the same message that "Now you are on the mend and will continue to improve I want you to remember that Dr. Foster says it is so important to make efforts. Efforts and daily and constant prayer must go together."[33]

Perhaps Julia developed independent views and considerable courage because she did not marry and, having an independent trust income, had little need to bend to any man's views. Julia's strong religious faith—irritating as its persistent expression may have been—and her belief that one had to do God's work by serving others probably helped her to understand her life and to give it meaning.[34] Although she was born and always lived as a lady, working for the glory of God gave Julia Elliott a sense of certitude that she was engaged in a useful occupation.

In 1883 S. Raffalovich wrote to William Graham Sumner from
Paris to congratulate him on a book he had written. Raffalovich, expecting to be very critical, had reviewed the book for a journal but had
found only good things to say. No doubt flattered, Sumner responded
to Monsieur Raffalovich who now revealed the first name of Sophie. Apparently mystified and titillated, Sumner responded once again by ask-
ing how S. Raffalovich could both write on political economy and be a
woman, and so a correspondence of several years' duration began.
Sophie repeatedly invited Sumner and his wife to visit her family and
herself as soon as possible in Paris, ''a lovely town yet, before it is
spoiled by the iron tower and other atrocities.''[35] Sumner did visit her
eventually, when she was the bride of William O'Brien, Member of Parliament from Ireland and radical advocate of Irish Home Rule.

Sophie Raffalovich O'Brien was different from the other women in
this discussion; she was not American and not, strictly speaking, Victorian, although she did become for a time a subject of the Queen. Yet
in a significant sense as a woman in Western culture she faced virtually
the same disabilities as they, and she was sensitively and sometimes
amusedly aware of the stereotypical ways in which men responded to
women, especially to intellectual women like herself. She was also
aware, as were Celeste Bush and Chet Sumner, that whatever success she
attained depended perhaps as much upon what men thought of her as a
woman as upon her own talent and dedication to hard work. Nevertheless, her training had helped her understand the need for useful occupation and even limited success in a field that men dominated.

Mademoiselle Raffalovich, born in 1859, belonged to a wealthy
and cosmopolitan Russian Jewish emigre family, members of which
were immersed in intellectual affairs and public life. Sophie's mother,
Marie Raffalovich, an obviously forceful woman and a sympathizer with
the Irish cause, first corresponded enthusiastically with O'Brien, sent
him an expensive volume on the Huguenot persecutions, invited him to
visit the family in Paris, and in various ways encouraged O'Brien's relationship with Sophie. Like Sophie, an older brother studied political
economy but then became important in Parisian financial circles, while
her younger brother was a promising poet. Sophie herself had published
and translated reviews and articles. Late in the 1880s she would publish
a book on Jeremy Bentham and translate another on Richard Cobden.
She was proficient in at least French and English and was beginning to
learn Russian.

In trying to explain ''that anomaly, a woman who takes an interest
in political economy,'' Sophie stressed that she was in no way irritated,
as Sumner had feared, but rather a little proud that he should address

her as Mr. and refer to her masculine traits. "I think that a country woman of yours who would object to *masculine* when it is so kindly meant," Sophie wrote disarmingly, "would show herself anything but *strong* minded. Besides weakness of mind," Sophie continued wryly, "she would show herself greatly deficient in psychological insight."[36]

Sophie explained that she had been educated in France, "but rather as a French boy, than a French girl" because she had wanted to help her brother with his lessons. And yet her comments on her love of learning suggest that she studied for reasons other than sisterly affection or duty: "English literature was like a new and beautiful country, and we plunged into it with the utmost delight. Political economy gave me the same delicious experience of finding what I wanted. It answered so many doubts and puzzles, that even the most dry parts were a source of joy." "I am afraid," Sophie concluded, that "I have lost any good opinions you may have of me, by this proof of the feminine perversity that will mix sentiment where it has nothing to do, and is capable of evolving a religious enthusiasm from the dismal science" of economics.[37]

In the preceding comment, Sophie showed herself sensitively aware of presumed sex differences and at least indirectly commented on the limitations she had felt because of her sex, even in a relatively liberal family and social environment. She explained to Sumner that "When one is very young the idea of doing the same work as men is very delightful. I remember it reconciled me to geometry for which I had not the least taste" until her brother persuaded her to give it up because of her bad temper on geometry days. "But," she wrote, "the feeling of having been defeated was very nasty—however political economy is such a delightful study." Over the years, Sophie had learned to recognize the social distinction betwen men's and women's work; but it seems that she continued to act on the belief that playing a sex role was of secondary importance to the real business of life, which was to learn. Of a special class of Sumner's students who were "young ladies," she wrote that "If they begin with the idea they are doing men's work, I think they will soon forget all about it, in the mere enjoyment of it."[38]

When Sophie Raffalovich married the Catholic William O'Brien in 1890, she converted to his faith and to the prescribed Victorian female role of faithful helpmeet. Her published reminiscences after her husband's death in 1928 stress that she joyfully accepted an obedient and secondary role to the great and good man who was her husband.[39] And although as Mrs. O'Brien she continued to write, she turned from work in economics to books and articles that focused primarily on her husband and on the charms of Ireland.

But Sophie O'Brien, in becoming a radical politician's wife, also continued to support the cause of Ireland that she had upheld before their marriage in such Parisian journals as *Le Soir*. One is tempted to believe that Sophie and her mother were drawn to O'Brien, the charismatic man of action and politics, because he could fight openly for causes that they could support only privately or pseudonymously in print. Her father, once a banker and Odessa grain exporter in Russia, had opposed the marriage but relented eventually, Sophie wrote, and promised to "allow me the same income as if it was he who had chosen my husband." Much of that very handsome income went to support William O'Brien and the Irish cause, at least until the Bolshevik Revolution considerably depleted the Raffalovich family fortune. Sophie, who managed the accounts, decided which causes the O'Briens could afford to support.[40]

Contemporaries, the many letters that Sophie and her husband exchanged over the years, and her memories all suggest "a singularly happy marriage." Perhaps it was so partly because Sophie, while worshipful, refused to be overawed by her husband; she persistently supported woman's suffrage although O'Brien voted against it in the House of Commons. In 1912 she published a book on *Unseen Friends,* which admiringly discussed the lives and works of such women writers as Charlotte Bronte, Margaret Oliphant, Christina Rossetti, and certain Catholic nuns who had founded charitable institutions. To Sophie O'Brien, these women were inspring because they had maintained their religious piety, domestic virtues, and traditional femininity, and had kept "aloof from 'the woman's movement' and from undesirable celebrity and newspaper puffing," while nevertheless engaging in useful occupations. Their own work had enabled them to support themselves and a family, or to help the unfortunate, or to satisfy their "intellectual ambition" in literary endeavors.[41]

Years earlier, in discussing her younger brother, who had "really the faculty of doing some original work by and by," Sophie had mentioned only talent, but she may have been aware of her handicap as a woman when she wrote that "We must be content with useful work, such as is within the reach of the average. And political economy teaches one to appreciate usefulness, and reconciles one to modest work, when ambition is impossible." "After all," Sophie wrote in a letter of the following year, "to live well is the harder, nobler task, than facing death, and a more useful one to humanity." Like the other women in this study, Sophie Raffalovich O'Brien found comfort in knowing that a woman could maintain the feminine virtues of the lady while being useful in the world.[42]

Although not rebels, feminists, or New Women, the women discussed in this chapter developed the ability to escape a sense of aimlessness that women, especially ladies, often experienced in the late nineteenth century. Whether they married or remained spinsters, they were committed to the belief that they must be engaged in useful and fulfilling occupations—whether remunerative employment, volunteer work, or the creative arts. They were committed to an ethic of work. Consequently their problem was how to be both ladies and useful—to be useful ladies.

In a sense the problem was less difficult to solve than might appear, if a woman were not a feminist rebel who sought to invade the male professions. If she were willing to accept work that men judged appropriate, a woman could find employment that her society deemed useful and respectable. Almost predictably the five women under discussion took up the feminine occupations of dressmaking, teaching, writing, and charity work.

Another less predictable development is that they threw themselves into their woman's work with considerable energy and tenacity. Celeste Bush, an excellent teacher, was a dogged and inspired advocate for a professionalized teaching staff and an improved educational system. Alice Sumner, a strong-minded disciplinarian, successfully directed a school, managed her household, and expanded her helpmeet role to include advising the father of American football. Chet Sumner could have been a drudging dressmaker; instead she created gowns and cloaks and taught herself painting. Surely Julia Elliott's need as a lady to feel useful in God's work helps explain the fervor with which she urged religion upon others. Sophie Raffalovich actually took up the male discipline of political economy for a time, although she found it necessary to use a pseudonym or the evasive S. Raffalovich, and after marrying she continued to write on a variety of subjects.

Although they did not publicly challenge men's prerogatives or professions, and although they did not choose career rather than marriage if chance offered, these women functioned in their work somewhat like New Women. They came to enjoy a sense of personal independence and satisfaction as useful ladies imbued with the work ethic. Whether this is true of those many other women who are not easily categorized as ladies, New Women, feminists, or working women is a matter for investigation.

7

Planning and Progressivism: Wacker's Manual of the Plan of Chicago

THOMAS J. SCHLERETH

To Chicagoan Walter Dwight Moody, "the completion of the Plan of Chicago was the most important civic event in the history of the city." If implemented, Moody maintained the 1909 metropolitan plan prepared by Daniel H. Burnham and Edward H. Bennett would enable Chicago to become nothing less than "the center of the modern world."[1] No small claim for a city hardly seven decades old, but not atypical braggadocio for a midwestern metropolis already notorious for its special brand of civic and architectural boosterism.

Moody, a former general manager of the Chicago Association of Commerce and the first managing director of the Chicago Plan Commission (CPC), made his boast in a strangely titled, now largely unread work called *Wacker's Manual of the Plan of Chicago: Municipal Economy.*[2] First published in 1911, this curious volume in the history of American city planning literature went through several editions during the decade (1911–1921) that Moody superintended the promotion of the Burnham/Bennett Plan. The book's misleading title prompted contemporaries as well as a few modern scholars mistakenly to attribute the work's authorship to Charles Wacker, prominent Chicago brewer turned real estate developer, financier, civic leader, and first chairman of the CPC. Moody's middle and surname also occasionally prompted confusion with that of the popular Chicago evangelist Dwight L. Moody whose tabernacle and ancillary structures (bible college and institute, bookstore, and radio station,) still dot Chicago's near northside cityscape.

THOMAS J. SCHLERETH, University of Notre Dame, Notre Dame, Indiana.

Who was Walter Dwight Moody? Why did he write a best-seller and ascribe it to another man? What were the work's principal ideas? What might such ideas reveal about the philosophy and the practice of turn-of-the century urban planning in Chicago and the nation? What might the intellectual history of this segment of the American city planning movement add to our understanding of the main currents of American intellectual history?

Walter Dwight Moody's occasional mistaken identity with Dwight Lyman Moody contains one clue to his character. In his efforts in "putting the Plan across," W. D. Moody openly acknowledged that he did so with all the zealotry of "the clergyman and the pedagogue." In an era when many reformers had previous clerical backgrounds (Richard Ely or Graham Taylor) or, as Henry May has demonstrated, personal religious motivations (John Bates Clark or Charles H. Cooley) behind their attempt to bring about social and political change, Walter Moody's evangelical fervor to promote urban planning as the redemption of American cities seemed perfectly in step with many of his fellow progressives.[3]

Moody's career began not in salvation but in sales. The title of one of his early publications can serve as a capsule biography. On a 1907 book cover he proudly proclaimed himself as one of those *Men Who Sell Things*, the book being the *Observations and Experiences of Over Twenty Years as a Travelling Salesman, European Buyer, Sales Manager, Employer*. Drummer, promoter, adman, business college teacher, showman, Moody personified the late nineteenth-century American whom Daniel Boorstin has labelled "the Go-Getter" and whom both Burnham and Wacker saw as "a hustler, a man who knows how to do things and to get the greatest amount of publicity out of a movement."[4]

To such a man the CPC entrusted the monumental task of making every Chicagoan fully plan conscious. The objective was to reach the one and one-half million citizens who could not afford the prohibitively expensive (twenty-five dollars), lavish, limited first edition of two thousand copies of the Plan published by the Commercial Club.[5] Handsome though it was, filled with evocative sketches by Jules Guerin and Jules Janin in both color and black and white, Burnham and his Commercial Club associates recognized that the Plan of Chicago was little more than sagacious advice from people with no official power. In accepting one of the limited edition copies, Mayor Fred Busse, who would later create the CPC, was careful to note that the plan's proposals were not hard and fast and would not necessarily result in immediate changes. The unofficial nature of the venture, however, inspired Charles Eliot, the retired president of Harvard, to comment:

> That a club of businessmen should have engaged in such an undertaking, and have brought it successfully to its present stage, affords a favorable illustration of the workings of American democracy. The democracy is not going to be dependent on the rare appearance of a Pericles, an Augustus, a Colbert, or a Christopher Wren. It will be able to work toward the best ideals through the agency of groups of intelligent and public spirited citizens who know how to employ experts to advantage.[6]

To sell the plan that they had commissioned experts to produce, the Commercial Club members, through their control of the CPC, employed another expert to promote the plan. Walter Moody, professional organizer, one of the new breed of public executives who made careers out of managing civic organizations, assumed this responsibility. As early as 1909 Moody had been approached by Charles D. Norton, later assistant secretary of the treasury under William Howard Taft, to publicize the plan as the exclusive promotional property of the Commercial Club. When the plan was presented to the city and a public agency, the Chicago Plan Commission was created by a municipal ordinance. Moody's talent was again solicited—this time by the CPC's first chairman, Charles H. Wacker. Moody accepted the task of mobilizing a comprehensive promotional campaign to match the sweeping metropolitan scope of the plan itself.[7]

Although he never pretended to be a technical planner like Burnham or Bennett, Moody did consider his task of "the scientific promotion of scientific planning" to be equal in importance to whatever was accomplished on the drafting table or in the architectural office. He defined city planning as "the science of planning the development of cities in a systematic and orderly way." Furthermore, he divided city planning into "two distinct and widely separate scientific branches. The first, or technical branch, embraces architecture and engineering. The second, which is promotive, is likewise scientifically professional and could be truthfully termed the dynamic power behind the throne of accomplishment."[8]

The terms scientifically professional indicated another characteristic that Moody shared with many other thinkers of his era. As David Noble, Samuel Hays, and Charles Forcey have argued, many Progressives believed strongly in the efficacy of the scientific method guided by professional expertise to achieve social change.[9] Walter Moody shared this assumption, not only in his promulgation of the Chicago Plan but also in his promotion of the new profession of city planning. The special identity that Herbert Croly claimed for architects, that Frederick Winslow Taylor coveted for industrial engineers, and Louis Brandeis wished firmly established for lawyers and businessmen, Moody sought for city planners. Like his contemporary colleagues in city planning, Charles Mulford Robinson and John Nolen, he endeavored to contribute to what Burton J. Bledstein has named the late nineteenth- and early twentieth-century culture of professionalism. Moody's decade of work with the CPC, his numerous magazine and newspaper articles, and his two major books were methods whereby he sought to make the profession of city planning a vehicle of urban reform. [10]

Publicity was the key to Moody's reformism. In debt to the social scientific advertizing techniques he borrowed from the pioneering social psychologist Walter Scott Dill, a fellow Chicagoan who later became president of Northwestern University, Moody made his appeal for implementation of the 1909 plan to each of the assorted interest groups and power blocs in Chicago.

Of the multiple constituencies to be persuaded of the necessity of the plan, Moody felt most confident of the city's capitalists; after all, had it not been an informal competition to determine who would actually sponsor a city plan that forced the merger of Chicago's Merchants and Commercial Clubs? By the time the Commercial Club turned over the Burnham Plan, its members had invested over a half-million dollars in the enterprise. Of the general electorate, Moody was less sure. His first major publication as managing director of the CPC sought to reach this city-wide, adult audience. A ninety-page, hardbound reference work titled *Chicago's Greatest Issue: An Official Plan* was distributed to over 165,000 Chicago property owners and tenants who paid twenty-five dollars or more in rent; the booklet is usually credited with countering the initial critiques of the plan (such as G. E. Newcomb's caustic *Chicago Replanned* [1911] and the protests of the Twelfth Street Property Owners Association) and with securing support for the passage of the first plan bond issue (the widening of Twelfth Street) proposed to the Chicago voters in 1912. [11]

Within the first six months of administering the CPC, Moody moved to institute a city planning study program in the Chicago schools. Daniel Burnham had suggested this move; he felt that for comprehensive urban planning to succeed "children must grow up dreaming of a beautiful city." Burnham, who had been extremely disappointed when his 1905 plan for San Francisco failed to be implemented because of inadequate promotion and subsequent citizen apathy, hoped to achieve his educational objective by lectures and the distribution of literature in the city schools. Moody had bigger plans. Believing as he did that "the ultimate solution of all the major problems of American cities lies in the education of our children to their responsibilities as future owners of our municipalities and arbiters of their governmental destiny," he proposed introducing an accredited course on the Chicago Plan into the city's public school curriculum. The course would be a part of Moody's program for scientific citizen making.[12]

To assist in such civic nurture, Moody wrote the first city planning textbook to be used in American schools. He named the text *Wacker's Manual*, because he believed that the people "should come to know intimately the individual who to a large extent held the destiny of the city in his hands." He felt it imperative for the populace to have the same confidence and knowledge about their plan leader, Charles Wacker, chairman of the CPC, as their plan.

Influenced by the work of German educators who had been instructing children in urban planning since the 1880s, he designed his manual and its accompanying teacher's handbook for use in the second semester of a civics course already operating in the final term of Chicago's public grammar schools. The eighth grade was selected because many contemporary educational psychologists contended that children were thought to be most impressionable at that stage of growth, and because after grammar school, many would drop out of school. While writing the manual, Moody sought help from the University of Chicago faculty, the staff at the Chicago Historical Society, and the Art Institute. He persuaded Ella Flagg Young, city superintendent of schools, to have the Board of Education officially adopt and purchase (at thirty-four cents a hardbound copy) the 1911 first edition for use in the spring of 1912. Eventually over fifty-thousand copies of the manual were printed. They were read not only by Chicago school children but also by their parents.

While by no means as stunning in diversity of pictorial media or aesthetic quality, the manual aspired to make as powerful a visual impact as had the plan. The manual included over 150 charts, maps, and pictures (many reproduced from the plan) as compared with the plan's 142 illustrations. Similar to the parent plan, nearly a third of the manual's graphics were of foreign urban design. Color renderings in both Burnham's treatise (where they were largely the work of Jules Guerin) and Moody's textbook were hazy, subdued pastels, connoting a tranquil, sunlit environment for Chicago which corresponds with an equally unreal absence of automobiles, pollution, and congestion in these projected visual utopias of Chicago's future.

Moody further modeled his 137-page primer along organizational lines roughly parallel to the 164-page, octavo-size plan. He divided the textbook into four major topics: (1) general urban planning philosophy and nomenclature (chapters 1–3); (2) a historical survey of city planning since antiquity (chapters 4–7); (3) Chicago's historical, geographic, economic, and civic development, including the origins of the 1909 plan (chapters 8–10); and (4) a detailed exegesis of the plan's main components—transportation network, street system, Michigan Avenue redevelopment, park system, civic center (chapters 11–16).

Of the "four great educational mediums" he produced in advancing the Plan of Chicago, Moody considered his manual to have the most long-range influence. Along with almost every previous American educational reformer—Benjamin Rush, Horace Mann, Henry Barnard, Francis Parker—he believed that the promise of an enlightened, public-minded citizenry rested with the current school age generation. An educator for several years in Chicago's La Salle Extension University, Moody claimed his manual "recognized the need for bringing out in the children of our cities a sharp, clear, vivid interest in those cities, in their history, their growth, in their present and their future." The manual can be considered one of the earliest urban histories for use in the secondary schools; moreover, its visual and verbal coverage of the American and European urban built environment introduced eighth graders to civic art and public architecture—areas of the fine arts that progressive educators usually found neglected in most American classrooms.[13]

Moody's manual shared with fellow Chicagoans Francis Parker and John Dewey the desire to create a larger classroom by relating school and society. Like Parker and Dewey, Moody sought to adjust education, through the discipline of city planning, to the interests of young people and to tie what he called civic learning to the real world outside the classroom.[14] The manual's injunctions to use the city as part of the curriculum were perfectly consonant with Dewey's principles of integrating *The School and Society*. Although in practice he exhibited none of the innovative pedagogical techniques that Dewey and his followers advocated, Moody completely agreed in theory with progressive education's concern that schooling should fit the needs of the child rather than the demands of tradition.

Perhaps the greatest common ground shared by Moody as a promoter of planning education, and Dewey as a proponent of progressive education, was their common assumption regarding the correlation between education and politics. Dewey, in *Education and Democracy* (1916)—a major educational manifesto of progressivism—commented, "we may produce in the schools a projection in the type of society we should like to realize and by forming minds in accord with it generally modify the larger and more recalcitrant features of adult society." Likewise, Moody, in *Wacker's Manual* (1911) proposed to "prepare the minds of our children to grasp and lay fast hold upon the science of city planning for the future glory of Chicago and the prosperity and happiness of all her people."[15]

Along with providing a pioneering pedagogy for disseminating "the principles and practices of scientific planning," Moody quite unabashedly wrote his primer to inculcate what he variously termed community patriotism, united civic interest, civic patriotism, and community virtue. In the manual "the work of citizen building and city planning" were synonymous since Moody saw the plan and its implementation across the cityscape as the artifactual evidence that "gave the people of Chicago a way to express in solid form their progressive spirit."[16]

In an article in *Century Magazine* assessing the "White City and Capital City," Daniel Burnham specifically identified himself and his city planning with the Progressive movement. Architectural historian Thomas Hines has recently pointed out the ramifications of Burnham's reformist liberal Republicanism, particularly its influence on the shape and substance of the 1909 plan.[17] Such progressivism became further pronounced when Moody translated the plan into a manual.

Moody, basically a supporter of capitalistic individualism (he had been the executive director of the Chicago Association of Commerce before joining the CPC), also saw the need—perhaps in the interest of conserving that economic system—for greater social collectivization and municipal cooperation among individual citizens. Long-range, large-scale city planning would, he admitted, proscribe certain rights and prerogatives of the city dweller. Moody worried that in early twentieth-century American cities such as Chicago rampant individualism perhaps had gone too far and that the system's inherent atomism was rapidly destroying communal urban life.[18]

To meet this dilemma, Moody advocated major environmental and architectural change as an important component of the larger reform movement that contemporaries and later historians would call Progressivism. In short, he argued in both the manual and in his later writings for a greater combination of central planning and voluntary individual cooperation. His friend, Bernard W. Snow summarized this view in an address honoring the CPC in 1910: "Every generation has its burdens. To this is given the duty of curbing the individualism and establishing the collectivism of Democracy."[19]

Walter Moody promulgated a political Progressivism that historian Stow Persons has labelled neodemocracy.[20] Nonpartisan, believing in the political role of public opinion, anxious to separate electoral politics from public administration, Moody's writings are a perfect case study of an early twentieth-century neodemocrat in action. With his fellow Progressives, Moody was willing to revise his original ideal of social progress as achievable solely in individualistic terms and to concede to the state (particularly via a strong executive and numerous public commissions) the rapid expansion of its functions and powers. Moody, like Herbert Croly (who gave the Burnham Plan a highly favorable review in the *Architectural Review*), saw in neodemocracy a political philosophy that did not threaten the prerogatives of the expert. Along with Walter Lippmann he did not fear either a big leader (especially if he were a Burnham), or bigness in business, labor, or government. The public relations man who translated the philosophy of a business client such as Burnham, who always insisted: "Make no little plans, they have no magic to stir men's blood and probably themselves will not be realized. Make big plans; aim high in hope and work, remembering that a noble, logical diagram once recorded will never die," could hardly see bigness as a bogey.[21] Nor could he deny the power of the word, especially the printed word, in shaping democratic political thought and action. A reformer who had written a half dozen books, over forty pamphlets, position papers, reports, newspaper and magazine articles would not think otherwise. Finally, insistent that change came about by working through the established political system, Moody concurred in the direct democracy principles of a reformer like Frank Parsons and maintained "that the ballot box always precedes the city planner."

Since the ultimate implementation of the Burnham Plan depended upon widespread voter acceptance of each of its specific proposals, Moody saw his task as identical to that of Frederic C. Howe, who, in *The City: The Hope of Democracy* (1905), had argued for linking of all city planning reform with an extensive information and publicity program for adults and a comprehensive educational component within the schools for children. The Moody *Wacker's Manual* and his adult primer, *What of The City?* served these two purposes. They also contain evidence of at least two of the other important intellectual currents of late nineteenth- and early twentieth-century America: first, a quest for efficiency and order in personal, commercial, industrial, and political activity; second, the belief in the physical environment as a primary determinant of human behavior.

In a work subtitled "Municipal Economy," it comes as no surprise to find repeated pleas for greater centralization, the absolute necessity of eliminating all waste, the commercial value of beauty, and the civic efficacy of "good order, cleanliness, and economy." Actually many sections of Moody's tract could have been written by any number of Chicagoans—George Pullman, Marshall Field, Gustavus Swift—each of whom sought to impose entrepreneurial systems on the industrial and commercial landscape. This search for order as historian Robert Wiebe labels late nineteenth-century American history, pervades the manual, a work that also anticipates Walter Lippmann's *Drift and Mastery* in its demand for a "community patriotism to substitute order for disorder; and reason, common sense and action for negligence, indifference and inertia." Moreover, Moody's incessant arguments for the efficient use of public space strongly parallel Frederick W. Taylor's similar claims (published in the same year as the manual) for *The Scientific Principles of Management* in the organization of industrial space.[22]

"To make Chicago a real, centralized city instead of a group of overcrowded villages," Moody took to be a basic premise of the Burnham plan. Chicago's street and highway pattern, railroad network, cultural and civic activity would each have a center and in turn be a component of a new central city. The linchpin of this new urban core was a monumental civic center that would serve Chicago as the Acropolis had Athens, or the Forum had Rome, or St. Mark's Square had Venice—the very embodiment of the reformed civic life that Burnham and Moody hoped to see in Chicago. Although we have understandably lost sympathy for neoclassical expressions of institutionalized political power, the Progressives held that neoclassicism's unity, permanence, balance, order, and symmetry best proclaimed the symbolic and functional role of public buildings and communal spaces . A civic center—a unified cluster of "vast civic temples"—was what Moody called Burnham's proposed building group dominated by a colossal municipal administration building. It would typify the permanence of the city, record its history, and express its aspiration for reform. In Moody's estimate, the civic center would "give life to the spirit of unity in the city."[23]

In the process of centralization, congestion and waste would be eradicated. Moody warned his young readers in his manual that "the *elimination of waste is the World's Greatest Scientific Problem*," and in his manifesto for adult voters he suggested various ways by which scientific planning would solve this international dilemma: zoning controls, public health regulations, uniform building codes, standardized construction materials and designs.[24] A pet Moody project was his proposal, set forth in a pamphlet titled *Fifty Million Dollars for Nothing!* (1916), wherein he outlined how the people of Chicago could obtain thirteen hundred acres of lakefront parks, playgrounds and watercourses by recycling the city's garbage and waste material—old bricks and mortar, excavation soil, street sweepings, cinders and ashes. In twelve years, estimated Moody, Chicago taxpayers would have new parklands along the lakefront worth fifty million dollars, at no cost whatsoever.

As both Samuel Haber and Samuel Hays demonstrate in their respective investigations of the gospel of efficiency in the scientific management and conservation movements, Progressives like Moody, Burnham, and their associates became enthralled with the principles of efficiency, standardization, and centralization in civic life because they had already attempted to implement such principles in business life. Although they looked to Europe for their aesthetic inspiration—particularly to that of Baron Georges Eugene Haussmann and the French Ecole de Beaux Arts—their planning ideas reflected primarily the order and systemization they prized in their own businesses. For example, Frederic Delano, a Commercial Club Plan Committee member who had made his way up to the presidency of the Wabash railroad at age twenty-two, maintained that in his mind, "a comprehensive city plan represented a natural progression from his own idea of centralization of the Chicago passenger railroads."[25]

During a decade that produced studies on the "Elimination of Waste in Education," "Scientific Management in the Churches," and "The Waste of Private Housekeeping," it is hardly a novelty that Moody should refer to his plan as an instrument of "the City Practical" as opposed to "the City Beautiful" with which it was often confused. A rational, unified, efficient, scientific, practical plan, he insisted, was the sole way to "bring order out of the chaos incident to rapid urban growth."[26]

To the elements of education and efficiency that have been suggested thus far as crucial to Moody's strategy for civic reform must be added a third feature—environmentalism. Like many of his generation, Walter Moody believed in a modified ecological determinism. Taken as he was with the emergence of American social science in the latter half of the nineteenth century and confident of its beneficial applications to "the science of city planning," he maintained that the "physical conditions which make for good health, good order and good citizenship must be made clear to our children." Convinced that "splendid material upbuilding" of the metropolis would yield "a social, intellectual and moral upbuilding of its people," Moody stated a simple environmental equation: "City building means man building." Following an evolutionary analog used earlier by Chicago novelist Henry Blake Fuller to explain the progressive development of "a higher type of

Chicagoan'' in cultural achievements, Moody predicted a parallel social evolution to follow upon the advent of social scientific urban planning in the Prairie City.[27]

Such city planning could not come too soon in Moody's judgment. "The physical conditions of people in the cities as compared with the people of the open country is deteriorating," he warned his young readers, because "city life is an intense life, many times more wearing upon the nerves than country life." Quoting various social scientists, he also charged that the unplanned and unkempt city "saps the energy of men and makes them less efficient in the work of life." Moreover, it was "this strain of city life which increases insanity and brings weaknesses of many kinds to shorten life and deprive people of their vigor." Heady stuff for mere 14-year-olds but only one example of the manual's argument that the physical environment conditions public behavior.[28]

Several of the manual's proposals to correct "the marked deterioration of the physique" of urban dwellers bear a striking resemblance to the theories of American psychiatrist George M. Beard, discoverer of neurasthenia or nervous weakness. Beard believed that environmental tensions, particularly when acerbated by the stress of urbanization, modernization, and technological innovation, were the chief causal factors in the etiology of mental illness. In his most famous book, *American Nervousness,* Beard claimed that the incidence of mental disorders was unusually high (and growing even more so) in late nineteenth-century urban America. There had been no nervous exhaustion or physical deterioration, for example, in those cities of ancient Greece or Rome that Burnham and Moody held up as exemplars of ordered, planned, urban design. These ancient civilizations, Beard contended, lacked five characteristics peculiar to nineteenth-century civilization: steam power, the telegraph, the periodical press, the sciences, and the mental activity of women. In each of these aspects of modernity, Beard felt America was a quarter century more advanced than any European country.[29]

As early as the time of Benjamin Rush, American physicians had almost as a matter of course acknowledged that the unique pace of American life (its competitiveness, its religious pluralism, its lack of stability in social status) was somehow related to America's higher rate of mental illness. After the Civil War two other ideas—the concept of evolution and the increase in the population and number of American cities—had been added to this traditional belief in the relationship between American civilization and psychological and physical health. Beard accepted and amalgamated both evolution and urbanization into his interpretation of American nervousness. Charles Rosenberg notes Beard maintained that the conquest of neurasthenia need involve no change in man himself, just his environment. The technology that had produced the telegraph, the railroad, and the factory had already begun to provide other technological innovations that helped to reduce the tensions of American experience. Here Beard cited as specific examples the elevator, the sewing machine, and the Pullman palace car.[30]

Moody, although there is no evidence that he ever met or read Beard, shared his belief in evolution and in urban neurasthenia. Like Beard he looked to the continued advance of material and technological progress to offset evils of the American urban environment. City planning, in Moody's view, naturally provided one panacea whereby urbanites could overcome or at least mitigate ecological determinism. In the school text he also called a physical geography, Moody, with an analogy he borrowed from Frederick Law Olmsted, argued that urban parks and forest preserves could be "compared with the lungs of a person, as the means by which the city and its people get the stimulus of fresh air so necessary to normal well-being." Much like Olmsted, who argued for orderly park design as a method of social control and urban reform, Moody envisioned the parks of the 1909 plan as crucial components in alleviating stress, overcrowding, and congestion. In the Chicago city parks the masses supposedly would find an environment conducive both to activity and to contemplation.[31]

Critics of Burnham's plan and Moody's manual complained that the plan did not do enough to alleviate the social evils that afflicted numerous Chicagoans: lack of housing, schools, or adequate sanitation. Charges of elitism and lack of concern for public improvements at the neighborhood level were directed at a plan that admittedly and primarily dealt with elaborate transportation systems, monumental aesthetic centerpieces, and symmetrical street facades. In several respects the Chicago that Burnham had planned and that Moody promoted was a metropolis for businessmen; yet ironically, with the exception of the central business district, there were no carefully designated areas for commercial expansion throughout the rest of the city. Nor were there any model tenements for workers, much less model neighborhoods. Not that Moody was oblivious to Chicago's housing or social problems. Slums were mentioned in both the manual and the plan but only briefly. Once in the plan, for example, it was suggested that "it is no attack on private property to argue that society has the inherent right to protect itself [against] gross evils and known perils" by imposing restrictions on overcrowding, enforcing sanitary regulations, and limiting lot coverage. Mel Scott has discovered an assertion in the plan that if private enterprise cannot rehouse persons forced out of congested quarters, the city itself may have to do so "in common justice to men and women so degraded by long lives in the slums that they have lost all power of caring for themselves.'' But this daring idea only appears as an afterthought in the Burnham/Moody philosophy of the city, tucked away surreptitiously, at best a very minor chord in a grand symphony of magnificent boulevards, imposing structures, and splendid parks. The housing concerns of other Progressives such as Lawrence Veiller and Jacob Riis in other cities and New York did not exist among most of their counterparts of the Burnham/Moody persuasion in Chicago.[32]

Moody's writings reveal many of the myopias of the contemporary neodemocratic mind. He had little notion of the demographic, racial, and ethnic changes that were going to sweep over neighborhoods in a city such as Chicago. He was far too sanguine about the coexistence of the city and the automobile. Furthermore, he tended to exaggerate the belief that the conservation of wasted energy and resources alone would solve urban problems or that ordered civic spaces, efficient circulatory systems, and grandiose natural landscapes would yield contented, prosperous, virtuous citizens. Had social problems been stressed more directly in Moody's translation of Burnham's plan as they were in the St. Louis city plan of 1907, perhaps nothing of the Chicago 1909 plan would have been implemented. So argues historian Robert Akeley who is persuaded that had Moody not downplayed the social reform dimension of what would have eventually had to accompany any genuine municipal rejuvenescence, the success of the physical proposals and the image of the plan as a comprehensive program of civic renaissance would have been seriously jeopardized. Akeley also feels that ''Chicago planning salesmanship was based upon enthusiasm and commitment, rather than on calculated exploitation.''[33]

Moody assuredly was an enthusiast. ''No one has ever equaled him in promoting city planning, convincing an entire metropolis of its value, and winning support of a particular plan from voters and public officials alike.''[34] An ingenious and skillful propagandist, he promulgated the necessity of scientific city planning in ways other than the *Wacker Manual.* Thousands of pamphlets, mailings, circulars with titles like ''Chicago Can Get Fifty Million Dollars for Nothing!'' ''Reclaim South Water Street For All The People,'' ''Pull Chicago Out of the Hole—United Action Will Do It!'' and ''Economic Readjustment From a War to a Peace Basis'' were his work.

As adroit with other communication media as he was with publications, he developed an extensive stereopticon slide library illustrating all aspects of the Burnham plan and many examples of city planning throughout the world. Over the ten years that he gave slide lectures on city planning all over Chicago and around the country, he estimated he had talked to approximately 175,000 people. Under his direction the Chicago Plan Commission made its own movie, "A Tale of One City," a two-reeler contrasting the existing conditions of Chicago with the 1909 plan proposals. The first documentary film on city planning ever produced, it opened in Chicago (a city that in 1915 still hoped to become the movie capital of the country) to a sell-out crowd at the Majestic Theater. Shown in fifty theaters in the Chicago metropolitan area and then in other United States cities, over 150,000 people saw the film during its premier year of 1915.

Finally in 1919 Moody wrote a 440-page treatise titled *What of The City?* where much of the history of the Chicago Plan Commission as well as his own history in the planning movement was recounted. Probably his most sophisticated analysis of Chicago city planning within the context of the national urban planning movement, the book's highly autobiographical content also reveals much about Moody the plan promoter; it, along with the manual, summarizes his main political and planning ideas. Whereas the manual had proselytized on the local level, *What of The City?* sought nationwide converts; the former publication Moody designed to reach the generation of the future, still occupying Chicago's classrooms; the latter book he prepared for the continuing adult education of his own generation throughout the country's cities.

To talk of converts and proselytizing recalls an initial characterization of Walter Moody made earlier in this chapter. W. D. Moody, it will be remembered, was occasionally confused with fellow Chicagoan D. L. Moody. A later historian of American city planning, while not mistaking the two men, aptly calls Moody an evangelist of planning whose civic bible was the 1909 plan that spread the gospel of municipal reform "with the aggressiveness of a salesman and the fervor of a religious zealot."[35]

Within this context Moody might be compared to William Thomas Stead, editor of the Anglo-American *Review of Reviews* who a decade earlier had written another municipal reform tract, *If Christ Came to Chicago!* (1894). Stead's bestselling expose of municipal corruption and his program for urban reform included in a final chapter ("In the Twentieth Century") an inclusive city plan to implement comprehensive civic reform. A detailed comparison of Moody's primer and Stead's intriguing city plan for making Chicago "the ideal city of the world," while pertinent to this discussion, will not be done here; mention is made merely to suggest that Moody's techniques were by no means novel to the Chicago reform effort that sought to improve the city by altering the cityscape.[36]

Moreover, W. T. Stead, a Congregational minister who preached civic and social reform at meetings of the city's Central Music Hall in the wake of the World's Columbian Exposition, could only have smiled with approval at one of Moody's last official acts to promote the Burnham plan. In early 1919 Moody wrote *Seed Thoughts For Sermons*, a seven-page appeal to the city's clergymen to recognize the humanitarian and social value of the Chicago plan that had been written a decade earlier. Numerous clergy followed Moody's injunction to preach the value of comprehensive planning to their congregations on January 19, 1919, the date chosen as Plan of Chicago Sunday throughout the city. Later, that day was alluded to as Nehemiah Sunday because so many ministers had used Nehemiah's description of the rebuilding of Jerusalem and the temple as their text. Many congregations also displayed the Chicago flag on their churches while others sang hymns such as "Work, for the Night Is Coming!" Stead would have loved it.[37]

The British reformer would also have endorsed Moody's career as a propagandist, particularly Moody's crucial role in effecting the transition whereby a private plan drawn up by a private club became a public ordinance to be implemented by a public commission that in turn hired as its managing director a former publicist for private enterprise who became a public civil servant who wrote a public school textbook. Had Stead lived to see a copy, he would have approved of Moody's manual, a book that can serve the historian as a tracer element to reveal some of the less familiar intellectual history of the vast effort surrounding the 1909 plan.

The legacy of the Burnham plan and Moody's promotion of it is multiple. In terms of actual alteration of the physical cityscape, it has been estimated that over $300 million in public construction can be directly attributed to the inspiration of the plan. Moody's numerous publications contributed to the literature of the city planning profession, prompting a demand for the services of city planners in cities all over the nation. Finally, because of Moody's salesmanship of Burnham's idea, the Burnham plan became *the* paradigm for the American city planning movement for the next generation. It was this model of the City Practical that future planners and politicians in Chicago and elsewhere built on, adapted, or rebelled against in their collective task of what Moody called the "science of city planning and citizen building."[38]

8

E. Franklin Frazier and the Problem of Assimilation

DALE R. VLASEK

DURING an extremely productive career E. Franklin Frazier wrote numerous examinations and analyses of the Afro-American experience ranging from sociological studies of the black family to programs for racial advancement to polemics against the black bourgeoisie. Beneath the diversity of his thought, one theme united all of his work— a concern for the assimilation of the black man into American life. The concept of assimilation, unfortunately, is one of those notoriously imprecise ideas that plague American social science. As many scholars have noted it has meant different things to different people at different times. And Frazier's use of the term was no exception. Although his commitment remained constant his definition of assimilation changed over the course of his career in response to external conditions and contemporary ideas.

Initially, like many members of the black middle class, Frazier perceived assimilation in terms of acculturation, integration, and amalgamation. In order to become assimilated blacks had to acquire the cultural and behavioral patterns of white society; enter the social, economic, and political life of the nation on the basis of human equality; and, if they so desired, intermarry with whites. Consequently, during the 1920s he devoted much of his efforts to creating a program that would eliminate black cultural deficiencies and end segregation. Later as Frazier became a mature professional sociologist his perceptions changed. Because of his training in the Chicago School of Sociology he came to see acculturation, integration, and amalgamation as part of an

DALE R. VLASEK, University of Iowa, Iowa City, Iowa.

all-pervasive race relations cycle that was working itself out in American life. Through his investigations he documented the acculturative and integrative effects of urbanization and industrialization and anxiously recorded the cycle's slow movement toward completion. Finally, after years of watching blacks move from cultural inferiors to a minority group on the verge of assimilation Frazier was disillusioned to find that they were still outside of American life. By the mid-1950s his theoretical and substantive examinations of international race relations had led him to the realization that assimilation required a psychological and cultural fusion of blacks and whites into a new cosmopolitan entity. Within American society he found that the black middle class and the American system of race relations resisted the fusion process. And drawing much of his style from similar contemporary critiques of the middle class and race relations he criticized them both. [1]

Understanding this theme of assimilation is the key to understanding Frazier's social thought. Students of his work have long been aware of the existence of this concern, but they have overlooked its complexity and changing nature. Moreover, some of his critics have misread it as a bias, leading to the distortion and denigration of much of Afro-American culture and tradition. The purpose of this study is to trace the development of Frazier's conception of assimilation together with its attendant programs for black advancement and relate them to intellectual currents in both the black and white communities. For only by seeing the dynamics of his thought can one gain an appreciation of Frazier's scholarship, place it in a proper relationship with his times, and recognize his contributions to American social science. [2]

Although Frazier never spelled out exactly what he meant by assimilation it is clear that he derived much of his early conception of it from black society. Born to middle-class parents in Baltimore, Maryland, in the fall of 1894, he was heir to a legacy of acculturation and integration. For the upper and middle classes of the late nineteenth and early twentieth century the solution to racial problems lay in the acceptance of white middle-class culture. Continually reminded by whites of the backwardness of the race, they worked diligently to appear as middle-class Americans. They practiced the manners and morals of Victorian America; they trained and educated their children in the tradition of gentility; they avoided anything, particularly ungrammatical speech and immorality, that might be reminiscent of the Afro-American folk culture; and they admonished those members of black society who failed to follow their lead. At the same time, the upper and middle classes envisioned an integrated world as the goal of the race and they resisted any attempt to increase segregation and discrimination. In Frazier's hometown, for example, they initiated a series of partially successful boycotts against Jim Crow railroad cars and steamship lines and joined with other Maryland blacks to defeat three separate attempts at statewide disenfranchisement.[3]

These same lessons were delivered to Frazier a little closer to home. His father James Edward Frazier was a patriarch in the best sense of the word. He was a hardworking man with an abiding interest in the integrity, success, and upward mobility of his children. Perhaps because he never had the opportunity to receive a formal education and had taught himself to read, write, and calculate, he had an almost religious faith in the efficacy of education. He never tired of reminding his five children that they could avoid the humiliations he occasionally suffered by obtaining a good education. Apparently the message was accepted. For despite his death at an early age, three of his sons became professionals—one an academician, one a lawyer, and one a physician—his daughter a nurse, and his remaining son a businessman.[4]

Besides being concerned with his own family, James Frazier was intensely interested in the problems and progress of the Afro-American. He subscribed to a variety of black newspapers and magazines and read the editorials of the leading racial spokesmen. He kept a scrapbook for his children highlighting the critical affairs of the day and insisted that they discuss them with him. He filled the dinner conversation with a vigorous condemnation of Baltimore's Jim Crow proceedings. And he wrote letters of denunciation not only to the local papers but to papers as far away as Atlanta, Georgia. In a house filled with such spirit Franklin Frazier could not help but be touched.[5]

Starting with this legacy Frazier's own conception of assimilation developed as he grew to maturity. After graduating from Howard University in 1916, he spent three years as a teacher in various segregated schools in the South. Later in the early 1920s, after receiving a Master of Arts degree in sociology from Clark University, he accepted a position in Atlanta as an instructor in sociology at Morehouse College and the director of the newly founded Atlanta School of Social Work. During these years he had the opportunity to observe the problems of the Afro-American firsthand; as he watched he began to flesh out his own idea of black assimilation and to devise a program that might lead to its fulfillment.

Frazier legitimized his early ideas by formulating a general theory about societal organization and evolution. As a young scholar he had read Franklin Giddings's *The Principles of Sociology* and he drew upon it heavily to argue that race relations in the United States were based upon anachronistic principles characteristic of an earlier stage of social evolution. Societies, he explained, had evolved through three stages with each stage having its own principle of social cohesiveness. Primitive society, for example, organized itself along kinship lines. But when it began to expand and conquer other groups it reorganized itself around the lines of authority in order to subordinate specific groups of people. This authority or subordination was institutionalized by the establishment of hereditary classes endowed with certain privileges and rights. With the coming of the revolutionary era and industrial capitalism, society reorganized itself along the modern principles of social equality and citizenship. Under these principles a person had rights and privileges not as a member of a hereditary group but as an individual member of society.[6]

In America, however, societal evolution had stalled. At approximately the same time that the new principles had begun to operate, blacks entered the social order as slaves. The introduction of a hereditary subordinate group restored the archaic authoritarian principles and reinstated the practice of assigning rights by class. Even after emancipation, American society continued to treat blacks as members of a separate and subordinate caste, not only denying their status as citizens, but also, Frazier wrote, denying their existence as human beings.[7]

Frazier felt that the solution to this problem was two-fold. First, blacks had to demand that American society recognize the modern principles of social organization and treat them as citizens and humans. Secondly and simultaneously, they had to work to end those things that had facilitated their banishment to a caste outside of American life. As Frazier viewed matters, the former was dependent upon the latter. Whites would not willingly or passively accept blacks as equals. They would yield only to forceful demands and political pressure and these could be more effective if blacks could eradicate those factors that created their subordinate status.[8]

Black subordination, according to Frazier, rested on three intertwined circumstances. First, blacks were racially different from whites; that is, their Negroid characteristics, while not representing any innate barriers to social equality, had acted as symbols of the other elements of subordinate status. Second, blacks were economically dependent upon whites. The pattern of American economic development determined that most blacks lived in poverty, worked for white employers, bought from white merchants, and rented from white landlords. Third, and most important, because of an incomplete assimilation of American culture, isolation from the cultural mainstream of American life, and inadequate educational and cultural facilities, blacks had a lower level of culture than whites. Together these things were denying blacks access to American society. They posed barriers to assimilation and to overcome them Frazier not only urged pride in racial characteristics and racial heritage but proposed to accelerate the acculturation process and to reduce economic dependence.[9]

As early as 1920 Frazier identified acculturation as one of the central problems of black advancement. In a study of black longshoremen in New York City, he explained that their already depressed existence was worsened by their failure to adopt the values and habits of urban life. He felt they could benefit from a sane program of Americanization similar to the one used on immigrants. Later as he became more familiar with the problems of newly urbanized blacks through his position in Atlanta, Frazier became more adamant and direct. The chief need of southern blacks, he repeatedly declared, was socialization. Many blacks, he wrote, were "ignorant," not only illiterate but incognizant of the basic social skills, traditions, knowledge, and ideals which most Americans possessed. Torn away from their native African culture by slavery, blacks had had neither the time nor the opportunity to completely assimilate white western culture. As a result they appeared as either culturally backward or "poor imitations" of white men. If blacks were to advance they had to complete the assimilation process. For unlike other racial or ethnic groups they did not have a culture outside of American life to draw upon. And if they chose to shut themselves off from western culture, Frazier insisted, their development would be arrested and they would remain on the level of "barbarism."[10]

Frazier recognized, however, that the completion of the assimilation process required some sort of program or institutional tool to reach the mass of incompletely assimilated blacks. And after a brief search in which he rejected a number of traditional and unconventional institutions, he settled on the time-honored approach of assimilation through economic activity. This idea of course was not original with Frazier. Any number of racial and ethnic spokesmen had suggested similar ideas before. But Frazier's proposal did have its new and unique aspects. Frazier had long been aware of the black economic plight. His observations of the effects that the agricultural, mercantile, and financial systems of the South had on blacks together with his contacts with the degraded and impoverished life of urban blacks led him to categorize blacks as "the most preyed upon of the economically dependent classes." This concern encouraged and promoted a youthful interest in socialism and Marxist ideology. Like many young Americans in the years before the First World War, he had been an active member of the Intercollegiate Socialist Society. Later, during his research for his master's thesis, he encountered the designs for black economic independence through collective action proposed by people like A. Phillip Randolph, Chandler Owen, and Marcus Garvey and came away impressed. This interest was strengthened still further in 1921 when he had the opportunity to see a collective economy at work. Supported by a fellowship from the American-Scandinavian Foundation, he spent a year studying the rural cooperatives of Denmark. During the course of his visit, he found that these enterprises had raised Danish farmers from "poverty and dependence" to "self-respect and comfort." Frazier was so pleased by their success at bringing "wealth to the inhabitants" that he hoped to introduce similar institutions to America. He was confident that cooperative organizations could not only help blacks escape economic dependence but also eliminate cultural deficiency.[11]

As Frazier envisioned it, these cooperatives could take a variety of forms. For black farmers he suggested the formation of collective marketing associations and credit unions. And for both rural and urban blacks he proposed consumer-controlled stores. But regardless of what form they took cooperatives were potentially powerful weapons in the battle to achieve assimilation. First, cooperatives would enable blacks to gain economic independence. Because they were relatively simple to operate, financially feasible given the limited capital of the black community, and economically viable in the world of corporate power, cooperatives would give Afro-Americans a firm position in the modern economic system. Black consumers, Frazier wrote, could be served by black stores drawing on black suppliers and hiring black workers. Blacks would become in effect the producers and distributors of their own wants and needs in the marketplace and the facilitators of employment opportunities in fields long denied to the race.[12]

More importantly, cooperatives could give "the colored population as a whole an education in business" and thus act as a stimulus to acculturation. Many black businessmen had failed, Frazier explained, because they were ignorant of the simplest concepts of capitalism. Like the grocer who sold stock to meet his payroll they were incompetent to act as entrepreneurs and cooperatives could correct this situation. Moreover, cooperatives could train blacks in the essentials and practices of democracy, something that was badly needed for a people denied political participation. Above all, cooperatives could mean an increase in white-collar, clerical, and skilled employment. By moving into these new jobs blacks would begin to acquire a sense of self-respect and assertiveness. They would learn to be self-reliant, industrious, thrifty, and task-oriented, or in other words, they would acquire the economic values of the white middle class.[13]

The thrust of Frazier's proposal, then, was to use economic participation as a tool for acculturation and eventual integration. And although he personally favored collective rather than individual action, he was more concerned with the resultant economic and cultural benefits than with the precise type of economic organization. When acculturated and economically secure groups emerged through the efforts of individual entrepreneurs he was more than willing to accept them as representatives of black progress. He felt that they validated his assumptions concerning the obstacles to assimilation. In 1925 he found such a group in Durham, North Carolina, and he proudly displayed it as proof that acculturation and economic independence were major steps on the way to ending racial discrimination and achieving assimilation.

Durham was a city of remarkable economic development. Black entrepreneurs, led by John C. Merrick, founder of the North Carolina Mutual Life Insurance Company, owned or controlled a brickyard, a lumber mill, an ironworks, a textile mill, as well as a number of banks, realty companies, and drug stores. They were so successful that they had made Durham "the capital of the black middle class," and in doing so had demonstrated a potential for cultural transformation and an improvement in race relations.[14]

The achievements of Durham's entrepreneurs proved to Frazier that Afro-Americans could adopt the bourgeois mentality and cultural values of western civilization. He explained that Durham's black businessmen had discarded the traditional black cultural patterns and had internalized the spartan and frugal virtues of the struggling bourgeoisie. Like ambitious businessmen anywhere they made hard work and long hours their rule, not out of necessity, but out of the desire to expand their businesses and to invade new fields. Moreover, their personal values and behavior were indistinguishable from their white counterparts. They valued progress and respectability, detested waste and immorality, and spent their wealth on fine homes, expensive automobiles, and Newport vacations.[15]

In addition, Durham showed that when blacks had a cultural life similar to whites and a secure economic position, racial tensions were diminished. While racial discrimination had not vanished in Durham, it had moderated slightly. White businessmen, Frazier insisted, acknowledged and supported the economic accomplishments of the black entrepreneurs. Moreover, they recognized the existence of common values beneath skin color. They knew that the Durham middle class respected property rights and "would no more vote for Debs than they."[16]

Frazier realized that Durham was unique in many ways. The "savage" racial prejudice of the lower South was absent and direct interracial competition was minimal. But nevertheless it confirmed his belief that economic development, cultural acquisition, and racial integration were closely linked. And if economic activity could reap such benefits in North Carolina it might provide the leverage to open up the rest of the nation to black advancement.[17]

As the 1920s drew to a close Frazier began to have some doubts about the efficacy of economic development as a force for assimilation. Originally he had hoped that economic activity would be advantageous for the entire race. But he discovered to his chagrin that those blacks who acquired middle-class wealth and a middle-class mentality acted like members of the capitalist bourgeoisie. "A Negro businessman," Frazier wrote, "who gets out of the white man's kitchen or dining room rightly regards himself as escaping slavery." But once out he maintained "himself by exploiting the Negro who remains in the kitchen" and took "consolation in the feeling that if he did not exploit him a white man would."[18]

At approximately the same time that Frazier became disillusioned with economic activity as an avenue for assimilation he discovered a new one. In 1927 after leaving Atlanta in the midst of a furor created by his authorship of an article that likened the mental processes of racism to those of insanity, he took up graduate studies at the University of Chicago. There under the direction and tutelage of the nation's leading sociologists and social theorists he came to see the problems of the Afro-American as part of a larger social and cultural phenomenon. And with that new conception he was able to envision the forces of twentieth century life restructuring American race relations and ensuring the assimilation of the Afro-American.[19]

Among the many research interests and methodological innovations of the Chicago School, Frazier found the race relations theories of Robert E. Park most impressive. For not only did they legitimize his earlier thinking by revealing that assimilation was the inevitable outcome of an irreversible social process but they also provided him with a scientific model that he could follow in order to realize his racial goals.

Park had abandoned the earlier sociological theories concerning race and had conceptualized race relations as part of a dynamic process, progressing in a cyclical fashion, moving through four stages—contact, competition, accommodation, and assimilation—and ending with the creation of a homogeneous society. For Park the race relations cycle was akin to an immutable natural law; various factors might combine to slow or stop it temporarily but it would move on to its conclusion. The cycle began when two races met through commercial or geographic expansion. As they attempted to live together they inevitably began to compete over the limited amount of resources available. Eventually this conflict was resolved through the institution of slavery, a caste system, or a segregated society. Regardless of what form accommodation took, it was followed by the cultural, social, political, and at times biological merger of the two races into an assimilated society. In America, Park explained, blacks and whites had progressed to a stage of accommodation and no further. Assimilation had begun under slavery but with the coming of emancipation a period of racial conflict ensued and a new form of accommodation emerged.[20]

In general, Frazier agreed with Park's assumptions concerning the breakdown of assimilation during reconstruction; but he also believed that he had evidence that the process had started up again, not on the plantations of the South but in the industrial cities of the North. The massive wartime migrations of rural blacks to industrial jobs in the northern cities had created a social and cultural climate conducive to assimilation. Upon entering the city the incompletely assimilated Afro-American was liberated from the social controls and community organizations that had ordered his life in the South. In their place he gained increased communication with the larger society, an opportunity for social mobility, and new sources of social control. At the same time, he was able to abandon unskilled and degrading work for employment in the professions, public service, or industry. And in doing so, he joined economic or occupational groups having goals and values identical to comparable groups within white society. In short, urbanization and industrialization were transforming blacks into dark-skinned Americans.[21]

Frazier's fascination with the powers of the city is not surprising. For just as the University of Chicago was the nation's leading center of race relations studies it was also the nation's center for urban sociology. By borrowing ideas—like Park's thesis that the city was a great sifting and sorting mechanism that selected and segregated people according to factors like race, cultural level, vocation and ambition; William I. Thomas's and Florian Znaniecki's concept of social disorganization as a portent of reorganization; and Ernest W. Burgess's supposition that the seeming irrational growth of American cities could be seen as a series of concentric circles or zones—Frazier was able to fashion a theory of urbanization and industrialization as assimilating forces.[22]

In his dissertation (later published as *The Negro Family in Chicago*, 1932) and in a number of articles, Frazier illustrated the acculturating powers of the city. Using the black family as a representative unit, he examined the cultural levels within the black community in relation to the inherent organizational structure of both the ghetto and the larger metropolis. Unlike other scholars, he portrayed the ghetto as a microcosm of urban social organization rather than an undifferentiated conglomeration of blacks. And within its confines, he found that black families underwent the identical processes of disorganization and reorganization, selection and segregation that occurred in the large metropolis. The outcome, moreover, was essentially in conformity with the gradients for urban growth described by E. W. Burgess. The urban structure through its sifting and sorting mechanisms produced an ecological pattern revealing the varying degrees of acculturation to white middle-class norms. Newly arrived blacks settled in the deteriorated areas near the central city. But after a period of cultural disorganization and reorganization, accompanied by economic improvement, they moved out toward the periphery. Correlating this intraghetto migration with occupation and family patterns, Frazier found that the farther blacks located away from the center of the city, the more they were employed as professionals, public servants, and skilled workers, and the more their family structure and habits approximated those of the white middle class.[23]

Starting with these ideas, Frazier built an extremely successful career as a sociologist. Teaching first at Fisk University in Nashville, Tennessee, and later at Howard University in Washington, D.C., he spent the next twenty-five years examining on an ever-enlarging scale how urbanization and industrialization were furthering the assimilation of the Afro-American. In 1937 he studied the black community of Harlem and found the identical processes of acculturation operating in New York City. In 1939 he ambitiously traced the organization and structure of the black family throughout its existence in the United States and concluded that city life along with the industrialization of the black work force was producing black middle-class Americans. In 1940 he identified the middle class as the most assimilated of the Afro-American population. And later that same year he proclaimed that even the South, the bastion of racism, was very slowly succumbing to the twin pressures of urbanization and industrialization.[24]

Finally in his magnum opus, *The Negro in the United States* (1949), Frazier declared that the urban-industrial forces of twentieth century life had transformed Afro-Americans and redefined their position in American society. Through urbanization blacks lost their mental and cultural isolation, liberated themselves from the petty restrictions of the small town, gained a sense of racial consciousness, entered the political system, joined the ranks of the industrial and white-collar work forces, and eventually adopted the habits of the white majority. Through increased economic participation and membership in interracial labor unions blacks acquired both economic independence and a voice in the economic affairs of the nation. Through the expanding role of the federal government blacks became the recipients of much needed economic and social aid. Through the diplomatic struggles of the Cold War for the loyalty of the former colonial nations, the United States was compelled to place more importance on the solution of its own racial problem. And finally through the mass communications media and increased public awareness many whites came to see American race relations as a crisis confronting the nation as a whole. Blacks, as Frazier saw it, were now a racially conscious minority group, supported by allies in the form of the federal government and enlightened public opinion, and standing on the verge of entering American life.[25]

Frazier was not alone in his optimistic assessment of American race relations. By the late 1940s most of his fellow social scientists had abandoned the earlier ideas about race and were confident that their investigations could lessen racial and ethnic hostilities and promote intergroup harmony. Through works like Gunnar Myrdal's *An American Dilemma* (1944) they proclaimed their belief in the ultimate elimination of racial injustice. In addition, Frazier's ideas were verified by his own personal and professional successes. At a time when black sociologists had to travel by Jim Crow railway cars to attend professional meetings and use the freight elevator to reach the lecture halls, his well-deserved scholarly reputation secured for him the presidency of the Eastern Sociological Association (1944) and later the American Sociological Association (1948).[26]

As America moved into the 1950s and 1960s, Frazier's hopeful prediction seemed to becoming true. The nascent civil rights movement began to challenge the segregated society of the South; the Supreme Court destroyed the legal underpinnings of discrimination; and the federal government moved, albeit slowly and reluctantly, to guarantee black social and political equality. But during these years when one might expect Frazier to be encouraged by these developments, his intellectual mood and scholarship revealed an increasing bitterness and pessimism. Between the mid-1950s and his death in 1962 he lashed out repeatedly in vitriolic attacks against the black middle class, the black intellectual, and by inference the American system of race relations. Some investigators have suggested that this represented a return to his youthful Marxism, while others have hinted that he abandoned assimilation for cultural pluralism. Neither is true. Frazier's new attitude reflects a new definition of assimilation.[27]

By the late 1950s Frazier had come to feel that assimilation required more than acculturation, integration, and occasionally amalgamation. It needed an additional psychological and cultural transformation that would mesh the two races into a new cosmopolitan entity.

Although this process remained nameless for Frazier, it is apparent that he conceived of it as a fusion. First, blacks and whites had to psychologically accept each other as equal members of the larger community, disregarding any racial differences. Second, both races had to merge their social heritages, cultural traditions, and racial contributions into a new social, cultural, and racial society that retained elements of both groups. According to Frazier, this fusion process had taken place in a number of areas. He cited the example of the brunette schoolchildren of France linking themselves ancestrally to the blond, blue-eyed Gauls without any sense of their own brown hair and dark eyes. Similarly in Brazil, African descendants thought of themselves as Brazilian and Latin rather than Afro-American.[28]

His discovery of this additional process stemmed from an increasing sophistication in his understanding of race relations. During the 1940s and 1950s Frazier undertook a series of theoretical investigations of international race relations. From these studies he emerged with a broader perspective on American race relations. He stopped viewing American society through the eyes of an American black man and came to realize that there were alternatives and options to the way in which the pattern of American race relations had developed. In Brazil, for example, he was impressed by a society that had evolved so completely as a "fusion of white, black, and red" that there was no "race problem." While in Africa he found a native elite that had readily accepted the education, technology, and economics of the West but refused to relinquish its African identity and cultural heritage.[29]

But when he examined American society to see if a similar process had occurred he was disappointed. While acculturation and integration were taking place, fusion was not. White Americans, he explained, refused to accept the humanity of blacks. Although whites had reluctantly allowed blacks admission into the political, economic, and cultural life of the nation, they failed to see them as mature, intelligent, and rational human beings. Even worse, the black middle class in its desire to be accepted as American had discarded its own cultural heritage and racial traditions and unquestioningly and sometimes inappropriately adopted those of white society. Instead of recognizing their Afro-American folk culture, as embodied in the black church and Negro spiritual, and their genteel traditions, as descended from the antebellum house servants, as sources of cultural strength and racial pride, the middle class rejected them as demeaning and old-fashioned. In short, neither condition was fulfilled and assimilation appeared to have failed.[30]

For Frazier this failure of assimilation was symbolized by the emergence of a pathological group which he labeled the black bourgeoisie. The members of the black middle class because of their cultural and economic achievements had traveled furthest along the race relations cycle of any group within the black community. But cut off from their own cultural roots and rejected by white society they lived in a sort of limbo. Neither part of the black world nor wholly accepted by the white, the black bourgeoisie were in "the process of becoming NO-BODY."[31]

The black bourgeoisie, Frazier reasoned, realized their anomalous position and compensated for it by erecting a wall of irrational behavior and conspicuous consumption. They created a make-believe world in which they were brilliant entrepreneurial capitalists in a powerful and growing Afro-American economy and the sought after leaders in a glittering and lavish black social set. By ignoring the realities of modern capitalism, the insignificance of black businesses, and the salaried occupations of most of the middle class, the black bourgeoisie sought affiliation with the power and status of the white economic elite. Like the Pullman porter, who, while owning only his own home and eighty dollars worth of stock, rejected the New Deal because it forced men of property like himself to support lazy workingmen, they imagined themselves as the black equivalents of white upper-class society. Even worse, Frazier lamented, they tried to act the part in their social lives. The black bourgeoisie entertained in a grand style with extravagant parties, dinners, dances, debutante balls, and the like in order to exhibit their luxurious homes, expensive automobiles, fine clothes, and costly jewelry.[32]

Their strenuous efforts were not sufficient to insulate them from the realities of being black and unassimilated in white America. Their make-believe world was only a facade masking some very serious psychological and cultural problems. The black bourgeoisie, according to Frazier, were permeated with a debilitating self-hatred. Rejected by white society because of their race, members of the middle class denigrated their African origins, effaced their Negroid characteristics through hair-straighteners and skin bleachers, and demeaned the Afro-American culture of the masses. Furthermore, they had an unrealistic image of themselves and their role in society. The black press, in particular, catered to middle-class society and filled its pages with descriptions of its social life and wealth. The press routinely inflated the black bourgeoisie's petty accomplishments, turning police magistrates into judges, mediocre professors into significant scholars, and minor political appointments into major racial achievements. Even so, the black bourgeoisie were intensely insecure. Many of them, Frazier explained, were so afraid of losing status within their narrow world that they buried themselves in debt to maintain their high levels of consumption. Others, recognizing both their inability to compete in the larger society and their vested interest in segregation, resisted any attempts to destroy the ghetto and integrate blacks into white society. Finally, the black bourgeoisie suffered from cultural confusion. Because of their abandonment of Afro-American values and their failure to enter the white world their behavior—particularly in regard to religion and sex—was irregular, contradictory, and at times hypocritical.[33]

It should be noted that Frazier's ideas about the black middle class and American race relations reflected certain trends within American sociology. During the years immediately prior to the appearance of his critiques, studies like David Riesman's *The Lonely Crowd* (1950), C. Wright Mills's *White Collar* (1951), and William H. Whyte's *The Organization Man* (1956) were lamenting, each in its own way, the mediocrity and pretentiousness of middle-class society. At the same time, other social scientists were revealing the brutal impact of American race relations on the Afro-American personality. In works like Abram Kardiner's and Lionel Ovesey's *The Mark of Oppression* (1951) and Stanley Elkins's *Slavery: A Problem in American Institutional and Intellectual Life* (1959), blacks were depicted as displaying peculiar behavior patterns and personality traits as a result of racial discrimination and degradation.[34]

For Frazier, however, the pathological behavior of the black bourgeoisie merited more than mere social criticism. The very existence of the black bourgeoisie indicated to him that the most assimilated segment of black America had gone astray; the race relations cycle had misfunctioned; and something needed to be done about it. The solution to this situation, as he saw it, was to awaken in the black community a sense of its Afro-American identity, cultural heritage, and racial traditions. Blacks had to be made aware of those qualities that made them unique and encouraged to retain them as they entered the white world. Unfortunately, the people best suited for this difficult task, the black intellectuals, had failed in their racial duty.

Black intellectuals, Frazier wrote, had been "seduced by the dream of final assimilation" and readily accepted the "annihilation of the Negro—physically, culturally, and spiritually." Like their counterparts among the black bourgeoisie, the intellectuals were cut off from their own traditions and heritage. And nothing symbolized this more than their use of Gandhianism as an ideological justification for nonviolence in the civil disobedience movement. Despite the clear evidence that the dynamics of civil rights had firm roots in the black religious experience and Afro-American folk culture, blacks thought so little of them that they turned to an alien tradition for a rationale. "When Negroes are forced to face hostile white mobs," Frazier observed, "they do not sing Indian hymns, they sing Negro spirituals and the hymns of their fathers which embodied the faith of their fathers in a hostile world."[35]

To rectify their past neglect Frazier urged black intellectuals to undertake a careful exploration of the Afro-American experience in both its African and American dimensions. By uncovering the negative effects of slavery and racism as well as the positive contributions of the Afro-American heritage they would be in a position to "save the soul" of the black man. Through literature, art, music, history, and drama they had to produce a new and more appropriate identity, self-image, and sense of personality. This task, as Frazier saw it, was far more than a simple production of group pride. It was an integral, if not vital, stage in the assimilation process. If blacks did not gain a sense of their own personal worth and merge their social heritage into the larger American heritage in the same way that other ethnic groups had done in the past then assimilation would never occur.[36]

Not long after he published his castigations of the black intellectuals, Frazier told a younger colleague that he planned to write one more book—a final study about the future of the Afro-American in which he would try to clarify the difference between integration and assimilation. Unfortunately, he never had the chance to finish his task. Within two months he suffered a fatal heart attack on May 17, 1962. But even in the final weeks of his life he was still concerned with the issues that had governed his career from its inception. He was still trying to clear the way for the assimilation of the Afro-American.[37]

As a young man he had defined the problem of assimilation in terms of acculturation and integration and devised an economic program to enable blacks to acquire the cultural habits of the white middle class and to enter the larger economic world. Later as a Chicago sociologist he saw the forces of American life assimilating blacks through the progress of a race relations cycle. Finally, through his investigations of international race relations he came to redefine assimilation as a process requiring a psychological and cultural fusion absent in American life. His concern for assimilation was neither as simple as some accounts of his thought have held nor as destructive of Afro-American culture as others have maintained. For Frazier assimilation was a complex phenomenon, ever changing and ever elusive.

NOTES

Preface

1. Robert A. Skotheim, *American Intellectual Histories and Historians* (Princeton: Princeton University Press, 1966).
2. See, for example, John Higham and Paul K. Conkin, eds., *New Directions in American Intellectual History* (Baltimore: Johns Hopkins University Press, 1979).
3. David W. Noble to Hamilton Cravens, Nov. 14, 1980.

Introduction

1. Robert A. Skotheim, *American Intellectual Histories and Historians* (Princeton: Princeton University Press, 1966), pp. 264 ff. Persons reviewed the book in the *Journal of American History* 53(1967):786–87.
2. Stow Persons, ed., *Evolutionary Thought in America* (New Haven: Yale University Press, 1950), p. v.
3. *Journal of Religion* 29(1949):66.
4. The widely read and often criticized *Theory and Practice of Historical Study: A Report of the Committee on Historiography*, Social Science Research Council Bulletin no. 54 (New York, 1946) is a key document.
5. See, for example, the essays in John Higham and Paul Conkin, eds., *New Directions in American Intellectual History* (Baltimore: Johns Hopkins University Press, 1979).
6. *Mississippi Valley Historical Review* 34(1948):672–73.
7. Ibid.
8. *American Historical Review* 53(1948):345–46. We have noted earlier in this essay the high praise Sidney Mead gave the book in his review in the *Journal of Religion* 29(1949):66.
9. John Lydenberg in the *New England Quarterly* 32(1959):117.
10. Irvin G. Wyllie in *Mississippi Valley Historical Review* 55(1958):488–89.
11. *American Literature* 31(1959):95–98.
12. John Higham, *Writing American History: Essays on Modern Scholarship* (Bloomington: Indiana University Press, 1970), p. 69.
13. Arthur A. Ekirch, Jr., *American Intellectual History: The Development of a Discipline*, American Historical Association Pamphlet no. 102 (Washington, D.C., 1973), pp. 38–39.
14. *Journal of American History* 61(1974):150–52.
15. *New England Quarterly* 47(1974):328.
16. Russell B. Nye in *American Literature* 46(1974):226–27. The similarly commendable, if slightly reserved review of Wallace Evans Davis appeared in the *American Historical Review* 79(1974):1238–39.
17. Stow Persons, "The Cyclical Theory of History in Eighteenth Century America," *American Quarterly* 6(1954):147–63.
18. Cushing Strout, ed., *Intellectual History in America: Contemporary Essays on Puritanism, the Enlightenment, and Romanticism* (New York: Harper & Row, 1968), 1:147.

Part 1

1. "Social Darwinism and the American Businessman," *Proceedings of the American Philosophical Society* 103(1959):629–35.
2. Michael C. Coleman, "Not Race, But Grace: Presbyterian Missionaries and American Indians, 1837–1893,"*Journal of American History* 67(1980):41–61.

Chapter 1

1. Moses Coit Tyler, "President Witherspoon in the American Revolution," *American Historical Review* 1(1896):672. Tyler's discussion was largely biographical and descriptive; he did little to analyze Witherspoon's revolutionary thought. Works on Witherspoon's Scottish intellectual background are: William Oliver Brackett, "John Witherspoon: His Scottish Ministry" (Ph.D. diss., University of Edinburgh, 1935); George Eugene Rich, "John Witherspoon: His Scottish Intellectual Background" (D.S.S. diss., Syracuse University, 1964); Wayne William Witte, "John Witherspoon: An Exposition and Interpretation of His Theological Views As the Motivation of His Ecclesiastical, Educational and Political Career in Scotland and America" (Ph.D. diss., Princeton Theological Seminary, 1953). Works on Witherspoon's thought in Scotland and America are: Douglas Sloan, *The Scottish Enlightenment and the American College Ideal* (New York: Columbia University Teachers College Press, 1970), pp. 103–45; Miles L. Bradbury, "Adventure in Persuasion" (Ph.D. diss., Harvard University, 1967);'James D. Casteel, "Professors and Applied Ethics: Higher Education in a Revolutionary Era, 1750–1800" (Ph.D. diss., George Peabody College for Teachers, 1964); Roger J. Fechner, "The Moral Philosophy of John Witherspoon and the Scottish-American Enlightenment" (Ph.D. diss., University of Iowa, 1974). The standard biography of Witherspoon is still Varnum Lansing Collins, *President Witherspoon: A Biography*, 2 vols. (Princeton: Princeton University Press, 1925).
2. See suggestive article by John Clive and Bernard Bailyn, "England's Cultural Provinces: Scotland and America," *William and Mary Quarterly* 3d ser. 11(1954):200–213.
3. Witherspoon's university education is discussed in Fechner, "Moral Philosophy," pp. 41–87.
4. On Hutcheson see older works by Robert Scott, *Francis Hutcheson: His Life, Teaching and Position in the History of Philosophy* (Cambridge: Cambridge University Press, 1900) and Gladys Bryson, *Man and Society: The Scottish Inquiry of the Eighteenth Century* (Princeton, Princeton University Press, 1945). More recent works that treat Hutcheson as a philosopher are: S. A. Grave, *The Scottish Philosophy of Common Sense* (Oxford: Oxford University Press, 1960); Norman S. Fiering, "Moral Philosophy in America, 1650–1750, and Its British Context," (Ph.D. diss., Columbia University, 1969); and David Fate Norton, "From Moral Sense to Common Sense: An Essay on the Development of Scottish Common Sense Philosophy, 1700–1765," (Ph.D. diss., University of California, San Diego, 1966). On Hutcheson as a Real Whig political thinker see Caroline Robbins, *The Eighteenth-Century Commonwealthman: Studies in the Transmission, Development and Circumstance of English Liberal Thought from the Restoration of Charles II until the War with the Thirteen Colonies* (Cambridge, Mass.: Harvard University Press, 1959), pp. 185–95.
5. Elizabeth Flower and Murray G. Murphey, *A History of Philosophy in America* (New York: Putnam, 1977) 1:203–53; and David Fate Nortin, "Francis Hutcheson in America," in *Studies on Voltaire and the Eighteenth Century*, ed. Theodore Besterman (Oxford: The Voltaire Foundation, 1976), 154:1574–68; Gary Wills, *Inventing America: Jefferson's Declaration of Independence* (New York: Doubleday, 1978); Fechner, "Moral Philosophy," pp. 88–132.
6. Hugh Trevor-Roper, "The Scottish Enlightenment," in *Studies on Voltaire and the Eighteenth Century*, ed. Theodore Besterman (Geneva: The Voltaire Foundation, 1967), 58:1641–49.

7. Flower and Murphey, *History of Philosophy*, pp. xiv–xv.

8. Richard B. Sher, "Church, University, Enlightenment: The Moderate Literati of Edinburgh, 1720–1793," (Ph.D. diss., University of Chicago, 1979).

9. John Witherspoon, *Ecclesiastical Characteristics: or, The Arcana of Church Policy. Being An Humble Attempt To Open The Mystery of Moderation*, in *The Works of the Rev. John Witherspoon*, 4 vols. (Philadelphia: William W. Woodward, 1800–1801), 3:113.

10. Collins, *President Witherspoon*, 1:70–101.

11. On gentry mentality see Stow Persons, *The Decline of American Gentility* (New York: Columbia University Press, 1973), pp. 29–36; see also Francis L. Broderick, "Pulpit, Physics, and Politics: The Curriculum of the College of New Jersey, 1764–1794," *William and Mary Quarterly*, 3d ser. 6(1949):42–68.

12. For a discussion of other early American moralists of Witherspoon's era see Casteel, "Professors and Applied Ethics"; John Witherspoon, *Lectures on Moral Philosophy*, ed. Varnum Lansing Collins (Princeton: Princeton University Press, 1912), pp. 142–44; Francis Hutcheson, *Collected Works of Francis Hutcheson*, facsimile ed., 7 vols., by Bernard Fabian (Hildesheim, W.Ger.: Georg Olms, 1969). Hutcheson's *System of Moral Philosophy*, a two-volume work in the original 1755 edition, is in vols. 5 and 6 of Fabian's edition.

13. See Collins's introduction to his edition of Witherspoon's *Lectures*, xxi–xxii.

14. Fechner, "Moral Philosophy," pp. 172–74.

15. Witherspoon, *Lectures*, pp. 140–42; Hutcheson, *System*, 5:1–2.

16. Witherspoon, *Lectures*, pp. 4–10; Hutcheson, *System*, 5:1–14.

17. Witherspoon, *Lectures*, pp. 16–22.

18. Ibid., pp. 23–35.

19. Ibid., pp. 36–52.

20. Ibid., pp. 67–68.

21. Ibid., pp. 68–72.

22. Ibid.

23. Ibid., pp. 70–74; Hutcheson, *System*, 6:252–309.

24. Witherspoon, *Lectures*, pp. 74–79.

25. Ibid., pp. 87–90.

26. Ibid., pp. 90–94.

27. Ibid., pp. 98–99.

28. Bernard Bailyn, *The Ideological Origins of the American Revolution* (Cambridge, Mass.: Harvard University Press, 1967); Gordon Wood, *The Creation of the American Republic, 1776–1787* (Chapel Hill: University of North Carolina Press, 1969).

29. For a discussion of Witherspoon's revolutionary activities see Collins, *President Witherspoon*, 1:102–237, 2:3–118.

30. See Bailyn, *Origins of the American Revolution*, and Wood, *American Republic*, for these republican ideas.

31. Witherspoon, "Ignorance of the British with Respect to America," in *Works*, 4:289–91, 298–99 and "Thoughts on American Liberty," 4:298–99.

32. Witherspoon, "On Conducting the American Controversy," *Works*, 4:308.

33. Witherspoon, *Works*, 2:408.

34. Witherspoon, "The Druid," *Works*, 4:430.

Chapter 2

1. Two laudatory books that helped establish Bushnell's reputation as a great liberal theologian were: Mary Bushnell Cheney, *Life and Letters of Horace Bushnell* (New York: Harper and Bros., 1880), and Theodore T. Munger, *Horace Bushnell: Preacher and Theologian)* Boston: Houghton, Mifflin and Co., 1900). For one view of Bushnell as an extreme liberal, see Walter Marshall Horton, *Realistic Theology* (New York: Harper and Bros., 1934). Calvinism in Bushnell's thought is noted by Fred Kirschenmann, "Horace Bushnell: Cells or Crustacea?" in *Reinterpretation in American Church History*, ed. Jer-

ald C. Brauer (Chicago: University of Chicago Press, 1968), pp. 67–86. Vincent Daniel's "Nature and the Supernatural: A Study in the Development of the Thought of Horace Bushnell," (Ph.D. diss., Yale University, 1939) focuses on changes in his theology. See Howard A. Barnes, "Horace Bushnell: An American Christian Gentleman," (Ph.D. diss., University of Iowa, 1970) for bibliographical essay.

2. Mass theory is thoroughly explained in Stow Persons, *The Decline of American Gentility* (New York: Columbia University Press, 1973). Two earlier essays by Persons explain more concisely: "The Origins of the Gentry," in *Essays on History and Literature*, ed. Robert Bremner (Columbus: Ohio State University Press, 1966), pp. 83–119, and the pamphlet, *The Gentry in the United States* (Moscow: "Nauka" Publishing House, 1970). See also D. Alan Williams, "The Virginia Gentry and the Democratic Myth," in *Myth and the American Experience*, Nicholas Cords and Patrick Gerster, eds. (New York: Glencoe Press, 1973), 1:65–73. See Richard B. Morris, " 'We the People of the United States': The Bicentennial of a People's Revolution," *American Historical Review* 82(1977):1–19 for the view that the American Revolution had solid backing from lower classes who demanded and received what amounted to a social revolution.

3. For views critical of the current mass society, see Philip Selznick, "Institutional Vulnerability in Mass Society," in *America as a Mass Society*, Philip Olson, ed. (New York: Free Press, 1963), pp. 13–29, and Dwight McDonald, *Against the American Grain* (New York: Random House, 1952), pt. 1. For a more positive view, see Edward Shils, "The Theory of Mass Society," in *America*, Olson, ed., pp. 30–47. Leftist critiques include C. Wright Mills, *The Power Elite* (New York: Oxford University Press, 1956), and Herbert Marcuse, *Eros and Civilization* (Boston: Little, Brown, and Co., 1955). For a middle view and bibliography see Seymour Martin Lipset, *The First New Nation* (New York: Basic Books, 1963), Introduction. See also *Daedalus* 89(1960), and Daniel Bell, "The Theory of Mass Society: A Critique," *Commentary* 22(1956):75–83.

4. Persons, "Origins of the Gentry," p. 89; Murray Milner on status insecurity in *Intellectual Digest* (1972):72, and John Tomsich, *A Genteel Endeavor: American Culture and Politics in the Gilded Age* (Stanford: Stanford University Press, 1971), p. 14.

5. Joseph Barry, "Travels with Tocqueville: Traces of His America Persist," in *Annual Editions: Readings in American History*, 1:187–94.

6. Persons, *Decline of American Gentility*, p. 7, and *Gentry*, pp. 1–2. See also Paul B. Horton and Chester L. Hunt, *Sociology*, 3d ed. (New York: McGraw Hill, 1972), p. 396, Daniel Levine, *Varieties of Reform·Thought* (Madison: State Historical Society of Wisconsin, 1964), p. 3, and Selznick, "Institutional Vulnerability," p. 17.

7. Persons, *Gentry*, pp. 2–6, 10. Studies describing the decline of the gentry are: Richard Hofstadter, *The Age of Reform: From Bryan to F. D. R.* (New York: Vintage Books, 1955), especially Chap. 4; Geoffrey Blodgett, *The Gentle Reformers: Massachusetts Democrats in the Cleveland Era* (Cambridge, Mass.: Harvard University Press, 1966); John G. Sproat, *"The Best Man": Liberal Reformers in the Gilded Age* (New York: Oxford University Press, 1968); Fredric Cople Jaher, *Doubters and Dissenters: Cataclysmic Thought in America, 1885–1918* (London: Free Press of Glencoe, Collier-Macmillan, 1964); Henry F. May, *The End of American Innocence* (New York: Alfred A. Knopf, 1959); Christopher Lasch, *The New Radicalism in America: The Intellectual as a Social Type* (New York: Alfred A. Knopf, 1965).

8. Barnes, "Horace Bushnell: Gentry Elitist," *Connecticut History* 19(1977):1–24; Barnes, "The Idea That Caused a War: Horace Bushnell Versus Thomas Jefferson," *Journal of Church and State* 16(1974):73:83.

9. Cheney, *Life and Letters*, pp. 28, 54–56.

10. Sterling Library, Yale University, New Haven, Conn.

11. H. Sheldon Smith, *Changing Conceptions of Original Sin* (New York: Oxford University Press, 1955), p. 106; quoted in Sidney E. Mead, *Nathaniel William Taylor: Connecticut Liberal* (Chicago: University of Chicago Press, 1942), pp. 125–26; see James H. Moorhead, "Social Reform and the Divided Conscience of Antebellum Protestantism," *Church History* 48(1979):416–30, on Charles Grandison Finney's perfectionism, Clifford E. Clark, "The Changing Nature of Protestantism in Mid-Nineteenth Century America: Henry Ward Beecher's Seven Lectures to Young Men," *Journal of American*

History 57(1971):832–46, stresses Beecher's belief in the connection between conversion and character development, William R. Hutchison in "Cultural Strain and Protestant Liberalism," *American Historical Review* 76(1971):386–411, suggests that what motivated nineteenth-century liberal Protestants was a commitment to a common cultural style or pattern of cosmic or societal meaning, Lois W. Banner's "Religious Benevolence as Social Control: A Critique of an Interpretation," *Journal of American History* 60 (1973):23–41, concludes that the highest value of the post-Revolutionary generation of religious humanitarians went to men who scorned prevailing social customs; Smith, *Original Sin,* pp. 102, 134.

12. Bushnell, *Twentieth Anniversary: A Commemorative Discourse Delivered in North Church* (Hartford: Elihu Greer, 1853), pp. 12–13, 8; Bushnell, *Sermons for the New Life* (New York: Charles Scribner's Sons, 1916), p. 373; Cheney, *Life and Letters,* p. 92; Bushnell, *Sermons for the New Life,* p. 292.

13. Bushnell, "The Great Time Keeper," *National Preacher* 18(1844):4; Bushnell, *A Discourse on the Moral Uses of the Sea* (New York: M. W. Dodd, 1845), and "Uses and Duties of Stormy Sundays," *American Pulpit* 2(1846).

14. Bushnell, "Review of the Errors of the Times," *New Englander* 2(1844):143–75.

15. Bushnell, *Building Eras in Religion* (New York: Charles Scribner's Sons, 1903), pp. 356–85.

16. Bushnell, "The Evangelical Alliance," *New Englander* 5(1847):102–25.

17. Reprinted as "The Growth of Law," in Bushnell, *Work and Play* (New York: Charles Scribner's Sons, 1903), pp. 102–35; 78–80, 81, 118–21.

18. Catholicus (Benet Tyler), *A Letter to Dr. Bushnell of Hartford on the Rationalistic, Socinian and Infidel Tendency of Certain Passages in His Address Before the Alumni of Yale College* (Hartford: Henry S. Persons, 1843); Cheney, *Life and Letters,* p. 108; Tyler, *Letter,* p. 19.

19. Bushnell, "Spiritual Economy of Revivals of Religion," *Quarterly Christian Spectator* 10(1838):131–48, reprinted in *Views of Christian Nurture and of Subjects Adjacent Thereto* (Hartford: Edwin Hunt, 1847), pp. 123–46, 124–27, 130–34, 137–41.

20. Bushnell, "The Kingdom of Heaven as a Grain of Mustard Seed," *New Englander* 2(1844):600–619, reprinted as "Growth Not Conquest: The True Method of Christian Progress," in *Christian Nurture,* pp. 147–81.

21. Ibid., pp. 65; 1, 7.

22. Ibid., pp. 89, 91.

23. Barbara Cross, *Horace Bushnell: Minister to Changing America* (Chicago: University of Chicago Press, 1958), makes too much of Bushnell's social ambitions.

24. Bushnell, "Christian Comprehensiveness," *New Englander* 4(1848):81–111, reprinted in *Building Eras,* pp. 386–459, 410.

25. Cheney, *Life and Letters,* p. 191; Bushnell, *The Spirit in Man* (New York: Charles Scribner's Sons, 1870), pp. 39–40.

26. Cheney, *Life and Letters,* pp. 203, 552–53.

27. Bushnell, *God in Christ* (New York: Charles Scribner's Sons), pp. 20–25, 39.

28. Ibid., p. 48.

29. Ibid., pp. 43, 73, 81–82.

30. Bushnell, *God in Christ,* pp. 122–28.

31. Ibid., pp. 213, 249.

32. Kirschenmann, "Horace Bushnell," pp. 75–76, incorrectly stated that Bushnell allowed for no direct inspirations; Bushnell, *God in Christ,* pp. 342–43, 279–80, 294–95, 348–49.

33. Quoted in Clarence H. Faust and Thomas H. Johnson, *Jonathan Edwards: Representative Selections, with Introduction, Bibliography, and Notes* (New York: Hill and Wang, 1962), p. 107.

34. Bushnell, *God in Christ,* pp. 344–45.

35. *Princeton Review* 21(1849):296.

36. The best summary of the heresy controversy is Edwin Pond Parker, *The Hartford Central Association and the Bushnell Controversy* (Hartford: Case, Lockwood and Brainard Co., 1896).

37. Arthur O. Lovejoy, *Essays in the History of Ideas* (Baltimore: Johns Hopkins University Press, 1948), pp. 254–76; Cheney, *Life and Letters*, p. 499.

38. For a description of the excesses of the socioeconomic elite see Howard Mumford Jones, *The Age of Energy: Varieties of American Experience, 1865-1915* (New York: Viking Press, 1973), Chap. 3; Cheney, *Life and Letters*, pp. 234–35; Bushnell, *The Spirit of Man*, pp. 179, 181, 287, 293; Bushnell, *Sermons on Living Subjects* (New York: Scribner, Armstrong and Co., 1877), pp. 406, 416–417.

39. Bushnell, *Building Eras*, pp. 134, 129.

40. Bushnell, *Sermons for the New Life*, p. 65.

41. Ibid., pp. 330–333.

42. Bushnell, *Parting Words* (Hartford: L. E. Hunt, 1859), pp. 12, 15, 17–18.

43. Bushnell, *Nature and the Supernatural as Together Constituting the One System of God* (New York: Charles Scribner's Sons, 1907), Chap. 1.

44. Ibid., pp. 35–36.

45. Ibid., pp. 32–34, 37.

46. Ibid., pp. 177–78.

47. Bushnell, *Christian Nurture* (New Haven: Yale University Press, 1967), p. 13; Bushnell, *The Spirit in Man*, p. 88.

48. Bushnell, *The Vicarious Sacrifice, Grounded in Principles Interpreted by Human Analogies*, 2 vols. (New York: Charles Scribner's Sons, 1903), 1:172, 208–9, 218–19, 362–63.

49. Ibid., pp. 333, 335, 341.

50. *North American Review* 102(1866):558; Bushnell, *The Vicarious Sacrifice*, 2:40, 54, 63.

51. Charles H. Hopkins, *The Rise of the Social Gospel in American Protestantism* (New Haven: Yale University Press, 1940), p. 5; Kirschenmann, "Horace Bushnell"; Perry Miller, *Errand into the Wilderness* (New York: Harper Torchbooks, 1964), p. 202.

Chapter 3

1. Iowa State Teachers Association, *Proceedings*, 1878, in *Iowa Normal Monthly* 2(1879):183 (hereafter cited as ISTA, *Proceedings* and *IaNM*).

2. See David B. Tyack, "The Kingdom of God and the Common School," *Harvard Educational Review* 36(1966):447–49, 460, 466–69; James C. Carper, "A Common Faith for the Common School?: Religion and Education in Kansas, 1861–1900," *Mid-America* 60(1978):147–51, 160–61; John Pulliam, "Changing Attitudes Toward Free Public Schools in Illinois, 1825–1860," *History of Education Quarterly* 7(1967):202–4; Lloyd P. Jorgenson, *The Founding of Public Education in Wisconsin* (Madison: State Historical Society of Wisconsin, 1956), pp. 116–29.

3. For a discussion of the connections between Christianity, morality, and citizenship and Mann's solution to the problem of religious instruction, see R. Freeman Butts, *The American Tradition in Religion and Education* (Boston: Beacon Press, 1950), pp. 116–17 and Lawrence A. Cremin, *The American Common School* (New York: Teachers College, 1951), pp. 66–67, 70.

4. Iowa Department of Public Instruction, *School Laws of Iowa* (Des Moines: State Printer, 1872), p. 38 (hereafter cited as Iowa, *School Laws*). Also see "The Bible in the Public Schools, Optional with Teachers," *IaNM* 9(1886):220–22.

5. Robert Bellah, "Civil Religion in America," *Daedalus* 96(1967):7–8, 11–12,18. Also see Sidney Mead, "The Post-Protestant Concept and America's Two Religions," *Religion in Life* 33(1964):191–92, 197, 200.

6. Burton Confrey, *Secularism in American Education* (Washington, D.C.: Catholic Education Press, 1931), pp. 145–46; Samuel W. Brown, *The Secularization of American Education* (New York: Teacher's College, 1912), pp. 155–57; Donald Boles, *The Bible, Religion, and the Public Schools*, 2d ed., (Ames: Iowa State University Press, 1963), pp. 29–34, 58.

7. For census data see Leland L. Sage, *A History of Iowa* (Ames: Iowa State Univer-

sity Press, 1974), pp. 94, 201–2, 309–10, 314; U.S. Bureau of the Census, *Fourteenth Census*, 1920, vol. 3, *Population* (Washington, D.C.: Government Printing Office, 1922), p. 314; U.S. Bureau of Census, *Religious Bodies*, 1906, Bulletin 103 (Washington, D.C.: Government Printing Office, 1910), p. 54. The American Protective Association and Henry Bowers are discussed in John Higham's article, "The Mind of a Nativist: Henry F. Bowers and the A.P.A.," *American Quarterly* 4(1952):16–24, and Higham, *Strangers in the Land: Patterns of American Nativism, 1860–1925* (New Brunswick, N.J.: Rutgers University Press, 1955), pp. 62–63, 80–87, 108.

8. Joseph R. Gusfield, *Symbolic Crusade: Status Politics and the American Temperance Movement* (Urbana: University of Illinois Press, 1963), pp. 4–7, 11–12. Also see David B. Tyack, *The One Best System: A History of American Urban Education* (Cambridge: Harvard University Press, 1974), pp. 105, 109, 232, and Paul Kleppner, *The Cross of Culture: A Social Analysis of Midwestern Politics* (New York: Free Press, 1970), pp. 78, 167–68. For expressions of symbolic fears about immigrants, labor strikers, and radicals in response to the national social unrest of the 1880s and 1890s, see an address by Henry Sabin in ISTA, *Proceedings*, 1886, p. 58; "Editorial," *IaNM* 11(1888):4–5; "Editorial," *IaNM* 13(1889):1; A. R. Darling, "Thoughts on Moral Training," *IaNM* 18(1894):35; "Patriotism in the Schoolroom," *IaNM* 18(1894):147–48.

9. Iowa Department of Public Instruction, *School Report* (Des Moines: State Printer, 1876), pp. 208–9, 218–21, 224 (hereafter cited as Iowa, *School Report*). The percentages were compiled from the incomplete but only available statistics contained in this report.

10. On modernization see Keach Johnson, "Elementary and Secondary Education in Iowa, 1890–1900: A Time of Awakening," *Annals of Iowa*, pt. 1, 45(1979):101–2 and pt. 2, 45(1980):194–95; Tyack, *One Best System*, pp. 6–7. The percentages were compiled from the statistics printed in Iowa, *School Report*, 1921, 21, 108–9, 118–19, 126–27, 144–45, 148–49, 153, 300–301, 321. For comparative statistics on the physical development of schools in neighboring midwestern states, see U.S. Office of Education, *Report of the Commissioner of Education*, 1883–1884 (Washington, D.C.: Government Printing Office, 1885), pp. 316–23, and ibid., 1917, 2:66–80.

11. William McGuffey, *McGuffey's New Fifth Eclectic Reader* (Cincinnati: Van Antwerp, Bragg and Co., 1866), pp. 6–8, 40–44, 72–75, 83–85, 105–7, 150–53, 288–89, 306–7. For an Iowa argument that the use of McGuffey readers in schools proved that they were not Godless, see "Moral and Religious Instruction in the Schools," *Central School Journal* 10(1887):12. On the moral and religious content of schoolbooks, see Ruth Miller Elson, *Guardians of Tradition: American Schoolbooks of the Nineteenth Century* (Lincoln: University of Nebraska Press, 1964), pp. 39, 42–43, 62; John Nietz, *Old Textbooks* (Pittsburgh: University of Pittsburgh Press, 1961), pp. 53–54, 56–57; Richard D. Mosier, *Making the American Mind: Social and Moral Ideas in the McGuffey Readers* (New York: Columbia University, 1947), pp. 98, 122–23, 151–53. For evidence of such attitudes in Iowa, see Henry Sabin's Presidential Address, ISTA, *Proceedings*, 1878, in *IaNM* 2(1879):184–85; Anna E. McGovern, *Nature Study and Related Literature* (Cedar Rapids: Republican Printing Co., 1902), pp. iii, 12–13, 52–53, 58–59, 202, 345–46, 362.

12. Iowa, *School Report*, 1896, pp. 76–77; Iowa, *School Laws*, 1919, p. 784; Iowa, *Manual for Special Day Exercises* (Des Moines: State Printer, 1901), pp. 5–6, 52–53, 77; Bellah, "Civil Religion in America," p. 11; Merle Curti, *The Roots of American Loyalty* (New York: Antheneum, 1968), pp. 190–91.

13. William Shoup, *Graded Didactics for Teachers' Normal Institutes* (St. Paul: D. D. Merrill, 1889), p. 22; ISTA, *Proceedings*, 1886, pp. 36–37. For other examples, see J. L. Pickard, "Relation of Public Schools to Morality and Religion," *IaNM* 4(1881):317–22; D. Sands Wright, "Morals and Manners," *IaNM* 17(1904):273–75.

14. Iowa, *School Laws*, 1872, pp. 30–31; ibid., 1902, pp. 85–86.

15. O. C. Scott to Homer Seerley, Mar. 28, 1894, Seerley Personal Letter Files (unless otherwise indicated, University of Northern Iowa Archives, Cedar Falls); Henry Sabin to Homer Seerley, Aug. 7, 1899, Seerley Personal Letter Files.

16. Homer Seerley to editor of *Advance*, July 20, 1901, Seerley Personal Letter Book no. 4, pp. 31–34; Seerley to Dan F. Bradley, Sept. 28, 1903, ibid., p. 318; D. Sands

Wright, Diary, Sept. 21, 1918, p. 264 (University of Northern Iowa Archives, Cedar Falls); Wright, *Fifty Years at the Teachers College* (Cedar Falls: Iowa State Teachers College, 1926), pp. 65–67, 158–60, 168–72; T. P. Christensen, "Homer Horatio Seerley," *Annals of Iowa* 35(1960):378–80.

17. Roy C. Woods, "The Status of Co-operation between Church and Public Schools in Towns in Iowa under Five Thousand Population" (Master's thesis, University of Iowa, 1924), pp. 31, 57–58.

18. ISTA, *Proceedings*, 1916, pp. 57–65; D. Sands Wright, "Bible Study in High School," *Midland Schools* 30(1916):197; Wendell J. Hansen, "An Iowa Experiment in Public School Bible Teaching" (Ph.D. diss., University of Iowa, 1947), pp. 49–51, 54; Herbert Schneider, *Religion in 20th Century America*, rev. ed. (New York: Atheneum, 1964), p. 49.

19. ISTA, *Proceedings*, 1915, p. 15. Also see Wright, "Bible Study in the High School," *Midland Schools* 30(1916):197; ISTA, *School Credit for Bible Study, Religious Instruction, and Moral Training* (Des Moines: By the Association, 1916), p. 3; Iowa, *School Report*, 1922, p. 83; ISTA, *Proceedings*, 1922, p. 30; "Importance of Religious Education," *Midland Schools* 38(1924):357–58; Wright, *Bible Ethics for School and Home* (Cedar Falls: Record Press, 1926), pp. 29–31, 42, 74–77.

20. Wright, *Bible Ethics*, pp. 105, 108–9. For a similar attempt to base citizenship on Bible readings, see "American Citizenship Readings," *Midland Schools* 41(1926):129.

21. ISTA, *School Credit for Bible Study*, pp. 3, 5–6, 14–15; ISTA, *Proceedings*, 1916, pp. 65–66; Wright, "Bible Study in the High School," *Midland Schools* 30(1916): 197; Wright, Diary, June 28, 1917, p. 179.

22. ISTA, *Proceedings*, 1921, pp. 46–47; ibid., 1922, p. 30; ibid., 1924, p. 24, Iowa, *School Report*, 1922, p. 83; ISTA, *Proceedings*, 1925, pp. 35–36; ibid., 1927, pp. 113–14.

23. Ibid., 1924, pp. 24–26; "Importance of Religious Education," *Midland Schools* 38(1924):357–58.

24. Hansen, "Iowa Experiment in Public Bible Teaching," p. 61; ISTA, *Proceedings*, 1927, pp. 113–14; Seerley to Margaret Baker, Oct. 30, 1906, Seerley Private Letterbook no. 5, p. 139; Seerley to Rev. S. E. Yaggy, Mar. 11, 1915, Seerley Official Letterbook L3, pp. 409–11.

25. *Character Education Methods: The Iowa Plan* (Washington, D.C.: Character Education Institution, 1922), pp. 6–9, 12, 17–19, 23–24, 33–34, 38–40. For a discussion of the Iowa Plan and its place in history of character education and its relationship to civil religion, see Stephen M. Yulish, "The Search for a Civic Religion: A History of the Character Education Movement in America, 1890–1935" (Ph.D. diss., University of Illinois, Urbana, 1975), pp. 80–83, 109–14, 256–57, 262.

26. ISTA, *Proceedings*, 1927, pp. 113–14 (number of questionnaires sent and number and types of schools responding were not reported); Iowa Department of Public Instruction, *Course of Study for Elementary Schools* (Des Moines: State Printer, 1928), pp. 384–85; ISTA, *Proceedings*, 1929, pp. 60–61.

27. Tyack, *One Best System*, pp. 6–7, 109, 232, 241–42; Don S. Kirschner, *City and Country: Rural Responses to Urbanization in the 1920s* (Westport: Greenwood Publishing, 1970) pp. 112–13, 119–20.

28. On this point, see Bernard Wishy, *The Child and the Republic* (Philadelphia: University of Pennsylvania Press, 1968), pp. 139–40, 167–68; ISTA, *Proceedings*, 1925, pp. 34–35.

Chapter 4

1. Richard Hofstadter pioneered the study of the social applications of evolutionary ideas in *Social Darwinism in America* (Philadelphia: University of Pennsylvania Press, 1944), claiming wider adherence to an early and more narrowly accepted interpretation of Darwin than was warranted. Stow Persons, ed., *Evolutionary Thought in America* (New Haven: Yale University Press, 1950), broadened our understanding of the range of evolu-

tion's impact while "The Naturalistic Mind, 1865-1929," *American Minds: A History of Ideas* (New York: Holt, Rinehart, and Winston, 1958), analyzed the basic assumptions of scientific naturalism. Irving G. Wyllie, "Social Darwinism and the Businessman," *Proceedings of the American Philosophical Society* 103(1959):629-35, began the revision of Hofstadter's thesis during the 1960s and 1970s continued by Paul F. Boller, Jr., *American Thought in Transition: The Impact of Evolutionary Naturalism, 1865-1900* (Chicago: Rand McNally, 1969); Hamilton Cravens and John C. Burnham, "Psychology and Evolutionary Naturalism in American Thought, 1890-1940," *American Quarterly* 23(1971):635-57; and Robert C. Bannister, *Social Darwinism: Science and Myth in Anglo-American Social Thought* (Philadelphia: Temple University Press, 1979). Scientific racism, the theory of race grounded in naturalistic thinking, is traced in John Higham, *Strangers in the Land: Patterns of American Nativism, 1876-1955* (New Brunswick, N.J.: Rutgers University Press, 1955) and Thomas F. Gossett, *Race: The History of an Idea in America* (Dallas: Southern Methodist University Press, 1963). The influence of naturalism in anthropology can be followed in William Stanton, *The Leopard's Spots: Scientific Attitudes Toward Race in America, 1815-1869* (Chicago: University of Chicago Press, 1960); John S. Haller, Jr., *Outcasts from Evolution: Scientific Attitudes of Racial Inferiority, 1859-1900* (Urbana: University of Illinois Press, 1971); and George W. Stocking, Jr., *Race, Culture, and Evolution: Essays in the History of Anthropology* (New York: Free Press, 1968). Race ideas in American eugenics and their critique are traced in Mark H. Haller, *Eugenics: Hereditarian Ideas in America* (New Brunswick, N.J.: Rutgers University Press, 1963), and Kenneth Ludmerer, *Genetics and American Society: A Historical Appraisal* (Baltimore: Johns Hopkins University Press, 1972). Recent efforts to understand the broader significance of scientific naturalism in American society are found in Edward A. Purcell, Jr., *The Crisis of Democratic Theory: Scientific Naturalism and the Problem of Value* (Lexington: University of Kentucky Press, 1973); Hamilton Cravens, *The Triumph of Evolution: American Scientists and the Heredity-Environment Controversy, 1900-1941* (Philadelphia: University of Pennsylvania Press, 1978); Wyllie, "Social Darwinism and the Businessman"; Bannister, *Social Darwinism*.

2. George W. Stocking, Jr., "Lamarckianism in American Social Science, 1890-1915," *Journal of the History of Ideas* 23(1962):239-56; Scott, "The Social Lamarckian Crisis in American Reform Thought," *Proceedings of the Indiana Academy of Science* 85(1977):305-10.

3. Gossett, *Race*, and I. A. Newby, *Jim Crow's Defense: Anti-Negro Thought in America, 1900-1930* (Baton Rouge: Louisiana State University Press, 1965); for a brief review of the literature see Gossett, *Race*, pp. 409-30.

4. The historiography of American Protestant missionaries in Africa is limited and must be used with care. A standard general history of African missions is Charles P. Groves, *The Planting of Christianity in Africa*, 4 vols. (London: Lutterworth Press, 1948-1958), written from a British perspective. Friendly denominational coverage includes Clifford M. Drury, *Presbyterian Panorama: One Hundred and Fifty Years of National Missions History* (Philadelphia: Westminster Press, 1952); Robert G. Torbet, *Venture of Faith: American Baptist Foreign Mission Society, 1814-1954* (Philadelphia: Judson Press, 1954); Clifton J. Phillips, *Protestant America and the Pagan World: American Board of Commissioners for Foreign Missions, 1810-1860* (Cambridge: Harvard University Press, 1969). The early work of the American Board in South Africa is also treated in Alan R. Booth, *The United States Experience in South Africa, 1784-1870* (Cape Town: Balkerna Publishers, 1976). More critical assessments of the role of missions in Africa are found in Horton Davies and R. H. W. Shepard, eds., *South African Missions, 1800-1950: An Anthology* (London: Nelson and Co., 1954); Terence O. Ranger and John Weller, eds., *Themes in the Christian History of Central Africa* (Berkeley: University of California Press, 1972); Thomas O. Beidelman, "Social Thought and the Study of Christian Missions," *Africa* 44(1974):235-49. Robert Strayer's "Mission History in Africa: New Perspectives on an Encounter," *African Studies Review* 19(1976):1-15, provides a perceptive historiographic review of the literature to date, particularly of international coverage in African studies journals.

5. A survey of the decimal files and numerical file series in Record Group 59,

Records of the Department of State, National Archives, Washington, D.C., adds little to the discussion except to emphasize the quarrels and conflicts of American missionaries with European missionaries and colonial governments. Abundant primary manuscript materials are located in the Missionary Research Library, New York City; The Missions Library of the American Board of Foreign Missions, Boston; the Hoover Institution on War, Revolution and Peace, Stanford University; the Jenkins Library of the Southern Baptist Convention, Richmond, Va.; and more limited denominational holdings in the Methodist Church Board of Missions Library, New York City; and the Presbyterian Historical Society Library, Philadelphia. Valuable published guides include Missionary Research Library, *Dictionary Catalog of the Library* (New York: Missionary Research Library, 1968) and Robert Collins and Peter Duignan, *Americans in Africa: A Preliminary Guide to American Missionary Archives and Library Manuscript Collections on Africa* (Stanford: Hoover Institution, 1963). Michael C. Coleman reaches similar conclusions regarding the nonracist, although certainly imperialistic, views of white American missionaries to North American Indians in the midnineteenth century in "Not Race, but Grace: Presbyterian Missionaries and American Indians, 1837–1893," *Journal of American History* 67(1980):41–60; George M. Fredrickson, *The Black Image in the White Mind* (New York: Harper & Row, 1971), pp. 305–11.

6. Booth, *South Africa.*

7. Groves, *Christianity in Africa*, 3:129; James S. Dennis et al., *World Atlas of Christian Missions* (New York: Student Volunteer Movement, 1911), pp. 93–96.

8. "Supplement," *Missionary Review of the World* (hereafter cited as *MR*) 40(1917):814.

9. See William Searle, "Mission Work in South Africa," *MR* 23(1900):518–22; Arthur T. Pierson, " 'Kama The Good'—The Christian Chief of Africa," *MR* 24(1901):93–98; William Rainsford, "How Can Africa Be Civilized?" *Outlook* 93(1909):501–8; and William Clarke Bell, "Practicing the Social Gospel in Africa," *Missionary Herald* 70 (1924):468–69.

10. Melvin Fraser, "Brighter Side of Darkest Africa," *MR* 27(1904):454–57; Henry Richards, "Wonderful Story of Banza Banteke," *MR* 23(1900):818–25; Wilson S. Naylor, "Will Africans Ever Govern Themselves?" *World Outlook* 3(1917):9; W. C. Willoughby, "Study of Souls in Central Africa," *MR* 46(1923):13–19; Herbert Smith, "On the Edge of African Mentality," *MR* 51(1928):899–904.

11. "Among the Mongos of the Kongo," *MR* 26(1903):267–70; Walter Williams, "Fighting the Devil in Africa," *MR* 39(1916):597–601; Onar Hartzler, "Baluba Medicine and Religion," *MR* 57(1934):355–56.

12. Robert Milligan, "The Dark Side of the Dark Continent," *MR* 40(1917): 892–903; Rose Ryter, "Baby Clinics in West Africa," *MR* 57(1934):186–87; Cornelius Patton, *The Lure of Africa* (New York: Missionary Education Movement, 1917), pp. 8, 88–89.

13. Thomas Jesse Jones, *Education in Africa* (New York: Phelps-Stokes Fund, 1922); William Mackenzie, "Zululand a Century Ago," *MR* 59(1936):41–42, W. L. Smyser, "Those Missionary Folk in West Africa," *Asia* 33(1933):622–30, Royal J. Dye, "Darkest Africa Twenty Years Ago and Now," *MR* 26(1930):504–6, Wilson Naylor, "Africa Fifty Years Ago and Now," *MR* 51(1928):53–61. For the internal missionary debate on missions see William Ernest Hocking, *Re-Thinking Missions* (New York: Harper & Bros., 1932); Robert E. Spear, *Re-Thinking Missions Examined* (New York: Fleming Revell, 1933); Archibald A. Baker, *Christian Missions and a New World Culture* (Chicago: Willett, Clark Co., 1934); and Kenneth Scott Latourette, *Missions Tomorrow* (New York: Harper & Bros., 1936).

14. Scott, "American Images of Sub-Sahara Africa, 1900–1939," (Ph.D. diss., University of Iowa, 1968); *Ethnology of Africa* (Chicago: Field Museum, 1930), p. 20; *Culture Areas of Nigeria* (Chicago: Field Museum, 1935), pp. 385, 442–47; and *Anthropometry of the Ovimbundu* (Chicago: Field Museum, 1938). Anthropologists gathering artifacts for museums were particularly prone to argue from stages of material culture to evolutionary sequences of biological races.

15. *Negro Races: A Sociological Study* (New York: Macmillan Co., 1907), pp. 3–21,

449–55; *In Quest of Gorillas* (New Bedford, Mass.: Darwin Press, 1937), pp. 39, 51–54, 505–25; *African Game Trails*, 2 vols. (New York: Charles Scribner's Sons, 1910).

16. W. H. Leslie, "The Kongo, Twenty Years Ago and Now," *MR* 26(1903):675–78; Willis Ray Hotchkiss, "Heathen Darkness in Africa," *MR* 26(1903):931–35; Arthur T. Pierson, "Moral Darkness in the Dark Continent," *MR* 29(1906):567–70.

17. Sydney E. Ahlstrom, *A Religious History of the American People*, 2 vols. (New Haven: Yale University Press, 1975), 2:345–47; Samuel P. Verner, *Pioneering in Central Africa* (Richmond, Va.: Presbyterian Publications, 1903), p. 476; M. D. Williams, "Remodeling Society with Chisel and Plow," *World Outlook* 2(1916):5–6; Patton, *Lure of Africa*, pp. 172–76; James D. Taylor, "Missionary Situation in Bantu Africa," *MR* 42(1919):32–36; Ray E. Phillips, "Why Africa Turns from the Gospel," *Christian Century* 47(1930):80–82.

18. *Pioneering in Central Africa*, pp. 4, 83, 445.

19. D. C. Rankin, "Reign of Terror on the Kongo," *MR* 23(1900):341–44; "Portuguese Opposition to Missions," *MR* 44(1921):262–65; "Give the Nation the Facts About Liberia," *Christian Century* 51(1934):987–88; Arthur T. Pierson, "Editorial: Native Africa and Concessions," *MR* 23(1900):560; "Editorial: A South African Outrage," *Missionary Herald* 109(1913):435–36; Missionary letters to American consulates, State Department Correspondence, Record Group 59, National Archives.

20. Robert Nassau, *Fetishism in West Africa* (New York: Charles Scribner's Sons, 1904), p. 94; John Springer, *The Heart of Central Africa* (New York: Methodist Book Concern, 1909), p. 175.

21. Gertrude Hance, *The Zulu Yesterday and Today* (New York: Fleming Revell, 1916), p. 149; George Trull, *The Tribe of Zambe* (New York: Presbyterian Church, USA, 1917), pp. 76–85; Patton, *Lure of Africa*, pp. 127, 150.

22. See Nassau, *Fetishism*, and Robert Milligan, *The Fetish Folk of West Africa* (New York: Fleming Revell, 1912).

23. J. Merle Davis, *Modern Industry and the African* (London: Macmillan Co., 1933), pp. 107–8, and Julia Kellersberger, *Congo Crosses* (Boston: United Study of Foreign Missions, 1936), pp. 90–96.

24. Kellersberger, *Congo Crosses*, p. 19; John Wesley Haley, *Life in Mozambique and South Africa* (Chicago: Free Methodist Publishers, 1926), p. 145; Janet Miller, *Jungles Preferred* (Boston: Houghton Mifflin Co., 1931), pp. 19–25, 57, 172.

25. William Davis, *Ten Years in the Congo* (New York: Reynal & Hitchcock Co., 1938), pp. 3–4, 93–94, 133; Kellersberger, *Congo Crosses*, pp. 97–98, 120.

26. *Fetishism*, and *My Ogowe, A Narrative of Daily Incidents in Equatorial Africa* (New York: Neal and Co., 1914). Milligan's *Fetish Folk* is similar to Nassau's works.

27. *Pioneering in Central Africa*, pp. 116–17.

28. Snyder, "Some Peculiarities of the Natives of Central Africa," *MR* 26(1903): 183–88; Fraser, "Brighter Side," 455–56. My emphasis.

29. Milligan, *Fetish Folk*, pp. 14–15, 30–35, 42–58; Fraser, "Brighter Side," 456–57; Nassau, *My Ogowe*, p. 23.

30. Hance, *The Zulu*, pp. 41–54, 110; Jean Kenyon Mackenzie, *Black Sheep* (New York: Houghton Mifflin Co., 1916), p. 67; Helser, *In Sunny Nigeria* (New York: Fleming Revell, 1926), pp. 48–68.

31. Hance, *The Zulu*, p. 109; Walter Williams, "Christian Krus Who Have Stood the Test," *MR* 52(1929):116–24; Dye, "Darkest Africa," p. 505; Pierson, "Moral Darkness in the Dark Continent," *MR* 29(1906):569.

32. Verner, *Pioneering in Central Africa*, p. 350.

33. Mackenzie, *Black Sheep*, pp. 153–54; Trull, *Tribe of Zambe*, p. 39.

34. Kenneth Scott Latourette, "Real Issue in Foreign Missions," *Christian Century* 48(1931):506–8; J. T. Tucker, "Spiritual Self-Support in Africa," *MR* 51(1928):815–18; H. D. Davis, "Realistic Missions in a Realistic World," *MR* 61(1938):172–77.

35. "Men and Minerals in Katanga," *MR* 42(1919):421–26, and "Are Africans Worth Saving?" *MR* 51(1928):780–87; "Material Progress and the Africans," *MR* 59(1936):481–84.

36. *Modern Industry and the African*, pp. vii, 2–9.

37. Mathildge Dysart, "Fighting Superstition in Africa," *MR* 47(1924):421–24; Haley, *Life in Mozambique and South Africa*; Miller, *Jungles Preferred*; and Kellersberger, *Congo Crosses*, p. 85.
38. William Hudnut, "Building a Church in Africa," *MR* 45(1922):717–21; Mrs. John Springer, "How the African Preacher Preaches," *MR* 55(1932):140–43; C. S. Jenkins, "Hindrances to Missionary Work in Africa," *MR* 59(1936):525–27; A. E. Holt, "Unrest in the African Bible Belt," *Christian Century* 54(1937):709–10; John S. Hall, "Gospel Among Primitive People," *MR* 59(1936):466; Herbert Smith, "Pioneer Missionary Work in Africa," *MR* 59(1936):519–22.
39. *Congo Crosses.*
40. *The Bantu Are Coming* (New York: Richard Smith, 1931).

Part 2

1. Henry D. Shapiro, *Appalachia on Our Mind: The Southern Mountains and Mountaineers in the American Consciousness, 1870-1920.* (Chapel Hill: University of North Carolina Press, 1978) is an outstanding example of this latter genre.
2. See Margaret W. Rossiter, "Women Scientists in the United States Before 1920," *American Scientist* 62(1974):312–23; Rossiter, "The Female Research Associate, 1920–1940" (paper presented at History of Science Society, 1977); Rossiter, " 'Women's Work' in Science, 1880–1910," *Isis* 71(1980):381–98. I am indebted to Dr. Rossiter for the many insights she has shared with me from her forthcoming book on women scientists in America to 1940.
3. Hamilton Cravens, *The Triumph of Evolution: American Scientists and the Heredity-Environment Controversy, 1900-1941* (Philadelphia: University of Pennsylvania Press, 1978), pp. 157–274.

Chapter 5

1. Journal of Susan Warner, Aug. 2, July 30, 1851, Susan Warner Papers, Constitution Island Association, West Point, N.Y. This chapter stems from a study being completed on the novels and stories and the letters, diaries, and journals of the following nineteenth-century American women writers: Maria Cummins, Caroline Howard Gilman, Caroline Lee Hentz, Mary J. Holmes, Maria McIntosh, Sara Parton, Catharine Maria Sedgwick, E. D. E. N. Southworth, Harriet Beecher Stowe, Mary Virginia Terhune, Susan Warner, and Augusta Evans Wilson. The chapter was presented at the University Seminar for Feminist Inquiry, Dartmouth College, Nov. 20, 1980.
2. The adjective sentimental has been used to characterize a broad spectrum of antebellum literature. See Herbert Ross Brown, *The Sentimental Novel in America* (Durham, N.C.: Duke University Press, 1940). Recently the noun sentimentalist has been applied almost exclusively to these writers. The negative connotations associated with the term are given particular emphasis in Ann Douglas, *The Feminization of American Culture* (New York: Alfred Knopf, 1977). Douglas equates sentimentalization with feminization and, calling a plague on both houses, casts these writers (among other females) and their nineteenth-century male clerical cohorts in the role of villains, blaming them for a supposed decline from the strength and rigor of Calvinist culture and for paving the way for the subsequent rise of a consumer society. Nina Baym's *Woman's Fiction* (Ithaca, N.Y.: Cornell University Press, 1978) offers a less tendentious approach, but her literary focus suffers from a lack of historical context. I will save someone else the bother of pointing out that I, too, have used the term sentimentalist in previous articles. Increasing skepticism about the term's accuracy and usefulness led me to search for a more appropriate designation.
3. *Our Famous Women* (Hartford: A. D. Worthington and Co., 1886), p. 628. Quoted in a biographical sketch written by Kate Sanborn.

4. Stow Persons, *The Decline of American Gentility* (New York: Columbia University Press, 1973).

5. The commentary is based upon analyses of early nineteenth-century publishing including William Charvat, *Literary Publishing in America, 1790–1850* (Philadelphia: University of Pennsylvania Press, 1959); Hellmut Lehman-Haupt in collaboration with Lawrence C. Wroth and Rollo G. Silver, *The Book in America: A History of the Making and Selling of Books in the United States,* 2d ed. (New York: R. R. Bowker Co., 1972); Luke White, Jr., *Henry William Herbert: The American Publishing Scene, 1831–1858* (Newark, N.J.: The Carteret Book Club, 1943); John Tebbel, *A History of Book Publishing in the United States: The Creation of an Industry, 1630–1865* (New York: R. R. Bowker Co., 1972); Matthew J. Bruccoli, ed., *The Profession of Authorship in America, 1800–1870: The Papers of William Charvat* (Columbus, Ohio: Ohio State University Press, 1968).

6. James D. Hart, *The Popular Book: A History of America's Literary Taste* (New York: Oxford University Press, 1950), p. 67; Richard M. Bernard and Maris A. Vinovskis, "Beyond Catharine Beecher: Female Education in the Antebellum Period," *Signs: Journal of Women in Culture and Society* 3(1978):862. See also Tebbel, *Book Publishing,* p. 207.

7. Lyle H. Wright, "A Statistical Survey of American Fiction, 1774–1850," *Huntington Library Quarterly* 11(1938–1939):309; Robert E. Spiller et al., eds., *Literary History of the United States,* 3 vols., 3d ed., rev. (New York: Macmillan Co., 1963), 1:236.

8. "Bookselling: From Appleton's New American Cyclopedia," *American Publishers' Circular and Literary Gazette* 1(1858):391; "Notes on Books and Booksellers," *American Publishers' Circular and Literary Gazette* 1(1863):166–67 (the table from the *Boston Post* was reprinted here); Lyle H. Wright, "A Few Observations on American Fiction, 1851–1875," *Proceedings of the American Antiquarian Society* 65(1955):93, 102; *Nation* 14(1872):334–35.

9. Journal of Catharine Maria Sedgwick, Dec. 17, 1835, Catharine Maria Sedgwick Papers, Massachusetts Historical Society, Boston, Mass.; Sedgwick to friend, Feb., 1821, Sedgwick Papers.

10. Sedgwick to Sedgwick, May 25, 1822, Sedgwick Papers (Minot); Journal of Catharine Maria Sedgwick, Dec. 17, 1835, Sedgwick Papers.

11. (Boston: Marsh, Capen, Lyon & Webb, 1839), p. 210.

12. (New York: Harper & Bros., 1838), p. 24.

13. (New York: D. Appleton & Co., 1850), pp. 22–23.

14. Lyle H. Wright, *American Fiction, 1774–1850,* rev. ed. (San Marino, Calif.: Henry E. Huntington Library, 1948). Susanna Rowson was born in England of English parents in 1762, spent part of her childhood in the colonies, but returned to England and published three novels as well as poetry and criticism before crossing the Atlantic again in 1793.

15. Stowe to Georgiana May, n.d., in Annie Fields, ed., *Life and Letters of Harriet Beecher Stowe* (Boston: Houghton Mifflin and Co., 1897), p. 83.

16. See William Charvat's discussion of the tradition and its British origins in Bruccoli, ed., *Profession of Authorship.* The eighteenth-century male elite that provided the leadership for the Revolution usually adopted pseudonyms. Their reasons for doing so and the implications are explored in Gordon S. Wood, "The Democratization of Mind in the American Revolution," in *Leadership in the American Revolution,* papers presented at the Third Symposium, May 9/10, 1974 (Washington, D.C.: Library of Congress, 1974). The literary domestics also had their female predecessors. Eighteenth-century British women, whether amateur or professional in their literary endeavors, either adopted pseudonyms or published anonymously. They were probably similarly motivated. Briefly alluding to this phenomenon are Alison Adburgham, *Women in Print: Writing Women and Women's Magazines from the Restoration to the Accession of Victoria* (London: George Allen and Unwin, 1972) and J. M. S. Tompkins, *The Popular Novel in England, 1770–1800* (Methuen, 1969), Chap. 4.

17. Sedgwick to Mrs. Channing, 1822, Sedgwick Papers; Sedgwick to Sedgwick, Jan. 4, 1827, Sedgwick Papers; Terhune [Marion Harland], *Marion Harland's Autobiography* (New York: Harper & Bros., 1910), p. 264, and Terhune's statement in *Our Famous Women* (Hartford: A. D. Worthington & Co., 1886), p. 635; Terhune [Marion Harland], *Loiterings in Pleasant Paths* (New York: Charles Scribner's Sons, 1880), p. 132; Terhune, *Autobiography*, p. 240.

18. Terhune to Virginia Eppes Dance, Oct. 15, 1849, William R. Perkins Library, Duke University, Durham, N.C.; Terhune, *Autobiography*, p. 241; Terhune to W. E. Mitchell, July 22, 1893, Clifton Waller Barrett Collection, Alderman Library, University of Virginia, Charlottesville, Va.

19. John S. Hart, *The Female Prose Writers of America* (Philadelphia: E. H. Butler & Co., 1852), pp. vii–viii.

20. Hart, *Female Prose Writers*, pp. 49, 56–57, 387; Warner to Hart, Mar. 17, 1851, Maurice Family Papers, Southern Historical Collection, University of North Carolina, Chapel Hill, N.C.; Anna B. Warner, *Susan Warner* (New York: G. P. Putnam's Sons, 1909), p. 321; Susan Warner to Hart, Mar. 17, 1851, Maurice Family Papers; Hart, *Female Prose Writers*, p. 423.

21. Warner, *Susan Warner*, pp. 263, 346; Tebbel, *History of Publishing*, p. 308. The novel was reprinted sixty-seven times.

22. McIntosh to Cummins, Oct. 1, 1857, Barrett Collection.

23. The sources consulted for the biographical material on Parton include the Sara Parton Papers, Sophia Smith Collection, Smith College, Northampton, Mass.; James Parton, *Fanny Fern: A Memorial Volume* (New York: G. W. Carleton & Co., 1873); and Sara Parton's semiautobiographical novel, *Ruth Hall: A Domestic Tale of the Present Time* (New York: Mason Bros., 1855). James Parton's speculation is found in the *Memorial Volume*, p. 43.

24. The sources consulted on Southworth include the E. D. E. N. Southworth Papers, Manuscript Department, William R. Perkins Library, Duke University, Durham, N.C.; Southworth Papers, Manuscript Division, Library of Congress, Washington, D.C.; an autobiographical sketch by Southworth in Hart, *The Female Prose Writers of America*, 2d ed. (Philadelphia: E. H. Butler & Co., 1855); a biographical sketch in E. D. E. N. Southworth, *The Haunted Homestead* (Philadelphia: T. B. Peterson & Bros., 1860); and Regis Boyle's biography, *Mrs. E. D. E. N. Southworth, Novelist* (Washington: Catholic University of America Press, 1939).

25. The basic source for Hentz is the Hentz Family Papers, Southern Historical Collection, University of North Carolina, Chapel Hill, N.C.; Stowe to Eliza Cabot Follen, Feb. 16, 1853, Follen Miscellany, Massachusetts Historical Society, Boston, Mass. For further analysis concerning Stowe's practice of literary domesticity, see my "At War With Herself: Harriet Beecher Stowe as Woman in Conflict Within the Home," *American Studies* 19(1978):23–40.

26. Ibid.

27. William Perry Fidler, *Augusta Evans Wilson, 1835–1909* (University, Ala.: University of Alabama Press, 1951), p. 75; Terhune, *Autobiography*, pp. 363–64.

28. Fidler, *Augusta Evans Wilson*, p. 40; Sedgwick to Sedgwick, Feb. 4, 1836, Sedgwick Papers; Stowe to Stowe, July 11, 1853, Acquisitions, Stowe-Day Memorial Library and Historical Foundation, Hartford, Conn.; Stowe to sister [1838], Beecher Family Papers, Manuscripts and Archives, Sterling Memorial Library, Yale University, New Haven, Conn.

29. Hentz to Hart, Mar. 7 [1851], Simon Gratz Collection, Historical Society of Pennsylvania, Philadelphia, Penn.

30. Hentz to Hart, Nov. 13, 1851, Simon Gratz Collection; Hentz to Hart, Nov. 30, 1851, Miscellany, Boston Public Library, Boston, Mass.

31. Southworth to Bonner, [Dec., 1875], E. D. E. N. Southworth Papers, Manuscript Department, William R. Perkins Library, Duke University, Durham, N.C.

32. Parton [Fanny Fern], *Fern Leaves from Fanny's Portfolio* (Auburn, N.Y.: Derby and Miller, 1854), p. 100. The same defensiveness can be seen among the actual bluestockings a century earlier. Elizabeth Carter, the most highly educated of these late

eighteenth-century British women, was defended by her friend Dr. Johnson. Carter's domestic skills, he insisted, equalled her intellectual accomplishments: "My old friend, Mrs. Carter, could make a pudding as well as translate Epictetus from the Greek and work a handkerchief as well as compose a poem." Adburgham, *Women in Print,* pp. 134–35.

33. Wilson to Janie Tyler, Jan. 18, 1862, in Fidler, *Augusta Evans Wilson,* p. 66.

34. Wilson, *St. Elmo* (New York: Grosset & Dunlap, n.d., 1866), pp. 70, 200, 201; Terhune, *Phemie's Temptation* (New York: Carleton, 1869), pp. 183, 184–85.

35. Wilson, *St. Elmo* (New York: G. W. Carleton, 1866), pp. 238, 457; Terhune, *Phemie's Temptation,* p. 178.

36. Wilson to T. E. Cooke, Oct. 30, 1866, Library of Congress, Washington, D.C. I am indebted to former Dartmouth College student Ellen Meyer, for assistance in locating this source; Terhune, quoted in *Our Famous Women,* p. 636; Gilman to sister, Apr. 13, 1838, quoted in Mary Scott Saint-Amand, *A Balcony in Charleston* (Richmond, Va.: Garret & Massie, 1941), p. 111; Sedgwick to Mr. Wheaton, Mar. 15, 1829, Miscellany, Pierpont Morgan Library, New York, N.Y.

37. Terhune, *Autobiography* p. 485; Sedgwick to Kate Sedgwick, Feb. 16, 1835, Sedgwick Papers.

38. Hart, *Female Prose Writers,* p. 56.

39. The comment is quoted in a biographical sketch of Terhune by Sarah K. Bolton, *Successful Women* (Boston: D. Lathrop Co., 1888), p. 107.

40. The incident and quotation are found in a biographical sketch of Sara Parton written by Grace Greenwood. See *Eminent Women of the Age* (Hartford, Conn.: S. M. Betts & Co., 1869), pp. 83–84.

41. Stowe to Fields, July 27, 1868, James T. Fields Papers, Manuscripts Collection, Henry E. Huntington Library, San Marino, Calif.

42. Sedgwick to Kate Sedgwick, Dec. 14, 1830, Sedgwick Papers. In response to comments about *Hope Leslie,* Sedgwick also wrote to an admirer of the novel: "Literary occupation is rather a pastime than a profession with me." See Sedgwick Papers.

43. Sedgwick to Anna Jameson, Apr. 18, 1841, Sedgwick Papers.

Chapter 6

1. Significantly, nineteenth-century feminists and New Women who attacked the lady as a parasite thought of themselves as in some sense ladies. See Andrew Sinclair, *The Better Half: The Emancipation of the American Woman* (New York: Harper & Row, 1965), p. 120. And when nineteenth-century working-class women organized, they sometimes took such titles as New York City's Ladies Cordwainer's Society or Providence, Rhode Island's Lady Segar Makers. See Barbara Mayer Wertheimer, *We Were There: The Story of Working Women in America* (New York: Pantheon Books, 1977), pp. 88, 163. See also Philip Foner, *History of the Labor Movement in the United States,* vol. 1 (New York: International Publishers, 1947), pp. 108–11, for references to the early-nineteenth century Lady Shoe Binders of Lynn, Massachusetts, and the Ladies Shoe Binders Society of Philadelphia.

2. A sampling of the considerable literature includes Gerda Lerner, "The Lady and the Mill Girl: Changes in the Status of Women in the Age of Jackson," *Mid-Continent American Studies* 10(1969):5–15; Christopher Lasch, *The New Radicalism in America, 1889–1963: The Intellectual as a Social Type* (New York: Alfred A. Knopf, 1965), pp. 3–68; Helene E. Roberts, "The Exquisite Slave: The Role of Clothes in the Making of the Victorian Woman," *Signs: Journal of Women in Culture and Society* 2(1977):554–69; Anne Firor Scott, *The Southern Lady: From Pedestal to Politics, 1830–1930* (Chicago: University of Chicago Press, 1970); Sinclair, *Better Half,* pp. 113–36; Carroll Smith-Rosenberg, "The Hysterical Woman: Sex Roles and Role Conflict in 19th Century America," *Social Research* 39(1972):652–78; Barbara Welter, "Anti-Intellectualism and the American Woman: 1800–1860," *Mid America* 48(1966):258–70; Barbara Welter, "The Cult of True Womanhood: 1820–1860," *American Quarterly* 18(1966):151–74.

3. The New Woman has been discussed widely. See Carolyn Forrey, "The New

Woman Revisited," *Women's Studies* 2(1974):37–56; Robert W. Smuts, *Women and Work in America* (New York: Schocken Books, 1971), pp. 126–40; Peter Gabriel Filene, *Him-Her-Self: Sex Roles in Modern America* (New York: Harcourt Brace Jovanovich, 1974), pp. 15–32; Robert E. Riegel, *American Women: A Story of Social Change* (Rutherford, N.J.: Fairleigh Dickinson University Press, 1970), p. 240.

4. Leslie Woodcock Tentler, *Wage-Earning Women: Industrial Work and Family Life in the United States, 1900-1930* (New York: Oxford University Press, 1979), pp. 64–65, 74–77, 106–7; David M. Katzman, *Seven Days a Week: Women and Domestic Service in Industrializing America* (New York: Oxford University Press, 1978), pp. 266–67; Smuts, *Women and Work,* pp.84–87.

5. Studies of the Protestant or Puritan ethic in Western and American culture, from Weber, Troeltsch, and Tawney to later writers, have tended to discuss the phenomenon in terms of Calvinists, Puritans, and Americans, but to focus implicitly or explicitly on men. See Max Weber, *The Protestant Ethic and the Spirit of Capitalism,* trans. Talcott Parsons (New York: Charles Scribner's Sons, 1958); Ernst Troeltsch, *The Social Teaching of the Christian Churches,* trans. Olive Wyon, (London: George Allen & Unwin, 1931), 2:641–50; R. H. Tawney, *Religion and the Rise of Capitalism, A Historical Study* (New York: Penguin Books, 1926); Perry Miller, *The New England Mind: From Colony to Province* (Cambridge, Mass.: Harvard University Press, 1953), pp. 40–52. Notable recent exceptions are Daniel T. Rodgers, *The Work Ethic in Industrial America, 1850-1920* (Chicago: University of Chicago Press, 1978), pp. 182–209; Smuts, *Women and Work,* pp. 69–155; Filene, *Him-Her-Self,* pp. 60–76, who include useful discussions on attitudes toward work of leading feminists and of working-class women. The biographies and writings of late-nineteenth century feminists and New Women reveal the strength of their adherence to the work ethic. See Charlotte Perkins Gilman, *Women and Economics: A Study of the Economic Relation Between Men and Women as a Factor in Social Evolution,* ed. Carl N. Degler (New York: Harper & Row, 1966), pp. 157, 276, 317, 331–32, 337; Olive Schreiner, *Woman and Labor* (New York: Frederick A. Stokes Co., 1911), pp. 27, 44–45, 64–65, 298–99; Annie Nathan Meyer, ed., *Woman's Work in America* (New York: Henry Holt and Co., 1891). Meyer's volume includes the comments of almost twenty leading women in as many professional fields. By contrast to the preceding material, the present discussion examines the attitudes toward work of women who were neither notable, nor feminists, nor working-class in orientation.

6. Other investigators of women have made similar interpretations. See Rodgers, *Work Ethic,* pp. 182–209; Filene, *Him-Her-Self,* pp. 60, 70; Regina Markwell Morantz, "Making Women Modern: Middle Class Women and Health Reform in Nineteenth Century America," *Journal of Social History* 10(1977):493–94; Anne Firor Scott, "What, Then, Is the American: This New Woman?" *Journal of American History* 65(1978):679–703; Cindy S. Aron, " 'To Barter Their Souls for Gold': Female Clerks in Federal Government Offices, 1862–1890," *Journal of American History* 67(1981):835–53. Compare Stow Persons, *American Minds: A History of Ideas* (New York: Henry Holt and Co., 1958), p. 43: "The ethic of individual responsibility was perhaps the major legacy of Puritanism to American civilization."

7. Records, New Britain Normal School, Central Connecticut State College; Records, Connecticut State Library, Hartford.

8. Bush to William Graham Sumner, June 7, 1884, Oct. 21, 1883, William Graham Sumner Papers, Yale University Manuscripts and Archives, Yale University, New Haven, Conn.

9. Bush to Sumner, Dec. 15, 1899, Sumner Papers.

10. Bush to Sumner, Oct. 21, 1883, Nov. 15, 1901, Sumner Papers.

11. Bush to Sumner, Dec. 25, 1899, Dec. 15, 1899, Nov. 15, 1901, Sumner Papers.

12. Sumner to Sumner, May 1, [1874?], Apr. 12, 16, [1878?], Sumner Papers.

13. Sumner to Sumner, May 1, n.d., Sumner Papers.

14. Janet Camp Troxell to authors, Oct. 5, 1979; *New York Herald Tribune,* Dec. 19, 1934; *New York Times,* Dec. 19, 1934; Sumner to Sumner, Sept. 8, [1886?], Sumner Papers.

15. Sumner to Sumner, Tuesday, n.d., July 21, 1880, Sumner Papers.

16. Sumner to Sumner, Aug. 5, n.d., Dec. 27, n.d., Sumner Papers.

17. Sumner to Sumner, Aug. 31, [1886?], Sumner Papers.

18. *New Haven Register*, Sept. 16, 1979. Janet Camp Troxell to authors, Oct. 5, 1979.

19. *New York Herald Tribune*, Dec. 19, 1934; *New York Times*, Dec. 19, 1934; *New York Times*, July 30, 1935.

20. Joseph Sumner to W. G. Sumner, June 24, 1868, Sumner to Sumner, Dec. 20, 1863, Sumner Papers.

21. Sumner to Sumner, Dec. 10, 1865, June 26, [1883?], Oct. 2, 1867, Oct. 4, 1867, Sept. 28, 1866, Sumner Papers.

22. Sumner to Sumner, Sept. 28, 1866, Sumner Papers.

23. Sumner to Sumner, Sept. 30, [1867], Sumner Papers.

24. Sumner to Sumner, Oct. 25, 1868, Sumner Papers.

25. Sumner to Sumner, Feb. 23, 1868, Sept. 28, 1866, June 26, 1863, Nov. 8, 1863, Sumner Papers.

26. Sumner to Sumner, Sept. 20, 1867, Oct. 24, 1867, Sumner Papers.

27. Sumner to Sumner, Apr. 10, 1885, Sumner Papers.

28. Ibid.

29. Janet Camp Troxell to authors, Nov. 7, 1979; Elliott to Sumner, June 10, 1870, Sumner Papers.

30. Elliott to Sumner, May 11, [1870], Sumner Papers.

31. Elliott to Sumner, March 26, [1871], Sumner Papers.

32. Elliott to Sumner, Nov., 1889, Sumner Papers.

33. Elliott to Sumner, Aug. 2, 1900, July 25, 1900, Sumner Papers.

34. A member of the family circle remembers Julia Elliott as a religious fanatic who tried the patience of those around her. Janet Camp Troxell to authors, Nov. 7, 1979.

35. Raffalovich to Sumner, Nov. 17, 1883, Oct. 18, 1886, Sumner Papers.

36. Raffalovich to Sumner, Apr. 2, 1884, Sumner Papers.

37. Raffalovich to Sumner, June 25, 1884, Sumner Papers.

38. Raffalovich to Sumner, Jan. 31, 1887, Sumner Papers.

39. Sophie O'Brien, *Golden Memories: The Love Letters and the Prison Letters of William O'Brien*, vol. 1; *More Love Letters, Prison Letters and Others*, vol. 2 (Dublin: M. H. Gill and Sons, 1929).

40. O'Brien, *Golden Memories*, 2:45; Joseph O'Brien, *William O'Brien and the Course of Irish Politics, 1881-1918* (Berkeley: University of California Press, 1976), p. 101.

41. Michael MacDonagh, *The Life of William O'Brien, the Irish Nationalist: A Biographical Study of Irish Nationalism, Constitutional and Revolutionary* (London: Ernest Benn, 1928), p. 28; O'Brien, *Golden Memories*, 2:169.

42. O'Brien to Sumner, May 18, 1885, Mar. 30, 1886, Sumner Papers; Sophie O'Brien, *Unseen Friends* (London: Longmans, Green and Co., 1912), pp. 103, 230, 320.

Chapter 7

1. Daniel H. Burnham and Edward H. Bennett, *Plan of Chicago Prepared Under the Direction of the Commercial Club During the Years 1906, 1907, 1908*, ed. Charles Moore (Chicago: Commercial Club, 1909). A modern edition with an introduction by W. R. Hasbrouck has been issued in the DaCapo Press Series in Architecture and Decorative Arts, no. 29 (New York: DaCapo Press, 1970).

2. Walter D. Moody, *Wacker's Manual of the Plan of Chicago: Municipal Economy* (Chicago: Chicago Plan Commission, 1911), p. 3. As an example of a full-blown instance of Moody's proposed economic and cultural hegemony for Chicago, see his essay "Chicago Destined to Be the Center of the Modern World," *Municipal Engineering* 43, no. 3(1912):49-61 and in *The Bank Man* 7(1912):307-24.

3. Walter D. Moody, *What of The City? America's Greatest Issue: City Planning, What It Is and How to Go About It to Achieve Success* (Chicago: A. C. McClurg & Co.,

1919), p. 3; Henry May, *The Protestant Churches and Industrial America* (New York: Harper & Row, 1949), pp. 182-234.

4. Daniel Boorstin, *The Americans: The Democratic Experience* (New York: Random House, 1973), pp. 5-88; Chicago Plan Commission, *Proceedings* (Chicago: Chicago Plan Commission, 1911), p. 86. When Moody accepted the Managing Director position with the CPC, R. W. Butler, a member of the CPC wrote Daniel Burnham that "from this time forward the work will be pushed by the 'Chief of all Pushers'—Mr. Moody." Butler to.D. H. Burnham, Jan. 20, 1911, Burnham Papers, Art Institute of Chicago.

5. The origins, underwriting, and unveiling of the plan have been copiously documented: see Ira Bach, "A Reconsideration of the 1909 'Plan of Chicago,' " *Chicago History* 2(1973):132-41; Francoise Choay, *The Modern City: Planning in the 19th Century,* Planning and Cities Series (New York: George Braziller, 1969); Patrick Geddes, *Cities in Evolution: An Introduction to the Town Planning Movement and to the Study of Civics* (London: Williams and Norgate, 1915); Werner Hegemann and Elbert Peets, *The American Vitruvius: An Architect's Handbook of Civic Art* (New York: Architectural Book Publishing Co., 1922); Vilas Johnson, *A History of the Commercial Club of Chicago Including the First History of the Club by John J. Glessner* (Chicago: 1977); Lewis Mumford, *The City in History: Its Transformations, and Its Prospects* (New York: Harcourt Brace Jovanovich, 1961); John Reps, *The Making of Urban America* (Princeton, N.J.: Princeton University Press, 1965); Lois Wille, *Forever Open, Clear and Free* (Chicago: Henry Regnery Co., 1972).

6. Charles W. Eliot, "A Study of the New Plan of Chicago," *Century Magazine* 79(1910):418; also Perry Duis, *Chicago: Creating New Traditions* (Chicago: Chicago Historical Society, 1976), p. 49.

7. On the complicated machinations whereby "an alliance of businessmen, planners and politicians, by persuasion, pressure and politics" set the 1909 plan in motion, consult Michael P. McCarthy, "Chicago Business and the Burnham Plan," *Journal of the Illinois State Historical Society* 63, no. 3(1970):228-56; Moody, *What of The City?* pp. 329-32; *Chicago Tribune,* July 7, 1909; *Chicago Record-Herald,* Nov. 2, 1909.

8. Moody, *What of The City?* pp. 21-22.

9. David Noble, *The Paradox of Progressive Thought* (Minneapolis: University of Minnesota, 1958); Samuel Hays, *Conservation and the Gospel of Efficiency* (Cambridge, Mass.: Harvard University Press, 1959); Charles Forcey, *The Crossroads of Liberalism: Croly, Weyl, Lippmann and The Progressive Era, 1900-1925* (New York: Oxford University Press, 1961).

10. Robinson (1869-1917) and Nolen (1869-1935) also contributed to the literature of American city planning and the city planning profession. Robinson, who wrote three important books—*The Improvement of Towns and Cities* (1901), *Modern Civic Art* (1903), and *City Planning* (1916)—was the first appointee to the first university chair of civic design (Harvard) in the United States. Nolen, a founder and later president of the American Institute of Planners, wrote *Replanning Small Cities* (1912), *City Planning* (1916), and *New Ideals in the Planning of Cities, Towns and Villages* (1919). On the quest for professionalism, see Bledstein's *The Culture of Professionalism: The Middle Class and the Development of Higher Education in America* (New York: W. W. Norton, 1976), pp. 80-128, 287-332.

11. The most comprehensive assessment of the business community's involvement in the Chicago Plan is chronicled in Neil Harris, *The Planning of The Plan* (Chicago: Commercial Club of Chicago, 1979) and McCarthy, "Chicago Businessmen and the Burnham Plan," pp. 228-56; W. D. Moody, *Chicago's Greatest Issue: An Official Plan* (Chicago: Chicago Plan Commission, 1911); Executive Committee, Chicago Plan Commission, *Proceedings* (June 19, 1911), p. 237. Robert Akeley, "Implementing the 1909 Plan of Chicago: An Historical Account of Planning Salesmanship," (Master's thesis, University of Texas, 1973), pp. 185-87, calculates that there were 86 separate bound issues, totaling $233,985,000 falling within the recommendations of the plan.

12. W. D. Moody, *The Work of the Chicago Plan Commission During 1911* (Chicago: Address to the Commercial Club of Chicago, 1912), p. 10; *What of The City?* p. 50; "City Planning and the Public Schools," *American City* 6(1912):720.

13. In his highly autobiographical *What of The City?*, pp. 107–8, Moody listed his major educational achievements in advancing the plan: his work with the daily and the periodical press, his book *Chicago's Greatest Issue*, the various lecture series he coordinated, and the *Wacker's Manual*; *Wacker's Manual*, pp. 3–4. One product of Moody's teaching efforts was his ten-volume research series on *Business Administration: Theory, Practice and Application* (Chicago: La Salle Extension University, 1910–11).

14. On Parker's progressive pedagogy see Jack K. Campbell's well-researched life, *Colonel Francis W. Parker, The Children's Crusader* (New York: Teachers College Press, 1967) and Merle Curti's assessment in *The Social Ideas of American Educators* (Paterson, N.J.; Littlefield Adams, 1965), pp. 374–95; for Dewey's impact in Chicago, consult Katherine Mayhew, *The Dewey Schoool: The Laboratory School of the University of Chicago, 1896–1903* (New York: Oxford University Press, 1966).

15. Dewey, *Democracy and Education: An Introduction to the Philosophy of Education* (New York: Macmillan Co., 1916), pp. 100–102; *Wacker's Manual*, p. 10. Another example of the Progressives' interest in education and city planning reform is Randolph Bourne's discussion of the curriculum unit, "The City: A Healthful Place to Live," in *The Gary Schools* (Boston: Houghton Mifflin, 1916), pp. 117–19.

16. *Wacker's Manual*, pp. 4, 8, 97.

17. Burnham, "White City and Capital City," *Century Magazine* 63(1902):619–20; see also Burnham's speech, "A City of the Future Under a Democratic Government," *Transactions of the Town-Planning Conference, Royal Institute of British Architects* (Oct., 1910), pp. 368–78; Hines, "The Paradox of Progressive Architecture," *American Quarterly* 25(1973):427–48. For Hines's extended treatment of this facet of Burnham see *Burnham of Chicago: Architect and Planner* (New York: Oxford University Press, 1974), Chaps. 8 and 14.

18. Moody, *Wacker's Manual*, pp. 140–45; *What of The City?* pp. 412–30; also McCarthy, "Chicago Businessmen and the Burnham Plan," p. 233.

19. Commercial Club of Chicago, *The Presentation of The Plan of Chicago* (Chicago: Chicago Plan Commission, 1910), p. 29.

20. Stow Persons, *American Minds, A History of Ideas* (New York: Henry Holt and Co., 1958), pp. 349–52.

21. Burnham's famous credo is but another example of what David Burg calls "The Aesthetics of Bigness in Late Nineteenth Century American Architecture," in *Popular Architecture*, ed. Marshall Fishwick and J. Meredith Neil (Bowling Green, Ohio: Bowling Green University Popular Press, 1978), pp. 108–14.

22. *Wacker's Manual*, p. 4; *The Search For Order, 1877–1920* (New York: Hill and Wang, 1967), and an earlier study that buttresses the Wiebe thesis, Samuel P. Hayes, *The Response To Industrialism* (Chicago: University of Chicago, 1957); *Wacker's Manual*, 4, 17, 104, 8.

23. Burnham's proposed municipal building (see *Plan*, pp. 115–18) was modeled, in part, after Richard Morris Hunt's Administration Building at the 1893 World's Fair; *Wacker's Manual*, pp. 135–37.

24. Ibid., pp. 13, 66–70, *What of The City?*, pp. 38–60; *Wacker's Manual*, p. 69.

25. Haber, *Efficiency and Uplift: Scientific Management in the Progressive Era, 1890–1920* (Chicago: University of Chicago Press, 1964); Hays, *Conservation and the Gospel of Efficiency* (Cambridge, Mass.: Harvard University Press, 1959); Michael P. McCarthy, "Businessmen and Professionals In Municipal Reform: The Chicago Experience, 1887–1920" (Ph.D. diss., Northwestern University, 1970), p. 106; McCarthy, "Chicago Businessmen and the Burnham Plan," p. 231.

26. John Dewey, "Waste in Education," in *The School and Society*, in *The Middle Works of John Dewey, 1889–1924*, ed. Jo Ann Boydston, 2 vols. (Carbondale, Ill.: Southern Illinois University Press, 1976), 1:39–56; Shailer Mathews, *Scientific Management of Churches* (Chicago: University of Chicago Press, 1912); Charlotte Perkins Gilman, "The Waste of Private Housekeeping," *Annals of the American Academy of Political and Social Science* 48(1913):91–95. On the differences between the City Practical and the City Beautiful see Reps, *Making of Urban America*, pp. 331–39 and William H. Wilson, *The City Beautiful Movement in Kansas City* (Columbia: University of Missouri

Press, 1964), pp. 40–54; Moody's argument for the Burnham plan as primarily one of the City Practical can be found in *What of The City?*, pp. 15, 93.

27. *Wacker's Manual*, pp. 4, 80–81, 145; Henry Blake Fuller, "The Upward Movement in Chicago," *Atlantic Monthly* 80; "Chicago's Higher Evolution," *Dial* (1892): 205–6; *Wacker's Manual*, pp. 80–81.

28. Ibid., p. 133.

29. (New York: G.P. Putnam's Sons, 1881), p. 96; *Sexual Neurasthenia (Nervous Exhaustion): Its Hygiene, Causes, Symptoms, and Treatment, with a Chapter on Diet for the Nervous*, ed. A. D. Rockwell (New York: G. P. Putnam's Sons, 1884), p. 238n.

30. *No Other Gods: On Science and American Social Thought* (Baltimore: Johns Hopkins University, 1976), p. 107.

31. *Wacker's Manual*, p. 97; Geoffrey Blodgett, "Frederick Law Olmsted: Landscape Architecture of Conservative Reform," *Journal of American History* 62, no. 4(1976):869–89; Michael McCarthy, "Politics and the Parks: Chicago Businessmen and the Recreation Movement," *Journal of the Illinois State Historical Society* 65, no. 2 (1972):158–72; Peter J. Schmitt, *Back to Nature: The Arcadian Myth in Urban America* (New York: Oxford University Press, 1969).

32. *Plan of Chicago*, p. 105; Scott, *History of American City Planning*, p. 108; *Plan of Chicago*, p. 109; Roy Lubove, *The Progressives and the Slums: Tenement House Reform in New York City, 1890-1917* (Pittsburgh: University of Pittsburgh Press, 1962), pp. 217–56.

33. Akeley, "Implementing the 1909 Plan," pp. 52, iii.

34. Scott, *History of American City Planning*, p. 139.

35. Ibid., p. 140.

36. Stead, *If Christ Came to Chicago!* (Chicago: Laird & Lee, 1894), pp. 421–42; Akeley, "Implementing the 1909 Plan," p. 31, recognizes one similarity between the two reformers; they saw the Chicago citizenry as "full of a boundless elan and full of faith in the destiny of their city."

37. *Chicago Tribune*, Jan. 19, 1919.

38. Robert L. Wrigley, Jr., "The Plan of Chicago: Its Fiftieth Anniversary," *Journal of the American Institute of Planners* 26(1960):37. In Chicago, some of the most important progeny that have followed in the wake of the 1909 Burnham plan are: *Harbor Plan of Chicago* (1927); *The Outer Drive Along the Lake* (1929); *The Axis of Chicago* (1929); *Building New Neighborhoods: Subdivision Design and Standards* (1943); *Master Plan of Residential Land Use of Chicago* (1943); *Planning the Region of Chicago* (1956); *Development Plan for the Central Area of Chicago* (1958); *Comprehensive Plan* (1966); *Chicago 21* (1973); and *Riveredge Plan* (1974).

Chapter 8

1. Frazier's unspoken but implied differentiation of the assimilation process is similar to the distinctions drawn by Milton Gordon. Gordon described assimilation as a blanket term covering a multitude of subprocesses—the main ones being behavioral assimilation and structural assimilation. Behavioral assimilation is the process of cultural modification better known as acculturation, while structural assimilation refers to the entrance of the subordinate group into the social cliques, organizations, institutional activities, and general civic life of the receiving society. See Milton Gordon, *Assimilation in American Life* (New York: Oxford University Press, 1964).

2. There has been very little substantive examination of Frazier's social thought. For a sampling of the type of treatment his work has received see: G. Franklin Edwards, "Introduction" to E. Franklin Frazier, *On Race Relations* (Chicago: University of Chicago Press, 1968); G. Franklin Edwards, "E. Franklin Frazier" in *Black Sociologists: Historical and Contemporary Perspectives*, ed. James E. Blackwell and Morris Janowitz (Chicago: University of Chicago Press, 1974); Bart Landry, "A Reinterpretation of the Writings of Frazier on the Black Middle Class," *Social Problems* 26(1978):211–22. For a sampling of his critics see: Charles G. Valentine, *Culture and Poverty: Critique and Counter-Proposals*

(Chicago: University of Chicago Press, 1968); Oliver C. Cox, "Introduction" to Nathan Hare, *The Black Anglo-Saxons* (New York: Collier Books, 1970); L. Paul Metzger, "American Sociology and Black Assimilation: Conflicting Perspectives," *The American Journal of Sociology* 70(1971):631–32; Herbert Gutman, *The Black Family in Slavery and Freedom* (New York: Pantheon Books, 1976), and "Persistent Myths about the Afro-American Family," *The Journal of Interdisciplinary History* 6(1975):181–210. One reason why more studies have not been done is that Frazier's personal papers are not yet available for research. Frazier was an extremely productive scholar, writing over 120 articles and 8 books during his career. Such a large body of published work, I feel, is more than adequate to support an examination of the broad programs of an American intellectual.

3. An adequate view of upper- and middle-class acceptance of acculturation and integration can be gleaned from a variety of sources: W. E. B. Du Bois, *The Philadelphia Negro* (New York: Schocken Books, 1967), pp. 309–19; Kenneth Kusmer, *A Ghetto Takes Shape: Black Cleveland, 1870–1930* (Urbana: University of Illinois Press, 1976), pp. 91–112; David M. Katzman, *Before the Ghetto: Black Detroit in the Nineteenth Century* (Urbana: University of Illinois Press, 1973), pp. 135–74; St. Clair Drake and Horace R. Cayton, *Black Metropolis* (New York: Harcourt, Brace and Co., 1945), pp. 516–715; John Blassingame, *Black New Orleans: 1860–1880* (Chicago: University of Chicago Press, 1973), pp. 154–62; and particularly the works of August Meier, *Negro Thought in America: 1880–1915* (Ann Arbor: University of Michigan Press, 1963); "Negro Class Structure and Ideology in the Age of Booker T. Washington," *Phylon* 23 (1962):258–66; and "The History of the Negro Upper Class in Atlanta: 1890–1958," *Journal of Negro Education* 27(1959):130–39. For the activities of Baltimore's elite see: George W. Paul, "The Shadow of Equality: The Negro in Baltimore, 1864–1911" (Ph.D. diss., University of Wisconsin, 1972), pp. 346, 349–50, 257, 288; Margaret Law Callcott, *The Negro in Maryland Politics: 1870–1912* (Baltimore: Johns Hopkins University Press, 1969), pp. 105–7.

4. Frazier's father was a bank messenger for the Mercantile Trust Company in Baltimore. For those unfamiliar with black class structure the occupation might seem odd. But because of the skewed nature of black economic development such an occupation was prestigious and one so employed was considered to be "in banking." Arthur P. Davis, "E. Franklin Frazier: A Profile," *Journal of Negro Education* 31(1962):430–35; interview with Butler A. Jones, July 18, 21, 1972; J. Avery Smith, Kennsington, Md., Feb. 21, 1977, Feb. 26, 1979, to author.

5. Davis, "Profile," pp. 430–31; Edwards, *Black Sociologists*, pp. 88–89; Smith, Feb. 21, 1977, to author.

6. E. Franklin Frazier (hereafter EFF), "Social Equality and the Negro," *Opportunity* 3(1925):166–67; EFF, "What Is Social Equality?" *World Tomorrow* 9(1926):113.

7. EFF, "Social Equality and the Negro," pp. 166–67; EFF, "What Is Social Equality?" p. 113; EFF, "The Negro and Non-Resistance," *Crisis* 27(1927):213.

8. EFF, "Danish People's High Schools and America," *Southern Workman* 51(1922):429; EFF, "Social Equality and the Negro," p. 167.

9. EFF, "Social Equality and the Negro," p. 167. For an example of his thought regarding the development of racial pride see: EFF, "Racial Self-Expression," in *Ebony and Topaz*, ed. Charles S. Johnson (New York: National Urban League, 1927), pp. 119–21 and "Folk-Culture in the Making," *Southern Workman* 57(1928):195–99.

10. EFF, "A Negro Industrial Group," *Howard Review* 1(1924):230–31; EFF, "Three Scourges of the Negro Family," *Opportunity* 4(1926):210; EFF, "Is the Negro Family a Unique Sociological Unit?" *Opportunity* 5(1927):166; EFF, "How Present Day Problems of Social Life Affect the Negro," *Hospital Social Service* 13(1926):384; EFF, "Racial Self-Expression," p. 120; EFF, "A Note on Negro Education," *Opportunity* 2(1924):77.

11. Davis, "Profile," pp. 430–32; Edwards, "Introduction," pp. x–xi; EFF, "Co-Operatives: The Next Step in the Negro's Development," *Southern Workman* 53(1924):505; EFF, "New Currents of Thought Among the Colored People of America," (Master's thesis, Clark University, 1920), p. 69. For some indication of the impact of the

Danish trip on his early thought see: EFF, "Danish People's High Schools and America," pp. 424-30; EFF, "The Co-Operative Movement in Denmark, Part I," *Southern Workman* 52(1923):479-84; EFF, "The Co-Operative Movement in Denmark, Part II," *Southern Workman* 53(1924):123-30.

12. EFF, "Co-Operatives: The Next Step," pp. 505-9; EFF, "Some Aspects of Negro Business," *Opportunity* 2(1924):293-97; EFF, "New Currents of Thought," p. 69.

13. EFF, "Co-Operatives: The Next Step," pp. 506-7; EFF, "Some Aspects of Negro Business,," pp. 295-96.

14. EFF, "Durham: Capital of the Black Middle Class," in *The New Negro*, ed. Alain Locke (New York: A. and C. Boni Co., 1925), p. 333; Edwards, *Black Sociologists*, pp. 92-95.

15. EFF, "Durham," pp. 333-34, 338.

16. Ibid., pp. 339-40.

17. Ibid.

18. EFF, "Some Aspects of Negro Business," pp. 296-97; EFF, "La Bourgeoisie Noire," in *An Anthology of American Negro Literature*, ed. V. F. Calverton (New York: The Modern Library, 1929), p. 386.

19. The article that forced Frazier's departure from Atlanta was: "The Pathology of Race Prejudice," *Forum* 70(1927):856-62.

20. Stanford M. Lyman, *The Black American in Sociological Thought* (New York: G. P. Putnam's Sons, 1972), pp. 15-28, 35-36; Roland F. Wacker, "Race and Ethnicity in American Social Science," (Ph.D. diss., University of Michigan, 1975), pp. 5-47; Robert E. Park, "Our Racial Frontier in the Pacific," *Race and Culture*, vol. 1, *The Collected Papers of Robert Ezra Park*, ed. Everett C. Hughes, et al. (Glencoe, Ill.: Free Press, 1950), pp. 150, 207-20, 354; Fred H. Matthews, *Quest for an American Sociology: Robert E. Park and the Chicago School* (Montreal: McGill-Queens University Press, 1977), pp. 151-70. For Frazier's reaction to Park's ideas see: EFF, "Sociological Theory and Race Relations," *American Sociological Review* 12(1947):265-71, and S. P. Fullinwider, *The Mind and Mood of Black America* (Homewood, Ill.: Dorsey Press, 1969), pp. 100-102.

21. EEF, *The Negro Family in Chicago* (Chicago: University of Chicago Press, 1932), pp. 242-44, 234, 252.

22. Robert E. Park, *Human Communities* (New York: Free Press, 1952), pp. 74, 86, 145-58, 79, 170; Barbara Klose Bowdery, "The Sociology of Robert E. Park," (Ph.D. diss., Columbia University, 1951), pp. 94-104; William I. Thomas and Florian Znaniecki, *The Polish Peasant in Europe and America* (New York: Alfred A. Knopf, 1927) 2:11, 27-31, 1303; Ernest W. Burgess, "The Growth of the City" in *The City* (Chicago: University of Chicago Press, 1925), pp. 50-55. For a critical analysis of Park and some of his students' contributions to urban sociology see: Maurice R. Stein, *Eclipse of Community* (Princeton: Princeton University Press, 1968).

23. EFF, *The Negro Family in Chicago*, pp. 117-219. See also: EFF, "Chicago: A Cross Section of Negro Life," *Opportunity* 7(1929):70-73; EFF, "The Negro Community: A Cultural Phenomenon," *Social Forces* 7(1929):415-20; EFF, "Occupational Classes Among Negroes in Cities," *American Journal of Sociology* 35(1930):718-38; EFF, "The Occupational Differentiation of the Negro in Cities," *Southern Workman* 57(1930):196-200.

24. EFF, "Negro Harlem: An Ecological Study," *American Journal of Sociology* 42(1937):72-88; EFF, *The Negro Family in the United States* (Chicago: University of Chicago Press, 1939), pp. 480-88; EFF, *Negro Youth at the Crossways* (Washington, D.C.: American Council on Education, 1940), pp. 46-174; EFF, "Negro Families and Negro Youth," *Journal of Negro Education* 9(1940):290-99; EFF, "The Role of the Negro in the South," *Social Forces* 29(1940):256-88.

25. EFF, *The Negro in the United States*, rev. ed. (New York: Macmillan Co., 1957), pp. 605, 704-5; EFF, "The Negro in the United States," in *Race Relations in World Perspective*, ed. Andrew W. Lind (Honolulu: University of Hawaii Press, 1955), pp. 351-55; EFF, "The New Negro," *Nation* 183(1956):7-8.

26. Wacker, pp. 133-35; Gunnar Myrdal, *An American Dilemma: The Negro Problem and Modern America:* (New York: Harper & Row, 1944), pp. xlvii-xlviii.

27. For an example of the first argument see: John Bracey et al. "Introduction" to *The Black Sociologists: The First Half-Century* (Belmont, Calif.: Wadsworth Publishing Co., 1971), p. 10, and St. Clair Drake, "Introduction" to EFF, *Negro Youth at the Crossways* (New York: Shocken Books, 1967), p. 14. For an example of the latter see: Gerald McWorter, "The Ideology of Black Social Science," in *The Death of White Sociology*, ed. Joyce Ladner (New York: Vintage Books, 1974), p. 178.

28. EFF, *Race and Culture Contacts in the Modern World* (New York: Alfred A. Knopf, 1957), pp. 338, 316-18.

29. EFF, "The Negro Family in Bahia, Brazil," *American Sociological Review* 7(1942):465-78; EFF, "Some Aspects of Race Relations in Brazil," *Phylon* 3(1942):295; EFF, "A Comparison of Negro-White Relations in Brazil and the United States," *Transactions of the New York Academy of Science*, Ser. 2, 6, 7(1944):251-69; EFF, "Brazil Has No Race Problem," *Common Sense* 11(1942):363-64; EFF, "The Impact of Colonialism on African Social Forms and Personality," in *Africa in the Modern World*, ed. Calvin W. Stillman (Chicago: University of Chicago Press, 1955), pp. 70-90; EFF, "Urbanization and Social Change in Africa," *SAIS Review* 3(1959):3-9; EFF, "Education and the African Elite," *Transactions of the Third World Congress of Sociology*, vol. 5, *Changes in Education* (Amsterdam: n.p. 1956), pp. 95-96; EFF, *Race and Culture Contacts*, p. 338.

30. EFF, *Black Bourgeoisie* (Glencoe, Ill.: Free Press, 1957), pp. 113-46; EFF, "The Negro Middle Class and Desegregation," *Social Problems* 4(1957):295; EFF, "The New Middle Class," in *The New Negro Thirty Years Afterward* (Washington, D.C.: Howard University Press, 1955), pp. 26-27, 30-31.

31. EFF, *Black Bourgeoisie*, p. 28.

32. Ibid., pp. 24-25, 115-24; EFF, "The New Middle Class," pp. 29-32.

33. EFF, *Black Bourgeoisie*, pp. 153-94, 210-12; EFF, "The Negro Middle Class and Desegregation," pp. 291-300; EFF, "Desegregation as an Object of Sociological Research," in *Human Behavior and Social Processes: An Interactionist Approach*, ed. Arnold Rose (Boston: Houghton Mifflin, 1961), pp. 608-11; EFF, *The Negro Church in America* (Liverpool: Liverpool University Press, 1961), pp. 1-46; EFF, "Human, All Too Human," *Survey Graphic* 36(1947):74-75, 99; EFF, "Negro, Sex Life of African and American," in *Encyclopedia of Sexual Behavior* (New York: Hawthorn Books, 1961), p. 774.

34. Charles Alexander, *Holding the Line* (Bloomington: Indiana University Press, 1975), pp. 133-37; Riesman, *The Lonely Crowd* (New Haven: Yale University Press, 1950), pp. 3-31, 113-72; Mills, *White Collar: The American Middle Classes* (New York: Oxford University Press, 1951), pp. 3-13, 215-82; Whyte, *The Organization Man* (New York: Simon and Schuster, 1956), pp. 7-59; Kardiner and Ovesey, *The Mark of Oppression* (New York: Norton, 1951), pp. 170-330; Elkins, *Slavery: A Problem in American Institutional and Intellectual Life* (Chicago: University of Chicago Press, 1959), pp. 81-144.

35. EFF, "The Failure of the Negro Intellectual," in *On Race Relations*, pp. 271-77.

36. Ibid., pp. 276-79; EFF, "What Can the American Negro Contribute to the Social Development of Africa?" in *Africa: Seen by American Negroes* (Paris: Presence Africaine, 1959), p. 278.

37. Hare, *Black Anglo-Saxons*, p. 35.

APPENDIX 1

Publications of Stow Persons

Prepared by H A R O L D   B.   W O H L

THIS bibliography of the published writings of Stow Persons is arranged by year and includes books, articles, reprints, and reviews in that order. Citations of reviews and reprints are in abbreviated bibliographical form.

1 9 4 3

REVIEW:

Adams, Brooks, *The Law of Civilization and Decay: An Essay on History* (New York, 1943), in *Chimera* 2(1943):61–64.

1 9 4 4

ARTICLE:

"The Americanization of the Immigrant." David F. Bowers, ed., *Foreign Influences in American Life.* Princeton: Princeton University Press, 1944, pp. 39–56.

1 9 4 6

REVIEW:

Curti, Merle, et al., *Theory and Practice in Historical Study* (New York, 1946), in *William and Mary Quarterly* 3(1946):600–602.

HAROLD B. WOHL, University of Northern Iowa, Cedar Falls, Iowa.

1 9 4 7

BOOK:

Free Religion: An American Faith. Yale Historical Publications, Miscellany 48. New Haven: Yale University Press, 1947, 168 pp.

1 9 4 8

REVIEW:

Greene, Evarts B., *Church and State* (Indianapolis, 1947), and Frank J. Klinberg, *A Free Church in a Free State: America's Unique Contribution* (Indianapolis, 1947), in *William and Mary Quarterly* 5(1948):445.

1 9 4 9

REVIEW:

Boorstin, Daniel J., *The Lost World of Thomas Jefferson* (New York, 1948), in *William and Mary Quarterly* 6(1949):318–21.

1 9 5 0

BOOK:

Ed., *Evolutionary Thought in America.* Special Program in American Civilization at Princeton University. New Haven: Yale University Press, 1950, x + 462 pp.

ARTICLE:

"Evolution and Theology in America." S. Persons, ed., *Evolutionary Thought in America* (New Haven: Yale University Press, 1950), pp. 422–53.

REVIEW:

Trinterud, Leonard J., *The Forming of an American Tradition: A Re-Examination of Colonial Presbyterianism* (Philadelphia, 1949), in *William and Mary Quarterly* 7(1950):287–89.

1 9 5 1

REVIEW:

Wish, Harvey, *Society and Thought in Early America: A Social and Intellectual History of the American People to 1865* (New York, 1950), in *William and Mary Quarterly* 8(1951):292–93.

1 9 5 2

BOOK:
Ed., *Socialism and American Life*. Princeton Studies in American Civilization, Number 4, 2 vols. Princeton: Princeton: University Press, 1952; Vol 1., xiv + 776 pp.; Vol 2., xiv + 575 pp. With Donald Drew Egbert.

ARTICLE:
"Christian Communitarianism in America." D. Egbert and S. Persons, eds., *Socialism and American Life* (Princeton: Princeton University Press, 1952), 1:125–51.

REPRINT:
"The Americanization of the Immigrant." D. F. Bowers, ed., *Foreign Influences in American Life*. New York: Peter Smith, 1952.

REVIEWS:
Handlin, Oscar, *The Uprooted* (Boston, 1951), in *William and Mary Quarterly* 9(1952):250–51.
Marcus, Jacob R., *Early American Jewry*. Vol. 1. *The Jews of New York, New England and Canada, 1649-1794* (Philadelphia, 1951), in *William and Mary Quarterly* 9(1952):447–48.
Sweet, William W., *Religion in the Development of American Culture, 1765-1840* (New York, 1952), in *Willliam and Mary Quarterly* 9(1952): 558–61.

1 9 5 3

REVIEWS:
Aaron, Daniel, ed., *America in Crisis* (New York, 1952), in *American Quarterly* 5(1953):178–80.
Guthrie, Dwight R., *John McMillan: The Apostle of Presbyterianism in the West, 1752-1833* (Pittsburgh, 1952), in *William and Mary Quarterly* 10(1953):486–87.
Martin, Kingsley, *Harold Laski* (New York, 1953), in *Mississippi Valley Historical Review* 40(1953):556–58.
Schneider, Herbert W., *Religion in Twentieth Century America* (Cambridge, 1952), in *Mississippi Valley Historical Review* 40(1953):350–52.
Van Wagenen, Jared, Jr., *The Golden Age of Homespun* (Ithaca, 1953), in *American Historical Review* 59(1953):227.

1 9 5 4

ARTICLE:
"The Cyclical Theory of History in Eighteenth-Century America." *American Quarterly* 6(1954):147–63.

REVIEWS:

Andrews, Edward D., *The People Called Shakers: A Search for the Perfect Society* (New York, 1953), in *William and Mary Quarterly* 11(1954):302–4.

Quint, Howard, *The Forging of American Socialism* (Columbia, 1953), in *American Journal of Sociology* 59(1954):406.

1 9 5 5

REVIEWS:

Barker, Charles A., *Henry George* (New York, 1955), in *Mississippi Valley Historical Review* 42(1955):346–47.

Mann, Arthur, *Yankee Reformers in the Urban Age* (Cambridge, 1954), in *Mississippi Valley Historical Review* 41(1955):729–31.

Smith, C. P., *Yankees and God* (New York, 1954), in *William and Mary Quarterly* 12(1955):494–97.

Williams, G. H., ed., *The Harvard Divinity School* (Boston, 1954), in *Theology Today* 12(1955):125–27.

1 9 5 6

REPRINT:

Evolutionary Thought in America. New York: G. Braziller, 1956.

REVIEWS:

Curti, Merle, *American Paradox: The Conflict of Thought and Action* (New Brunswick, 1956), in *Mississippi Valley Historical Review* 43(1956):521–22.

Shannon, David A., *The Socialist Party of America: A History* (New York, 1955), in *American Historical Review* 61(1956):665–66.

1 9 5 7

REVIEW:

Draper, Theodore, *The Roots of American Communism* (New York, 1957), in *Mississippi Valley Historical Review* 44(1957):572–73.

1 9 5 8

BOOK:

American Minds: A History of Ideas. New York: Henry Holt and Co., 1958, xii + 467 pp.

ARTICLE:

"Public Opinion—A Democratic Dilemma." *Stetson University Bulletin* 58 (1958):1–16.

1 9 5 9

ARTICLE:

"Darwinism and American Culture." *The Impact of Darwinian Thought on American Life and Culture.* Austin: University of Texas Press, 1959, pp. 1–10.

1 9 6 0

REVIEWS:

Bell, Daniel, *The End of Ideology: On the Exhaustion of Political Ideas in the Fifties* (Glencoe, 1960), in *American Quarterly* 12(1960):427–28.

May, Henry., *The End of American Innocence: The First Years of Our Own Time, 1912–1917* (New York, 1959), in *Mississippi Valley Historical Review* 47(1960):159–60.

Smith, Henry Nash, and W. M. Gibson, eds., *Mark Twain-Howells Letters: The Correspondence of Samuel L. Clemens and William Dean Howells, 1872–1910,* (2 vols., Cambridge, 1960), in *American Historical Review* 66(1960):177–78.

Van Zandt, Roland, *The Metaphysical Foundations of American History* (The Hague, 1959), in *American Quarterly* 12(1960):106.

1 9 6 1

ARTICLE:

"Religion and Modernity, 1865–1914." James Ward Smith and A. L. Jamison eds., *Religion in American Life, The Shaping of American Religion.* Vol. 1. Princeton: Princeton University Press, 1961, pp. 369–401.

REVIEW:

Spiller, R. E., and E. Larrabee, eds., *American Perspectives* (Cambridge, 1961), in *Journal of Higher Education* 32(1961):519.

1 9 6 2

REVIEW:

Seidler, Murray B., *Norman Thomas: Respectable Rebel* (Syracuse, 1961), in *American Historical Review* 67(1962):812–13.

1 9 6 3

BOOK:

Ed., *Social Darwinism: Selected Essays of William Graham Sumner.* Englewood Cliffs, N.J.: Prentice Hall, 1963, 180 pp.

REPRINT:

Free Religion—An American Faith. Boston: Beacon Press paperback, 1963, 162 pp.

1 9 6 4

REVIEWS:

Gatell, F. O., *John Gorham Palfrey and the New England Conscience* (Cambridge, 1963), in *Mississippi Valley Historical Review* 50(1964):699–700.

Gossett, Thomas F., *Race: The History of an Idea in America* (Dallas, 1963), in *Journal of Southern History* 30(1964):345–46.

1 9 6 5

BOOK:

Ed., *The Cooperative Commonwealth* by Laurence Gronlund. Cambridge: The Belknap Press of Harvard University Press, 1965, xxviii + 252 pp. A John Harvard Library Book.

REVIEW:

Baritz, Loren, *City on a Hill: A History of Ideas and Myths in America* (New York, 1964), in *American Historical Review* 70(1965):1227–28.

1 9 6 6

ARTICLE:

"The Origins of the Gentry." Robert H. Bremner, ed., *Essays on History and Literature.* Columbus: Ohio State University Press, 1966, pp. 83–119.

REPRINT:

Socialism and American Life. Princeton: Princeton University Press, Second Printing 1966.

REVIEWS:

Bell, Daniel, *The Reforming of General Education* (New York, 1966), in *Journal of Higher Education* 37(1966):524–25.

Fredrickson, George M., *The Inner Civil War: Northern Intellectuals and the*

Crisis of the Union (New York, 1965), in *Journal of Southern History* 32(1966):397–98.

1 9 6 7

REVIEWS:

Gay, Peter, *A Loss of Mastery: Puritan Historians in Colonial America* (Berkeley, 1966), in *American Historical Review* 72(1967):1479–80.

Skotheim, Robert A., *American Intellectual Histories and Historians* (Princeton, 1966), in *Journal of American History* 53(1967):786–87.

1 9 6 8

REPRINTS:

Evolutionary Thought in America. Hamden: Archon, 1968.

"The Cyclical Theory of History." Cushing Strout, ed., *Intellectual History in America,* 2 vols. New York: Harper & Row, 1968, 1:47–63.

"The Cyclical Theory of History in Eighteenth-Century America," with an afternote, in Hennig Cohen, ed., *The American Culture: Approaches to the Study of the United States.* Boston: Houghton Mifflin, 1968, pp. 112–28.

"Darwinism and American Culture." Cushing Strout, ed., *Intellectual History in America,* 2 vols. New York: Harper & Row, 1968, 2:1–9.

REVIEW:

Gilbert, James B., *Writers and Partisans: A History of Literary Radicalism in America* (New York, 1968), in *American Historical Review* 74(1968): 749–50.

1 9 6 9

ARTICLE:

"Thorstein Veblen: The Theory of the Leisure Class." Hennig Cohen, ed., *Landmarks of American Writing.* New York: Basic Books, 1969, pp. 247–55.

REVIEWS:

Boyer, Paul S., *Purity in Print: The Vice-Society Movement and Book Censorship in America* (New York, 1968), in *American Historical Review* 74(1969): 1378–79.

Somkin, Fred, *Unquiet Eagle: Memory and Desire in the Idea of American Freedom, 1815–1860* (Ithaca, 1967), in *Civil War History* 15(1969): 170–72.

Wilson, R. J., *In Quest of Community: Social Philosophy in the United States,*

1860-1920 (New York, 1968), in *Journal of American History* 56(1969): 151-52.

1 9 7 0

ARTICLE:

"The Gentry in the United States." XIII International Congress of Historical Sciences. Moscow: "Nauka" Publishing House, 1970.

REPRINT:

Socialism and American Life. Princeton: Princeton University Press, Third Printing 1970.

REVIEW:

Boller, Paul F., Jr., *American Thought in Transition: The Impact of Evolutionary Naturalism, 1865-1900* (Chicago, 1969), in *Journal of American History* 56(1970):923-24.

1 9 7 1

REVIEW:

Herrnstadt, Richard, ed., *The Letters of A. Bronson Alcott* (Ames, 1969), in *American Historical Review* 76(1971):196.

1 9 7 2

REVIEWS:

Berthoff, Rowland, *An Unsettled People: Social Order and Disorder in American History* (New York, 1971), in *Civil War History* 18(1972):57-59.

Desroche, Henri, *The American Shakers: From Neo-Christianity to Presocialism* (Amherst, 1971), in *American Historical Review* 77(1972):586-87.

1 9 7 3

BOOK:

The Decline of American Gentility. New York: Columbia University Press, 1973, viii + 336 pp. Awarded the Best Book Prize of Phi Alpha Theta, 1974.

REVIEW:

Mangione, Jerre, *The Dream and the Deal: The Federal Writer's Project,*

1935-1943 (Boston, 1972), in *Journal of American History* 60(1973): 496–97.

1 9 7 4

REVIEWS:

Perry, Lewis, *Radical Abolitionism* (Ithaca, 1973), in *Journal of American History* 60(1974):1117–18.
Strout, Cushing, *The New Heavens and New Earth: Political Religion in America* (New York, 1974), in *Journal of Southern History* 40(1974): 676–77.

1 9 7 5

BOOK:

American Minds: A History of Idea. Rev. and enlarged ed. Huntington, N.Y.: Robert E. Krieger Publishing Co., 1975, xii + 527 pp.

1 9 7 6

REPRINT:

The Decline of American Gentility. New York: Columbia University Press paperback, 1976.

REVIEWS:

Bender, Thomas, *Toward an Urban Vision: Ideas and Institutions in Nineteenth-Century America* (Lexington, 1975), in *American Historical Review* 81(1976):664–65.
Diggins, John P., *Up from Communism: Conservative Odysseys in American Intellectual History* (New York, 1975), in *Journal of American History* 63 (1976):764–65.

1 9 7 8

REVIEWS:

Keller, Morton, *Affairs of State: Public Life in Late Nineteenth Century America* (Cambridge, 1977), in *New York History* 59(1978):87–88.
Moorhead, James H., *American Apocalypse: Yankee Protestants and the Civil War, 1860–1869* (New Haven, 1978), in *Civil War History* 24(1978):276–77.
Numbers, Ronald L., *Creation by Natural Law: Laplace's Nebular Hypothesis in American Thought* (Seattle, 1977), in *Journal of American History* 65(1978):144.

1 9 7 9

REVIEW:

Higham, John, and Paul K. Conkin, eds., *New Directions in American Intellectual History* (Baltimore, 1979), in *Reviews in American History* 7 (1979):447–51.

1 9 8 0

REVIEWS:

Dusinberre, William, *Henry Adams: The Myth of Failure* (Charlottesville, 1980), in *Journal of American History* 67(1980):706–7.

Oleson, Alexandra, and John Voss, eds., *The Organization of Knowledge in Modern America, 1860-1920*, in *The Journal of Southern History* 46 (1980):440–41.

APPENDIX 2

Doctoral Graduates of Stow Persons and Dissertation Titles

1 9 5 1

ROBERT W. IVERSEN
Morris Hillquit, American Social Democrat: A Study of the American Left from Haymarket to the New Deal

SEYMOUR LUTZKY
The Reform Editors and Their Press

WALTER F. PETERSON
Social Aspects of Protestantism in the Midwest, 1870–1910

1 9 5 3

DONALD L. GRAHAM
Circuit Chautauqua, A Middle Western Institution

DWIGHT W. HOOVER
The Religious Basis of the Thought of the Elder Henry James

PHYLLIS NELSON YUHAS
George D. Herron and the Socialist Clergy, 1890–1914

EARL S. BEARD
Human Nature in Politics: A Study of Walter Lippmann

1 9 5 6

LEWIS F. WHEELOCK
Urban Protestant Reactions to the Chicago Haymarket Affair, 1886–1893

HAROLD B. WOHL
Charles Chauncy and the Age of Enlightenment in New England

1 9 5 8

WILLIAM H. CUMBERLAND   A History of the Jehovah's Witnesses

1 9 6 1

ARTHUR E. SODERLIND   Charles A. Beard and the Social Studies

1 9 6 2

JOHN A. DEJONG   American Attitudes toward Evolution before Darwin

CLIFTON E. HART   The Minor Premise of American Nationalist Thought

1 9 6 3

GEORGE H. DANIELS   Baconian Science in America, 1815–1845

MILTON B. POWELL   The Abolitionist Controversy in the Methodist Episcopal Church, 1840–1864

1 9 6 4

BRUCE CURTIS   The Middle Class Progressivism of William Graham Sumner

HAROLD BAUMAN   The Historiography of Carl L. Becker

1 9 6 8

CLIFFORD H. SCOTT   American Images of Sub-Sahara Africa, 1900–1939

JOHN P. COLEMAN   In Pursuit of Harmony: A Study of the Thought of Jesse Macy

ANN LEGER ANDERSON   Moorfield Story: An Intellectual Biography

1 9 6 9

HAMILTON CRAVENS   American Scientists and the Heredity-Environment Controversy, 1883–1940

THOMAS J. SCHLERETH	The Cosmopolitan Ideal in Enlightenment Thought: Its Form and Function in the Ideas of Franklin, Hume, and Voltaire, 1694–1790
HELEN RENA UPSON	Order and System: Charles Francis Adams, Jr., and the Railroad Problem
CARROLL ENGELHARDT	The Common School and the Ideal Citizen: Iowa, 1876–1921

1 9 7 0

HOWARD A. BARNES	Horace Bushnell: An American Christian Gentleman

1 9 7 1

STEPHEN E. BERK	The Church Militant: Timothy Dwight and the Rise of Evangelical Protestantism

1 9 7 2

DAVID HENRY DELEON	The American as Anarchist: A Socio-Historical Interpretation
BILLIE JEANNE STEVENSON	The Ideology of American Anarchism, 1880–1910

1 9 7 3

JOHN S. MCCORMICK	A Beleaguered Minority: The Young Intellectuals and American Mass Society, 1910–1920

1 9 7 4

MARY KELLEY	The Unconscious Rebel: Studies in Feminine Fiction, 1820–1880
ROGER J. FECHNER	The Moral Philosophy of John Witherspoon and the Scottish-American Enlightenment

1 9 7 5

DENNIS P. RUSCHE	An Empire of Reason: A Study of the Writings of Noah Webster

1 9 7 6

PAUL R. MEYER, JR.

The Transformation of American Temperance: The Popularization and Radicalization of a Reform Movement, 1813–1860

FREDRICK WOODARD

W. E. B. Du Bois: The Native Impulse: Notes Toward an Ideological Biography, 1868–1897

1 9 7 8

LARS HOFFMAN

William Rainey Harper and the Chicago Fellowship

DALE R. VLASEK

The Social Thought of E. Franklin Frazier

1 9 8 0

WENDY L. SCHLERETH

The Chap-Book: A Journal of American Intellectual Life in the 1890s

INDEX